Show AI—Don't Tell It

Build Buy-In with Visual Storytelling

DR. LISA PALMER

WILEY

To the women who have been my lifeline through decades of hard work and life's struggles: Mom, Angela, Bobbi, Delaine, Julie, and Wanda.
Because of your strength, love, and unwavering presence,
I have amazing children, a fulfilling career, and education that
I treasure. Saying thank you will never be enough. This book is
our shared legacy.

Contents

PART 3   Bringing AI to Life (Visualization as a Catalyst for Change)   173

PART 4   Appendices   249

Ready to dive deeper? Access more tools, checklists, and other exclusive book resources at **DrLisa.ai/snt-book-resources**.

Foreword

By Dan Roberts

Host of the Tech Whisperers Podcast

Author of Confessions of a Successful CIO

and Unleashing the Power of IT

The mantra of "developing the human side of technology" has guided me through four decades of helping leaders transform their workforce, tech functions, and companies. Having partnered with thousands of visionary CxOs, I've studied the mindset, success traits, and patterns that differentiate the good from the great leaders. What you find is a laser focus on getting the fundamentals right. You also find a series of big bets and answer-the-call moments that took vision and courage. These leaders are business first and are laser focused on their Big C: Customer.

They also lead with H.E.A.R.T. in recognizing how they show up with humility, empathy, adaptability, resilience, and transparency...while balancing the need to deliver results, hold people accountable, and have the hard conversations from the board and C-suite to peers and teammates.

That's why this book is such a breath of fresh air.

Show AI—Don't Tell It isn't a technical manual or another opportunistic play on the AI hype cycle. It's the leadership playbook for these times, rooted in real-world experience and grounded in the belief that transformation happens only when people feel it, see it, and trust it. And it's written by someone who knows that better than anyone I know.

Dr. Lisa Palmer brings what I call *The Dr. Lisa Factor*, a rare combination of practitioner experience, big tech scale, boardroom advisory chops, academic depth, and research rigor. She's been a CIO who knows the pressures of execution. She's been a trusted voice to C-suite leaders navigating disruption. And she earned her doctorate studying applied AI, resulting in the Five Pillars of AI Success, a framework that is helping countless organizations turn good AI intentions into business results.

Dr. Lisa understands what the best leaders already know: Bold AI Leadership is not about the latest algorithm ("a fool with a tool is still a fool!"). It's about people, building trust, communicating with clarity, and energizing teams around an exciting future.

That's why this book resonates so deeply with me. Not coincidentally, this book aligns perfectly with a set of characteristics I've observed across every great leader I've known. These leaders never allow themselves to get distracted by the latest bright shiny object. I call these the 7 Cs of Great

Leadership, and you will see how Dr. Lisa has masterfully woven these themes throughout her book. Let me highlight a few examples.

Customer: The best leaders put the customer at the center of their strategies. They ensure that everyone in the organization, from the front lines to the boardroom, is aligned around customer needs. Jeff Bezos famously called this "customer-back" thinking, and it has been one of Amazon's greatest differentiators.

Dr. Lisa makes that crystal clear. Her cautionary tale of the airline whose AI chatbot increased frustration, not loyalty, should be required reading for any leader. In contrast, her story of Starbucks' Deep Brew shows what happens when you start with the customer: personalized experiences, higher engagement, and direct revenue growth.

As PwC found, 73% of customers say experience drives buying decisions, yet 60% of AI projects fail because they ignore customer needs. This book's frameworks will help you avoid that trap. Dr. Lisa shows you how to align every AI effort with what your customers value, how to measure the right metrics, and how to ensure AI isn't just efficient, but delightful.

Culture: As Peter Drucker famously said, "Culture eats strategy for lunch." I've seen it happen over and over: organizations with perfect AI roadmaps fail because they didn't build a culture ready to absorb failure, iterate, and learn. Culture truly is the invisible force that determines success.

Dr. Lisa brilliantly devotes a chapter to building cultures where AI thrives. Imagine working in a place where curiosity replaces fear, experimentation is encouraged, and learning is capitalized. The book's case study contrasting Amazon's AI-embedded culture with a Fortune 500 retailer's failed rollout is a masterclass on why culture, not algorithms, determines success.

I especially love her Decision Evaluation Framework: simple, actionable questions that force cultural clarity before launching any initiative. Questions like "Will this democratize access?" or "Are we chasing signal or noise?" don't just guide AI, they shape the kind of culture you're building.

Cultivate: One of the greatest insights I've gleaned from great leaders is their genuine passion for setting their people up to thrive as a future-ready workforce. People/Talent are not the last pillar of their overarching strategy; they're the first. These leaders build workforce strategies that are more holistic, data-driven, and differentiated. They inspire ambition in their people. They know, grow, engage, retain, and attract the best workforces, setting their companies up to win.

Dr. Lisa shows that scaling AI isn't just about adding algorithms; it's about scaling your people's capacity to create value. Sarah Chen's journey reveals how AI pilots succeed when frontline employees become active participants, not passive users. The book's upskilling strategies—educating leaders, training cross-functional teams, and redefining roles to embrace Human + AI partnerships—are a blueprint for cultivating the agile, highly adaptive teams every organization needs.

And when resistance appears, Dr. Lisa demonstrates how AI literacy can turn skeptics into innovators, unlocking creativity across your workforce.

Courage: Fear is the enemy of progress. It's also the common denominator of courage, because without fear, there's no need for courage.

As I've studied successful transformations, there is always a "burn the ships" moment. There's that courageous act that signals to everyone that there's no turning back. That the path ahead, while uncertain, is the one we must take together.

Throughout the book, stories like Sarah's illustrate courage in action: transforming skepticism into trust, persisting through execution resistance, and building unstoppable momentum with the AI Performance Flywheel. Dr. Lisa operationalizes courage with practical tools like Visual Dartboarding, a way to move from abstract ideas to visual clarity that sparks alignment and action.

This book doesn't just tell you to be bold; it gives you a system for making bold decisions with speed and rigor, a necessity when AI moves faster than traditional decision cycles.

Change: The great leaders know how to take people on a journey, even when the road ahead is fraught with risk, unknowns, and the promise of hard work and long hours.

Driving lasting change takes a sustained top-down commitment and a strong, grassroots, bottom-up approach. It also takes what I call "winning the middle." Because middle management is the make-or-break layer. If you can move the middle from frozen to magic, you will have a greater likelihood of building and sustaining momentum.

The AI Performance Flywheel shows that success isn't a linear path. Rather, it's iterative and layered, cycling through foundation, execution, scale, and innovation. The Visualization Tool Decision Framework is a game-changer, helping leaders secure buy-in by turning complexity into clear, shareable visuals.

Southwest Airlines' iconic napkin sketch is the perfect metaphor: clarity and simplicity can launch billion-dollar ideas. Dr. Lisa shows how to apply that principle to AI adoption, recognizing that clear visuals create shared vision and unstoppable momentum.

Collaboration: "If you want to go fast, go alone. If you want to go far, go together." That proverb has never been more relevant. The journey ahead will require collaboration on a scale we haven't seen before, not just internally across functions, but externally with a growing ecosystem of partners, suppliers, and innovators.

AI is not a solo sport. It requires cross-functional collaboration at every level. The book's chapter on collaborative teams is one every CIO should bookmark. The story of John Deere integrating farmers, agronomists, and AI engineers proves how diversity of expertise transforms AI from a tech experiment into a business force.

Dr. Lisa's frameworks for orchestrating multiple AI initiatives across different maturity levels will help you avoid silos and tap into your organization's collective genius.

Communication: The best leaders differentiate themselves and their organizations by communicating with clarity. This is critical because we know confused minds don't act.

In the age of AI, clarity is more important than ever. We need everyone rowing in the same direction and at the speed of AI.

The most successful leaders don't just explain, they show. This book's relentless focus on visualization as a storytelling tool ensures AI doesn't remain an abstract mystery. Whether you're sharing opportunity maps with executives, risk heatmaps with boards, or customer journey maps with frontlines, Dr. Lisa gives you the visual tools to make your case. Once again, her frameworks will help you turn skepticism into engagement, hesitation into action, and disconnected ideas into enterprise-wide momentum.

Bringing It All Together: *Show AI—Don't Tell It* equips you with everything you need: a mindset grounded in human-centered business value, a strategy anchored in five success pillars, and an action plan that uses visual storytelling to drive alignment, execution, and innovation.

It reminds us that in the face of unprecedented technological acceleration, the leaders who win will be those who double down on the human side. Those who cultivate trust, clarity, collaboration, and culture at scale. Those who show the way *visibly, consistently, and boldly.*

This book closes with a powerful challenge: *start small, but make it visible.* Don't wait for the perfect moment, but instead, create momentum moments. Use these frameworks to make complexity simple, to turn AI from an initiative into a movement.

And above all, be the leader your organization needs now, the 7 Cs leader who can orchestrate transformation, inspire belief, and lead at the speed of AI.

Your teams are ready. Your stakeholders are watching. And the road ahead is wide open.

So here's my challenge to you:

Don't just talk about AI. Show it. Lead it. Build it. And let the results speak for themselves.

I'll be right here, cheering you on.

Bold AI Leadership: Lessons from a Hologram

A sports entertainment visionary, bursting with ideas to revolutionize fan engagement through AI, finds himself caught in a frustrating cycle. His inspired concepts for the future of sports tech are met with skeptical looks and tight purse strings. Sound familiar? It's the classic innovator's dilemma: how do you convince the cautious to invest in the extraordinary?

Enter our game-changing strategy. We didn't just pitch ideas; we brought them to life using our Show Not Tell approach. There was a collective gasp in the boardroom when our life-sized holographic chatbot materialized before their eyes, proudly sporting the team's colors and ready to interact with fans on game day.

But we didn't stop there.

We unveiled a 3D model that was part time machine, part LEGO set. As we scrolled through a timeline, stakeholders watched in awe as each new AI capability snapped into place, building a robust ecosystem of innovation. It wasn't just a presentation; it was a journey through the future of their business, with each step showing tangible, measurable outcomes.

The room felt electrified with possibility. Eyes widened, minds raced, and, suddenly, the "too risky" became the "can't miss." While our hologram wasn't the first step in their journey as foundational building blocks had to be laid first, it accomplished something incredibly valuable. It shattered the barriers of imagination, paving the way for practical, phased AI initiatives that everyone could get behind.

Fast-forward. The team knew that it was that visual experience, where a hologram rocked their jersey and an interactive 3D model showcased when and what business results they would get, that sealed the deal. In mere moments of Show Not Tell magic, skeptics became believers.

This story encapsulates what Bold AI Leadership looks like: leading with vision, overcoming skepticism, and building toward measurable success, one step at a time (see Figure P.1).

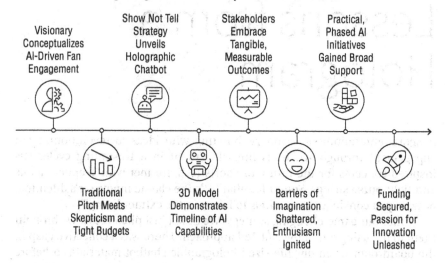

Igniting Innovation in Sports Entertainment

Visionary Conceptualizes AI-Driven Fan Engagement

Show Not Tell Strategy Unveils Holographic Chatbot

Stakeholders Embrace Tangible, Measurable Outcomes

Practical, Phased AI Initiatives Gained Broad Support

Traditional Pitch Meets Skepticism and Tight Budgets

3D Model Demonstrates Timeline of AI Capabilities

Barriers of Imagination Shattered, Enthusiasm Ignited

Funding Secured, Passion for Innovation Unleashed

FIGURE P.1   A hologram in team colors, coupled with a 3D timeline model, turned doubt into boardroom buy-in and ignited AI adoption.

Introduction: Why Leaders Need to Show Not Tell

Artificial intelligence is changing what leadership looks like. It's no longer enough to approve a budget and wait for results. Today's executives must guide strategy, build buy-in, and lead AI with the same clarity and conviction they bring to every other core part of the business. And yet, most leaders still struggle to answer one essential question.

How Do I Turn AI from Potential into Performance?

That's why I wrote this book. *Show AI—Don't Tell It* equips C-suite executives and business leaders with a pragmatic, proven system for turning AI initiatives into measurable business outcomes. The focus isn't on technical deep-dives. It's on what actually works when you need to align teams, secure funding, gain traction, and scale impact. I call this approach Bold AI Leadership, and it's built on three critical components (see Figure I.1):

- **Mindset:** The guiding principles that help leaders make confident, high-impact decisions about AI
- **Strategy:** The five success pillars that align AI with business value, customer outcomes, and organizational momentum
- **Action:** The visualization tools that make AI's impact visible, accelerate buy-in, and drive results at scale

Other books may talk about AI. This one shows you how to lead it boldly, pragmatically, and visibly.

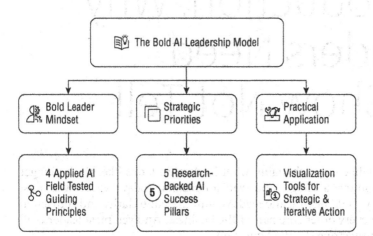

FIGURE I.1 The Bold AI Leadership Model illustrates how mindset, strategic priorities, and visualization tools drive concrete business results through AI.

What Makes This Approach Different

While many leaders are inspired by AI's potential, most struggle to communicate it in ways that spark action. Show Not Tell isn't just a storytelling technique; it's the key to making AI real inside the enterprise. I've seen firsthand how visual tools unlock alignment, especially in skeptical, siloed, or slow-moving organizations.

This book introduces tools, templates, and frameworks that I've used with hundreds of executive teams to:

- Translate AI strategy into business language
- Demonstrate ROI through early wins
- Turn resistance into momentum
- Align technical and non-technical teams around a shared path forward

The book is grounded in my Bold AI Leadership Model, developed through decades of real-world experience, research, and client work across industries. It's a playbook for forward-thinking leaders who are ready to move beyond the hype and show real business impact.

The Story That Sparked This Book

The inspiration for this book came from a real moment in the field: standing in a boardroom, helping a client use a holographic chatbot and a 3D timeline to bring their AI story to life. We didn't talk about models or data lakes. We *showed* how AI was saving time, reducing risk, and driving customer impact.

That single visualization flipped a room full of skeptics into believers and secured funding for one of the company's biggest strategic shifts. That experience became the seed for what I now teach every day: when you make AI's value visible, people move.

The Three-Part Structure

To make this system practical and repeatable, the book is divided into three parts, each focused on a key dimension of Bold AI Leadership: shaping the right mindset, establishing the strategic conditions for AI success, and driving action that delivers measurable results through visualization and momentum.

Mindset

The foundation of Bold AI Leadership is a confident, clear point of view. Part 1, "The Bold AI Leadership Mindset (The Four Applied AI Guiding Principles)," introduces the core beliefs and behaviors that separate reactive technology adopters from strategic AI leaders. You'll learn about the following:

- **Business Value:** Define a compelling vision grounded in measurable impact
- **Speed with Rigor:** Balance urgency with thoughtful execution
- **Simplicity:** Communicate AI clearly to earn trust and drive action
- **Human-Centricity:** Keep people at the center of AI strategy
- **The AI Performance Flywheel:** Apply my systematic approach to build and sustain momentum using structured execution

These chapters will help you craft a bold, business-grounded AI vision, balance urgency with execution discipline, communicate clearly to build trust, keep people at the center of change, and apply a repeatable system to turn vision into momentum.

Strategy

Once you have the mindset, you need a map. Part 2, "Strategic Priorities (The Five AI Success Pillars)," introduces my five research-backed strategic AI Success Pillars that keep AI initiatives aligned with enterprise priorities:

- **Business Value:** Solve real problems with measurable ROI
- **Customer-Centricity:** Focus AI efforts on experience, insight, and loyalty
- **Collaborative Teams:** Unite technical and business talent
- **Cultural Shifts:** Foster trust, literacy, and readiness
- **Data as a Strategic Asset:** Ensure quality, structure, and accessibility power your AI

Each pillar is explored through common pitfalls, practical frameworks, and real-world examples, so you can avoid false starts and build what lasts.

Action

Bold leadership demands more than belief; it demands execution. Part 3, "Bringing AI to Life (Visualization as a Catalyst for Change)," helps leaders bring their strategy to life by using visualization as a tool for alignment and momentum. It demonstrates how to:

- Win stakeholder buy-in
- Translate vision into clear execution paths
- Scale successful initiatives across the business

You'll learn how to apply visual storytelling and prototype-driven communication to overcome resistance, unify diverse teams, and scale momentum - whether you're leading a single AI pilot or transforming your entire operating model.

Who This Book Is For

If you're a CEO, CFO, CIO, COO, board member, or senior business leader who's expected to lead AI (but without a PhD in data science), this book is for you.

If you've ever asked:

- How do I get my board or executive peers to take AI seriously?
- What's the right way to frame AI investments around ROI?
- How do I build trust with my teams or confidence in our data?
- How do I scale what's working, while still experimenting and learning?

Then you're in the right place.

The Road Ahead

Throughout the book, you'll meet real and composite leaders like Sarah Chen of Central States Insurance Group - leaders dealing with the same challenges you face. Their stories bring the frameworks to life. You'll also discover parallels to disciplines like forecasting, behavioral economics, and systems thinking, because sometimes the best answers come from outside the AI echo chamber.

Above all, this book will challenge and equip you to:

- Lead boldly in the face of uncertainty
- Communicate clearly to inspire the skeptical
- Execute with speed, precision, and visual clarity to drive business impact

This isn't a tech manual. It's a leadership system. And it's how you'll transform AI from a buzzword into a business advantage, one win at a time.

The Road Ahead

PART 1

The Bold AI Leadership Mindset (The Four Applied AI Guiding Principles)

Part 1 introduces the foundational layer of the Bold AI Leadership Model: the mindset. To effectively lead AI initiatives, leaders need a clear and confident mindset, built upon four guiding principles: Business Value, Speed with Rigor, Simplicity, and Human-Centricity. I present these principles as the bedrock of successful AI adoption because they address fundamental challenges that organizations face.

I designed Business Value to establish the essential focus on delivering tangible results, ensuring that AI initiatives are driven by pragmatic innovation rather than technological hype. Speed with Rigor acknowledges the dynamic nature of today's markets, emphasizing the need for both agility and structure to achieve sustainable success. Simplicity is crucial for building trust and fostering widespread adoption by making AI approachable and understandable. Human-Centricity underscores the importance of prioritizing human capabilities and ensuring that AI augments humans, rather than replaces them. These four interconnected and mutually reinforcing principles equip executives to align their teams, make confident decisions, and drive AI initiatives that deliver measurable, lasting impact.

These principles - developed through deep concept exploration by myself and the founding team of my AI startup, drawing on our collective 110 years of technology experience, extensive market feedback, and insights from seasoned leaders across industries - are brought together and activated through the AI Performance Flywheel, introduced in Chapter 5. This repeatable system shows how Bold AI Leaders sustain momentum and turn strategic intent into measurable results. Grounded in modern, pragmatic realities, both the principles and the Flywheel have been refined and field-tested with hundreds of enterprises and public-sector clients.

In the following chapters, we'll explore each principle in detail, gaining actionable insights and real-world examples to guide your decision-making and empower bold leadership. I'll also lay the groundwork for practical application by including examples of visualization tools, equipping leaders with a clear understanding of how to communicate their AI vision effectively. These examples demonstrate how visualization can be applied to align with evolving goals and scale AI initiatives, a concept expanded in Part 3: Bringing AI to Life (Visualization as a Catalyst for Change). By the end of Part 1, readers will have the foundational mindset needed to confidently adopt the Bold AI Leadership Model, act boldly, and leverage visualization tools to foster alignment and inspire action.

CHAPTER 1

Business Value

Driving Business Success with Pragmatic AI Innovation

Both newcomers to AI and experienced practitioners face this core challenge. Organizations taking their first steps need to identify and prioritize opportunities where AI can create immediate value. Those already using AI must ensure their initiatives deliver measurable impact and align with strategic goals. This chapter provides a practical framework for both groups to transform AI from a promising technology into a proven driver of business success.

Introduction: The Foundation of Bold AI Leadership

This week, I spoke with the CIO of a multibillion-dollar mining company. He shared that they had recently invested millions in a big consulting company to help them "disrupt themselves." To their credit, they recognized that changing their business required a diversity of thought and approach that they couldn't accomplish alone. So, they brought in outsiders to help them innovate. Unfortunately, despite their investment of time, money, and opportunity cost, he was very disappointed in the results. In my many years as an executive advisor, I've heard this tale over and over again.

Why does this keep happening? True disruption requires laser focus on the opportunity that you're trying to grab or the problem you're trying to solve. You must hold fast to clarity of the *job that needs to be done*: on creating business value. The CIO was disappointed because the outcome that they gained was an iteration from where they started, an operational gain no doubt, but it wasn't the new business model he desired. Without clarity of purpose, even the best-funded efforts will falter.

Key Takeaways:

- **For Organizations Beginning Their AI Journey:** Start by clearly defining the business outcome you want to achieve, whether it's operational improvement or business model transformation. Focus on specific, measurable objectives rather than vague goals like "disruption." Some processes may be right for automation, while others need human-AI collaboration.

- **For Organizations Scaling AI:** Regularly reassess if your AI initiatives are delivering their intended business impact. Look for opportunities to both automate routine operations *and* transform how you do business. Balance quick operational wins with longer-term strategic innovations.

Admittedly, the focus on business value may seem obvious. Of course, leaders are focused on creating tangible value. That's the whole point, right? Yet, it's more complicated than it appears. Breaking free from the web of deeply entrenched mindsets, processes, policies, and "we've always done it this way" assumptions is no small task.

Organizations that are succeeding with AI approach every initiative with a relentless focus on outcomes. Some are targeting operational efficiencies (arguably the low-hanging fruit of AI). Others are using AI to create entirely new business models, add revenue streams, design innovative products, or transform customer experiences.

Take, for example, an FTSE 100 hospitality group in the United Kingdom that I studied in my doctoral research. Their leadership didn't look first to AI to cut costs or optimize existing processes. Instead, they set a bold goal: to drive revenue growth. This focus on the top line, rather than the bottom line, set them apart and positioned them for competitive advantage.

As Nikola Mrkšić, CEO of PolyAI - a voice AI company who landed this group as their first enterprise AI client - explained, "Revenue growth is magical. It gets people to move." And move they did, aligning their teams and unlocking the transformative potential of AI to propel their business forward. This example shows that AI isn't just a tool for operational improvements. It can be a driver of offensive strategies, fueling revenue growth, market expansion, and entirely new business models.

These two stories, the mining company and the hospitality group, highlight why Business Value is the foundation of the Bold AI Leadership Model. Whether you're streamlining operations or pursuing bold new growth opportunities, success depends on anchoring every AI initiative to tangible, measurable outcomes.

Both my professional experience and research fully support this conclusion. In fact, Business Value isn't just one principle of Bold AI Leadership; it's the most essential one. Every decision you make, every tool you implement, and every innovation you pursue must ultimately drive business value to succeed.

In this chapter, we'll explore how to do exactly that. You'll learn what Business Value means in the context of AI, the common pitfalls that prevent organizations from achieving it, and actionable steps to embed this principle into every initiative. Most importantly, you'll see how focusing on business value transforms AI from a buzzword into a true driver of measurable success.

Let's dive in.

Definition: Business Value in the Context of AI

At its core, Business Value is about outcomes that matter: measurable results that drive success. In the context of AI, it means anchoring every initiative to tangible goals like revenue growth, operational efficiency, or improved customer satisfaction. It's not just the technology itself; it's what that technology enables you to achieve.

This focus on Business Value is both simple and deceptively challenging. Of course, leaders know they need to create value. But too often, organizations lose sight of this fundamental principle. They get caught up in the excitement of new tools and possibilities and pursue projects that feel innovative but fail to deliver meaningful results.

In my experience and research, the organizations succeeding with AI approach every initiative with laser focus. They start by answering a basic but essential question: what is the job we're trying to get done? From there, they prioritize AI efforts that solve real problems, seize real opportunities, and drive real value. Then, they consistently ask and re-ask themselves this question as AI efforts progress. It's ridiculously easy to fall into old behavior patterns or to follow "shiny" technology paths. This disciplined approach ensures their AI efforts remain focused on outcomes that truly matter. These outcomes typically fall into three categories:

- **Driving Efficiency:** Automating processes, reducing costs, and freeing up resources for higher-value work
- **Enhancing Customer Experiences:** Personalizing interactions, improving satisfaction, and building loyalty
- **Creating New Revenue Streams:** Innovating products, expanding markets, and redefining business models

Business Value is the compass that keeps AI efforts on course. Without it, even well-funded initiatives risk becoming distractions. Leaders who embrace this principle know that harnessing AI doesn't mean chasing trends or building "toy projects" that fail to deliver. It means staying relentlessly focused on what matters most: creating measurable value that moves the business forward.

This principle is more than just a guiding idea; it's the foundation of Bold AI Leadership. It ensures that every decision, every project, and every investment is grounded in outcomes that make a real difference.

Pitfalls: The Risks of Losing Sight of Business Value

AI's transformative potential is undeniable, but the road to success is filled with traps that can derail even the best-intentioned. These pitfalls aren't just minor missteps. They squander valuable resources, erode stakeholder trust, and prevent organizations from realizing AI's true potential.

The pattern reveals itself consistently in boardrooms and executive meetings. Leaders, inspired by AI's promise but uncertain of the path forward, often lose sight of fundamental business principles. Without a clear vision of business value creation, organizations chase technical sophistication rather than practical outcomes. Pilot projects generate initial excitement but fail to scale. Resources drain away without meaningful returns. Eventually, enthusiasm gives way to frustration as promised outcomes remain elusive.

This section explores the most common pitfalls organizations face on their journey to becoming businesses fueled by AI, from the unmatched risks of inaction to the subtle trap of "toy AI" projects. I also address the dangers of business strategy misalignment, the inability to measure return on investment (ROI), missed opportunities for innovation, trust erosion among stakeholders, and why efforts stall at the pilot stage. By understanding these challenges, you'll be better equipped to navigate the complex terrain of AI adoption and position your organization for sustainable success.

Here's where things often go wrong.

Failing to Act

The greatest pitfall in AI adoption isn't chasing the wrong projects or failing to measure ROI; it's doing nothing at all. When I hear clients say "We're waiting to see what happens before we invest in AI," my response often surprises them: "I didn't realize you were so risk-tolerant." This catches them off guard because they believe they're avoiding risk by holding back.

The truth is, standing still in today's rapidly evolving markets is the ultimate gamble. While you wait, your competitors are leveraging AI to innovate, streamline operations, and deliver superior customer experiences. The gap between adopters and hesitators grows wider with each passing day, leaving the latter scrambling to catch up. Inaction doesn't just mean missed opportunities; it opens the door for disruption by bolder, more forward-thinking competitors. Every industry has its own "Blockbuster moment." The question isn't whether disruption is coming; it's whether you'll be the one driving it or the one left behind.

"Toy AI" Wastes Resources

Too often, organizations fall into the trap of what I call "toy AI projects" - flashy, experimental initiatives that look exciting in a demo but fail to deliver meaningful results. These projects may showcase cutting-edge AI capabilities, but they lack alignment with strategic goals and don't solve real business problems. Time, money, and talent are spent chasing shiny ideas that ultimately contribute little to the organization's success.

The allure of "toy AI" can lie simply in its novelty or be more nuanced. Projects that are technologically impressive or trend-driven are tempting to pursue, but they often distract from the real work of creating business value. The more insidious challenge presents itself when it seems like it's a well-aligned business investment.

The line between strategic investment and costly distraction can be deceptively thin. Consider Metaphysic, a company specializing in hyper-realistic synthetic media. They grabbed attention by creating incredibly life-like deepfake videos of celebrities like Tom Cruise for TikTok. Their viral deepfake demonstrations leveraged their core technical capabilities - exactly the kind of AI work they excelled at. This makes it a particularly instructive example, since it could have easily been justified internally as "playing to our strengths."

Yet despite aligning with their technical expertise, these attention-grabbing demonstrations consumed valuable resources without advancing strategic business goals. Instead of chasing social media moments, Metaphysic could have directed those same capabilities toward solving specific industry problems, like enabling personalized, high-quality content production at scale for film studios or advertising agencies. This would have transformed their technical prowess into sustainable revenue streams and market leadership.

This case highlights how subtle the "toy AI" trap can be: initiatives can appear strategically sound because they utilize your core capabilities yet still drain resources without creating real business value. Success requires not just technical alignment but ruthless focus on tangible business outcomes. The question isn't just "Can we do this well?" but "Will this drive meaningful results?"

Misalignment with Strategic Goals

When AI projects aren't tied to clear business objectives, they quickly drift off-course. I've seen teams pour months of effort into initiatives that have no connection to their company's strategic priorities. It's not that the technology is bad; it's that the focus is missing. Without alignment, AI becomes a collection of disconnected experiments that fail to gain leadership support or scale into something impactful. Even worse, this often leaves an organization-wide perception that AI is a waste of resources - a reputation hurdle that's hard to overcome and often lingers long after the project has failed, making it even tougher for forward-thinking leaders to secure approval for future AI initiatives.

Inability to Measure ROI

One of the biggest pitfalls I've seen with AI projects is the failure to set clear metrics for success. If you don't know how to measure business value, how can you prove it? Without defined ROI metrics tied to specific outcomes, it's impossible to gauge whether an initiative is delivering results. This lack of clarity leads to skepticism from stakeholders, makes it harder to secure funding for future projects, and leaves leadership questioning whether AI is a cost rather than an investment.

When organizations dive into AI initiatives without measurable targets, they lose the ability to evaluate progress or determine success. Projects may be technologically impressive, but if there's no tangible impact on efficiency, customer satisfaction, or the bottom line, their value remains invisible. Without clear metrics, leadership is left asking, "What did we actually accomplish?" And when that question can't be answered, the result is hesitation to support future AI investments.

This uncertainty creates a vicious cycle. Without proof of success, stakeholders grow skeptical, and future projects struggle to gain traction. Over time, the organization risks developing a reputation for failed AI efforts, making it even harder for forward-thinking leaders to get approval for bold new initiatives.

Contrast this with Intel's use of AI to manage spare parts, which is a prime example of how measuring ROI can build trust and momentum. By implementing an algorithm to automatically set inventory targets, AI that planners now trust 99% of the time, they achieved a 30% reduction in inventory and saved $600 million over two years. This wasn't just a showcase of impressive technology; it was a carefully aligned initiative designed to solve a real business challenge with clear, measurable outcomes.

Missed Opportunities for Innovation

When organizations lose sight of business value creation, they often fall into a common trap: their internal teams, sharing similar mindsets and biases, gravitate toward safe, incremental improvements or surface-level technology adoption. Bring together a group of smart, talented internal people, and they will undoubtedly increment their way to a better place than you're in today. But incremental gains are not the same as transformative change. This is why I consistently advise clients that breakthrough innovation rarely emerges from within. True disruption (the kind that reshapes markets) requires fresh, outside perspectives to challenge entrenched thinking and uncover blind spots.

These customer conversations always remind me of the famous Henry Ford quote: "If I had asked people what they wanted, they would have said faster horses." Disruption doesn't come from doing what's expected or sticking to what's comfortable. It requires stepping beyond familiar territory and envisioning a completely different future. Consider major market transformations like Netflix vs. Blockbuster or Uber vs. taxis. These seismic shifts didn't come from incumbents. They came from bold outsiders who reimagined the industry and seized opportunities others couldn't see.

The same principle applies to AI adoption. Instead of using AI to revolutionize customer experiences or create entirely new revenue streams, teams often default to tweaking existing processes or implementing technology without a clear purpose. The transformative power of AI - its ability to unlock entirely new possibilities and business models - often remains untapped.

Organizations need external catalysts to break free from shared mental limitations and imagine bolder futures. Without these outside voices, the most valuable opportunities often remain invisible, hiding in plain sight.

Erosion of Stakeholder Trust

When AI projects fail to deliver results, the ripple effects extend far beyond leadership's immediate disappointment. A lack of tangible outcomes can erode trust among two critical stakeholder groups: employees and customers. This loss of confidence makes it significantly harder to gain support for future initiatives, leaving organizations in a precarious position.

Employees are often the first to feel the impact when AI initiatives fall short. Without transparency or clear value, skepticism grows. Workers may view AI as a "black box" - a mysterious system making decisions they don't understand or trust. Worse, if AI is perceived as a threat to job security rather than a tool to enhance workflows, resistance is inevitable.

When employees aren't involved in the process, whether through training, input on system design, or understanding how AI improves their roles, they're less likely to buy into its success. Over time, this disillusionment can sap motivation and cause overt or covert resistance to future AI implementations.

Trust also erodes on the customer side when AI fails to meet expectations. For instance, customer-facing AI systems that provide subpar service or make errors can damage the company's reputation and reduce engagement. Customers expect AI to enhance their interactions through faster responses, personalized recommendations, or accurate support. When those expectations aren't met, it's not just the AI that's questioned; it's the organization as a whole.

Bench Accounting's sudden closure in December 2024 serves as a sobering lesson about the risks of poor AI implementation. The bookkeeping service had built its operations around machine learning automation, with human bookkeepers increasingly taking a back seat. When their AI systems stumbled, the company's lean support team, lacking deep accounting expertise, struggled to catch and correct mounting errors. Customer trust eroded as accuracy issues compounded, ultimately contributing to the company's collapse.

This case starkly illustrates how AI can become a liability when deployed without adequate human oversight and expertise. While automation promised efficiency gains, Bench's focus on technology-driven scale overshadowed the fundamental need for accuracy and customer service in financial services. Their story reminds us that AI should augment (not replace) human judgment in critical business functions, especially where trust is paramount.

Failure to Scale

Scaling AI beyond pilots remains a critical challenge for organizations. Despite promising technical demonstrations, many AI initiatives fail to expand because they can't demonstrate concrete business impact. This gap between potential and realized value creates a cycle where leadership hesitates to invest further, leaving transformative opportunities untapped. Here are critical reasons why AI initiatives fail to scale:

- **Value Definition Gap:** Organizations often struggle to connect AI capabilities to measurable business outcomes. Without clear ROI metrics, even successful pilots fail to secure the investment needed for broader deployment. Success requires shifting focus from technical achievements to tangible business impact.

- **Strategic Misalignment:** AI projects must directly advance core business objectives to gain leadership support. Initiatives that enhance customer experience, drive operational efficiency, or enable new revenue streams scale more successfully than those focused purely on technical innovation.

- **Data Foundation Weaknesses:** Scaling AI demands robust data infrastructure and governance. Poor data quality, limited access, or inadequate cloud infrastructure can cripple expansion efforts. Organizations must build a strong data foundation before attempting to scale.

- **Organizational Silos:** Traditional hierarchies often impede the cross-functional collaboration essential for AI scaling. Success requires seamless coordination between technical teams, domain experts, and business units through matrix organizational structures.

- **Cultural Barriers:** Scaling AI requires a cultural mindset that embraces learning, adaptability, and collaboration. Many organizations fail because of behaviors that reveal deep cultural resistance:

  - **Fear-Driven Decisions:** Teams, paralyzed by the fear of errors, impose excessive governance, demand perfect accuracy, and treat every setback as a crisis rather than a learning opportunity.

  - **Siloed Expertise:** Knowledge is hoarded within technical teams, leaving business units as passive customers instead of active collaborators. Domain experts are excluded from development, creating disconnects in execution.

  - **Change Resistance:** Teams cling to manual processes, defending outdated workflows and viewing AI as a threat rather than an enabler of progress.

  - **Misaligned Incentives:** Short-term metrics dominate, discouraging experimentation and cross-functional collaboration. Success is narrowly defined by technical metrics, not business impact.

  - **Quick-Fix Mindset:** Organizations chase immediate ROI without investing in learning, rush to complex solutions before mastering basics, and treat AI as a magic bullet rather than a capability that requires cultivation. In contrast, organizations that thrive with AI recognize learning itself as a form of ROI. They view experimentation and setbacks as opportunities to refine their capabilities, progressively building from simple solutions to more complex applications. This mindset shift creates the foundation for sustained success, enabling teams to scale AI initiatives with confidence.

The Hard Truth

The truth is, pursuing AI without a relentless focus on business value is a risky game. It's not enough to chase trends or try something new just to say you've done it. Leaders must anchor every effort to tangible, measurable outcomes that align with their strategic goals.

When organizations fail to prioritize business value, they waste resources, erode trust, and miss opportunities for meaningful innovation. But when they get it right? That's when AI becomes a driver of real change - solving problems, seizing opportunities, and delivering results that matter.

Actionable Steps: Embedding Business Value into Every AI Initiative

To transform AI from an abstract concept into a tangible, business-driving force, leaders must move beyond explanation to demonstration. Significant change, like that brought by AI, often feels intangible or overwhelming, making it difficult for people to grasp its potential and implications. This is why Show Not Tell is a cornerstone of Bold AI Leadership. By visualizing a clear future state and leveraging storytelling tools, leaders can ease the mental journey for their teams, helping stakeholders see the possibilities, understand the impact, and align around the path forward.

Think back to the hologram story from the book's preface. Imagine that boardroom filled with skeptical stakeholders, unsure of AI's potential to revolutionize their business. Then, a life-sized holographic chatbot appears, proudly sporting the team's colors and ready to interact with fans on game day. Complex problems are solved in real time, while AI handles routine tasks in the background. They aren't just hearing about AI's possibilities; they're seeing them. This vivid demonstration of the Human + AI Partnership transformed doubt into excitement, helping secure leadership buy-in for phased AI implementation. It's the difference between showing a flat floor plan on paper and walking someone through a fully rendered, interactive 3D model of a skyscraper. One is abstract and static; the other is immersive and transformative, making the future feel not just possible but inevitable.

This section outlines seven actionable steps to guide leaders in integrating Show Not Tell into every phase of their AI journey. By visually surfacing Business Value in every AI initiative, you'll turn skepticism into alignment and hesitation into action. My practical approach, centered on vivid demonstrations, measurable outcomes, and the Human + AI Partnership, is designed to help you turn AI potential into real-world business results:

1. **Define the Job to Be Done:** Clearly identify the core task or outcome you're trying to achieve.
2. **Align AI Projects with Strategic Goals:** Demonstrate how AI initiatives advance broader business objectives.
3. **Start with Minimum Viable Experiences (MVEs):** Begin with small, achievable steps to prove value.

4. **Measure ROI with Clear Metrics:** Establish how you will quantify the initiative's success.
5. **Foster Cross-Functional Collaboration:** Ensure seamless collaboration and alignment across teams.
6. **Embrace Iterative Learning:** Use early results to inform and continuously improve AI efforts.
7. **Cultivate an AI-Ready Culture:** Build an organizational environment that supports sustainable AI adoption.

The following narrative demonstrates how these steps can be applied to drive tangible business results.

Senior Operations Manager Swati faced a daunting challenge at Syntho-Fab, a sprawling manufacturing conglomerate: crippling inefficiencies, skyrocketing production costs, and consistently missed deadlines. She believed AI could revolutionize their outdated processes, but skepticism ran deep. To succeed, Swati knew she had to do more than implement AI; she had to *show* its value to her resistant team and budget-conscious executives. Driven by a set of seven actionable steps, Swati embarked on her journey.

Step 1: Define the Job to Be Done

To avoid chasing "toy AI" and ensure initiatives delivered real value, Swati began with a stark assessment of SynthoFab's problems. She stood before her whiteboard, three markers in hand, mapping out their pain points:

- $3.8M in excess inventory costs
- 40% production line downtime
- 65% on-time delivery rate
- 8-week average production delays

"We're not just bleeding money," she told her team. "We're losing market share every day we delay."

She drew a circle around one number: $3.8M. "This is where we start. Not with AI buzzwords, but with a clear problem to solve: optimizing our inventory and production flow."

Visualization Tip

To effectively Define the Job to Be Done, create a simple "Before & After" comparison of the current and future workflows. Use visuals like red arrows to highlight current inefficiencies and cost leaks, and green arrows to depict the streamlined, AI-optimized future. Clearly display key performance indicators (KPIs) to make the potential impact of AI undeniably clear.

Step 2: Align AI Projects with Strategic Goals

In the boardroom, Swati faced skeptical executives. "Another technology project?" the CFO frowned. "We need cost savings and revenue growth, not experiments."

Swati revealed her alignment map:

- **Corporate Goal:** 20% cost reduction by Q4
- **AI Solution:** Predictive inventory management
- **Expected Impact:** $2M savings in year 1

    → Reduced storage costs

    → Lowered waste

    → Optimized ordering

"This isn't about experimenting," she explained. "It's about hitting our numbers."

Visualization Tip

Visualize the alignment of AI projects with strategic goals using a "Goal-AI Solution-Impact" framework. For each AI initiative, clearly show the corresponding corporate goal, the AI solution implemented, and the expected business impact with measurable outcomes. This visual connects AI efforts directly to strategic priorities, demonstrating their contribution to the company's success.

Step 3: Start with Minimum Viable Experiences (MVEs)

Swati knew that a full-scale AI rollout would be too risky at this stage. They needed to test the waters, learn, iterate, and build confidence.

"We start small," Swati told her pilot team. "One production line. Two weeks."

She sketched their MVE:

- **Focus:** High-volume components only
- **Scope:** Warehouse A

- **Timeline:** 14 days
- **Success Metric:** 15% inventory reduction

"If we fail, we fail fast and learn. If we succeed..."
The Production Manager finished her sentence: "We scale."

Visualization Tip

To clearly communicate the value of your MVE, create a "Before & After Process Map." The "Before" side shows the current process for the chosen scope (e.g., a specific production line) and highlights the inefficiencies you aim to address. The "After" side visualizes the AI-enhanced process, demonstrating the expected improvements. Quantify the impact with the chosen success metric (e.g., a 15% reduction in inventory) to make the value tangible.

Step 4: Measure ROI with Clear Metrics

Swati knew that early, measurable results were crucial to build momentum. And that she'd have to prove hard ROI to ensure that more AI projects were undertaken later. (She had her eye on a new product design/development effort next!) So, after the first week of the AI-driven inventory optimization pilot, Swati's dashboard took shape:
Week 1:

- **Inventory Levels:** −8%
- **Storage Costs:** −$45,000
- **Order Accuracy:** 92%
- **Production Delays:** −15%

"Numbers don't lie," she told the steering committee. "And these numbers tell us we're onto something."

Visualization Tip

To effectively demonstrate ROI, create a "Before & After" visualization of key metrics. Show the "Before" state with baseline data and the "After" state with AI-driven improvements. Use visuals like side-by-side comparisons or a timeline to highlight the change. Quantify the difference with clear ROI figures (e.g., "AI reduced storage costs by $45,000 in the first week").

Step 5: Foster Cross-Functional Collaboration

Swati knew that AI initiatives often failed because of departmental silos. Data was trapped in separate systems, and teams rarely communicated effectively. To truly optimize SynthoFab's operations with AI, she understood that collaboration was essential. She couldn't have techies working in isolation; they needed input from those who understood the day-to-day realities of the business. To break down these walls and achieve a common goal of optimizing inventory and production flow, Swati gathered her cross-functional team members:

- James from Warehouse Operations
- Mei from Data Science
- Carlos from Production
- Sarah from Finance
- IT Systems Lead
- Quality Control Lead
- Shop Floor Supervisor
- HR Representative
- Supplier Relations Manager

"AI isn't just a bunch of algorithms," she explained, drawing connecting lines between their roles on a whiteboard. "It has the power to augment how we work together."

Each week, they huddled around real-time dashboards, spotting patterns in inventory, production flow, and financial data that human eyes had missed for years.

Visualization Tip

To clarify roles, responsibilities, and expected impacts in AI projects, adapt the RACI chart. RACI is a tool used to define who is **R**esponsible, **A**ccountable, **C**onsulted, and **I**nformed in a process. For AI initiatives, create a "RACI + Impact Chart" with these columns (see Figure 1.1):

- Role (e.g., Data Scientist, Business Analyst, Department Head)
- Responsibility (e.g., Data Preparation, Model Training, Business Requirements)
- Accountability (e.g., Model Accuracy, Data Quality, Business Outcome)
- Consulted (Who provides input)
- Informed (Who is kept updated)
- Impact (What specific impact is this role responsible for ensuring?)

RACI + Impact Chart: SynthoFab Inventory Optimization Project

Role	Responsibility	Accountability	Consulted	Informed	Impact (I am responsible for delivering)
Swati (Senior Operations Manager)	Project oversight, stakeholder management, resource allocation	Overall project success, ROI achievement	C-Suite, Finance, IT	Board, Shareholders	$3.8M cost reduction, 40% efficiency improvement
James (Warehouse Operations Lead)	Daily operations, process changes, staff training	Inventory accuracy, warehouse efficiency	Production team, Suppliers	Operations staff	32% inventory cost reduction, improved storage utilization
Mei (Data Scientist)	Model development, data analysis, algorithm optimization	Model accuracy, prediction reliability	IT, Operations	Project team	25% improvement in prediction accuracy, reduced stockouts
Carlos (Production Manager)	Production scheduling, resource optimization	Production efficiency, output quality	Warehouse team, Quality Control	Shop floor staff	45% production efficiency increase, reduced downtime
Sarah (Finance Analyst)	Cost tracking, ROI analysis, budget management	Financial reporting, cost control	Accounting, Operations	Management team	$2.8M validated cost savings, accurate forecasting
IT Systems Lead	Technical infrastructure, system integration	System uptime, data security	Data Science team, Operations	All users	99.9% system availability, seamless integration
Quality Control Lead	Quality standards, compliance	Product quality, compliance	Production, Operations	All departments	Reduced defects, maintained standards
Shop Floor Supervisor	Implementation oversight, team adoption	Daily execution, staff engagement	Production team, Operations	Shop floor staff	89% on-time delivery, improved workflow
HR Representative	Change management, training coordination	Staff readiness, skill development	All departments	All employees	Increased AI adoption, reduced resistance
Supplier Relations Manager	Supply chain coordination, vendor management	Supply chain optimization	Warehouse, Production	Vendors	Optimized ordering, improved vendor performance

FIGURE 1.1 SynthoFab RACI + Impact Chart.

Step 6: Embrace Iterative Learning

After three months of successful AI implementation, Swati's team encountered a significant challenge with direct business consequences. The AI model, which had been accurately predicting demand and optimizing production schedules, started to produce inaccurate forecasts. This wasn't just a technical glitch; it led to disruptions in the supply chain, as production schedules were thrown off, causing delays in fulfilling customer orders and increasing expedited shipping costs. Swati knew that AI systems aren't "set it and forget it"; they require ongoing monitoring and maintenance to prevent "drift" - a gradual decline in performance over time. So, instead of downplaying the issue or looking for someone to blame, she brought it to the forefront, framing it as a valuable opportunity to learn and refine the system.

So, instead of downplaying the issue, she brought it to the forefront, framing it as a chance to learn and refine the system.

Learning Loop:

- **Issue:** Seasonal variations skewing data (initially overlooked by the model).
- **Action:** Added weather data to model (to account for the seasonal impact).
- **Result:** 25% improvement in accuracy.
- **Next:** Expanding to global factors (like economic indicators). "Every setback is data," she reminded her team. "And data makes us better."

Visualization Tip

For business leaders, visualizing AI performance over time is essential. Use a "Learning Loop Visualization" to track key metrics relevant to business goals (e.g., forecast accuracy, cost savings, production efficiency). Show the initial performance, the point where performance declined ("drift"), the corrective actions you took, and the resulting improvements. This visual clearly demonstrates the value of iterative learning and helps secure continued support for AI initiatives.

Step 7: Cultivate an AI-Ready Culture

Swati understood that AI's success hinged on more than just technology; it required a fundamental cultural transformation at SynthoFab. She worked tirelessly to build trust, encourage collaboration, and empower employees to embrace AI as a partner.

Six months later, Swati stood in the same boardroom, but everything had changed:

- **Inventory Costs:** Down 32%
- **Production Efficiency:** Up 45%
- **On-Time Delivery:** 89%
- **Cost Savings:** $2.8M

Her proudest achievement was on the factory floor. Operators who once feared AI now used it daily, suggesting improvements and spotting opportunities.

"The technology was the easy part," she reflected. "The real transformation was in how we think and work."

Visualization Tip

The AI Transformation Split-Screen Dashboard (see Figure 1.2) powerfully illustrates the before and after states of AI integration in your organization. Think of it as a "transformation mirror" that reflects both where your organization started and what it has become. The split-screen format immediately shows stakeholders the contrast between traditional operations and AI-enhanced workflows, while the bottom metrics panel provides concrete evidence of improvement.

The dashboard combines three critical views:

- Direct role comparisons showing how AI transforms daily work
- Key performance metrics highlighting quantifiable improvements
- Collaboration patterns demonstrating enhanced cross-functional teamwork

This visualization is particularly effective for leadership presentations because it takes abstract concepts like "digital transformation" and "AI integration" and makes them tangible through specific examples and measurable outcomes. Use this dashboard early in your AI journey to show the potential future state, then update it with real metrics as your transformation progresses.

Pro Tip

Keep the metrics simple and impactful. Four to six key numbers that show clear improvement are more powerful than a complex array of statistics. Focus on metrics that matter to your specific audience: operational metrics for the operations team, financial metrics for the finance team, and so on.

SynthoFab's AI Transformation Journey

Cultural and Operational Evolution Dashboard

Before AI Integration	After AI Integration
Operations Manager: Manual scheduling, reactive problem-solving	**Operations Manager:** Strategic oversight, predictive optimization
Warehouse Staff: Physical inventory counts, paper-based tracking	**Warehouse Staff:** AI-assisted inventory management, digital tracking
Quality Control: Sample-based inspections, delayed reporting	**Quality Control:** AI-powered continuous monitoring, real-time alerts

Employee Satisfaction	Strategic Work Time	Employee Satisfaction	Strategic Work Time
65%	**30%**	**89%** ↑	**70%** ↑

Limited cross-functional collaboration	Enhanced cross-functional collaboration network

AI Adoption Rate	Monthly AI Suggestions	Process Automation	Time Saved
85%	**45**	**60%**	**25hrs**
Across all departments	From employees	Of routine tasks	Per employee/month

FIGURE 1.2   The AI Transformation Split-Screen Dashboard: Before and after view of organizational roles, metrics, and collaboration patterns, highlighting the tangible impact of AI integration on daily operations.

Real-World Story: Walmart's AI-Driven Search Improvement

To illustrate the Show Not Tell concept (demonstrating AI's value through tangible results), consider Walmart's AI-driven search improvement. This real-world story provides a compelling example of how a focus on Business Value, paired with actionable demonstrations, drives measurable success.

- **The Job to Be Done:** Improve online shopping experiences and drive revenue by delivering more relevant search results.
  - ○ **Current State:** Customers in international markets struggle with irrelevant search results that fail to account for linguistic and cultural nuances, leading to frustration and lost sales.
  - ○ **Future State:** An AI-powered search system optimizes relevance across multiple languages and cultural contexts, increasing customer satisfaction and conversion rates.

- **AI's Role:** Analyze customer behavior, optimize search algorithms, and adapt dynamically to new markets.
- **Human's Role:** Oversee algorithm adjustments, interpret analytics, and guide expansion strategies.
- **Outcome:** Walmart's AI-driven solution enhanced search precision, resulting in increased customer engagement, higher sales, and improved customer satisfaction in international markets. Leadership reported that all relevant KPIs - clicks, conversions, and revenue - showed significant improvement.

Visualization Tip

Create a "Customer Journey Split-Screen" showing two paths side-by-side. On the left: the current state with friction points highlighted in red (delays, errors, frustrations). On the right: the AI-enhanced experience with improvements in green (speed, accuracy, satisfaction). Add a metrics panel below showing key business impact: reduced errors, faster completion times, and improved customer satisfaction.

Key Takeaways:

- **For Organizations Beginning Their AI Journey:** Start with a clearly defined business problem where AI can create immediate value. Walmart's example shows how focusing on a specific pain point (search relevance) provides a clear metric for success. Consider starting with a single market or product line to prove value before scaling.
- **For Organizations Scaling AI:** Look for opportunities to extend successful AI implementations across new markets or use cases. Balance automation of routine tasks (like search optimization) with human oversight for cultural nuances and strategic decisions. Use early wins to build momentum for more ambitious transformations.

Visualization Tool Example for Business Value

Visualize AI's impact on customer experience with the Customer Experience Pulse (see Figure 1.3). This tool offers a real-time view of AI interactions shaping customer behavior, which allows for informed decisions, team alignment, and accelerated implementation. See Appendix A for implementation steps and key success indicators.

FIGURE 1.3 Customer Experience Pulse (basic example): See the real-time impact of AI on your business.

The Customer Experience Pulse Helps Leaders:

- Track and visualize how AI interactions shape customer behavior and business outcomes
- Utilize data points like Journey Interaction Metrics and Business Impact Metrics
- Leverage display formats like Interactive Journey Maps and Performance Indicators
- Understand update frequency and sample metrics for effective analysis

The tool is implemented through steps like Journey Mapping, Data Integration, Visualization Setup, and Feedback Integration, addressing common pitfalls such as Data Overload, Context Gaps, and Delayed Response. Success is indicated by Usage Metrics, Performance Impact, and Business Outcomes.

From Insight to Action

By providing a clear, real-time view of how AI shapes customer behavior, the Customer Experience Pulse empowers teams to make informed decisions, drive team alignment, and accelerate implementation. Remember, the goal isn't just to collect data; it's to inspire action. When teams can see how AI impacts customer behavior in real time, they're better equipped to make decisions that drive meaningful business outcomes. But what does true transformation look like? Let's consider this contrast.

Closing: Turning Vision into Action

Picture two scenes from the mining industry:

Scene 1: Present Day

A CIO stands in a control room filled with screens showing AI-powered dashboards. Despite millions invested, the results flash before him in frustrating increments: 2% efficiency gain here, 3% cost reduction there. "We're doing better," he sighs, "but not transforming."

Scene 2: The Possible Future

The control room now features a new display: "Digital Twin Marketplace - Revenue: $50M." The mining company has transformed its AI-powered operational models into a stand-alone product. A young engineer demonstrates their platform to a potential client: "See how our AI detected subtle vibration patterns in this haul truck fleet? That insight alone saved us $2M in prevented breakdowns." Behind her, screens show real-time equipment health scores from subscriber sites across three continents. The CIO smiles, remembering when their AI was just an internal cost-saving tool. Now it's generating subscription revenue that rivals their traditional mining operations. They're not just mining minerals anymore; they're mining their expertise.

The gap between these scenes illustrates this chapter's core message: AI success isn't built on technical capability alone. It's built on showing, not telling, what's possible. Remember the hologram from the book's preface? It didn't just present data. It transported stakeholders into a future they could see, touch, and believe in.

Think about your organization. What's your Scene 1 and Scene 2? What specific, vivid demonstration could bridge that gap? This chapter has equipped you with tools to make that future tangible, to move from abstract possibilities to concrete results. In the chapters ahead, we'll deepen this foundation, showing you how Bold AI Leaders turn visualization into transformation.

Key Takeaways:

- **For Organizations Beginning Their AI Journey:** Start by identifying your core expertise that could be monetized. Look beyond simple efficiency gains to identify potential new revenue streams. Begin with internal improvements that could later become external offerings.

- **For Organizations Scaling AI:** Consider how your AI solutions could create new business models. Look for opportunities to transform internal capabilities into marketable products or services. Balance operational improvements with strategic innovation that could open new revenue streams.

The future is already here, but it takes bold leaders to *show* others how to reach it.

Your Turn: Bold AI Leadership in Business Value

Business value must be at the heart of every AI initiative, yet many organizations struggle to clearly define, measure, and demonstrate this value to stakeholders. Whether you're just starting to explore AI's potential or working to optimize existing implementations, your success depends on your ability to connect AI capabilities directly to measurable business outcomes.

This exercise will help you systematically assess your current state, envision your future potential, and create a clear action plan that shows, not just tells, how AI can deliver tangible business value. Through structured evaluation and practical demonstrations, you'll learn to bridge the gap between technical capabilities and strategic business impact.

Assess: Where Are You on Your AI Journey to Create Business Value?

If You're Just Starting with AI:
- What are the most critical business problems or opportunities that could benefit from AI?
- How do you currently measure success in technology initiatives?
- What gaps exist between your current metrics and strategic goals?
- How do similar technology projects typically progress in your organization?

If You're Already Using AI:
- Are your AI initiatives primarily focused on efficiency, customer experience, or revenue growth?

- How effectively are your current AI projects delivering measurable business value?
- Where are you seeing incremental gains vs. transformative outcomes?
- How well do your AI metrics align with organizational strategic goals?

Reflect: Understanding Your Present and Future States

Your Present State (Scene 1):
- What metrics and outcomes dominate your current view?
- Where are you investing resources without clear business returns?
- What capabilities or expertise might be underutilized?
- If using AI, which projects need reprioritization or refocusing?

Your Future State (Scene 2):
- What transformative outcomes could AI help you achieve?
- How might current challenges become market opportunities?
- What new revenue streams or business models are possible?
- What would success look like in tangible, measurable terms?

Business Value Creation Strategy:
- How will you ensure every AI initiative ties to measurable business outcomes?
- What steps can strengthen the alignment between AI projects and strategic goals?
- How can you better Show Not Tell potential value to stakeholders?

Take Action: Making Business Value Tangible

For Organizations New to AI:
- **Create Your Value Map:**
  - Identify three top business challenges AI could address.
  - Define clear success metrics aligned with strategic goals.
  - Draft a simple visualization plan for stakeholders.

For Organizations Using AI:
- **Prioritize and Refocus:**
  - Select one AI project to revisit or reprioritize.
  - Adjust its focus to maximize business value.
  - Strengthen its alignment with strategic goals.

For All Organizations:
- **Build Your Value Framework:**
  - Establish clear measurement mechanisms.
  - Create regular checkpoints to assess progress.
  - Plan stakeholder engagement and feedback loops.

Your Bold AI Leadership Challenge This Week

Choose one immediate action.

If New to AI:
- Document your organization's detailed Scene 1 and ideal Scene 2.
- Identify one clear business problem where AI could create measurable value.
- Create a simple demonstration plan for stakeholders.

If Already Using AI:
- Select one AI project to reprioritize for greater business value.
- Map current AI metrics against strategic goals.
- Design a tangible demonstration of transformed business value.

All Organizations:
- Schedule a stakeholder meeting to share your vision.
- Create a simple visual showing the connection between AI capabilities and business outcomes.
- Define clear success metrics for your chosen initiative.

Remember

Bold AI Leaders focus relentlessly on business value. Success comes not from having the most advanced technology but from showing others how AI can transform challenges into opportunities and capabilities into value.

CHAPTER 2

Speed with Rigor

Balancing Agility and Structure for Sustainable Business Success with AI

From organizations making their first AI investments to those scaling mature implementations, today's market moves at a relentless pace. Those beginning their AI journey face pressure to start smart while moving quickly. Those with existing AI initiatives must accelerate while maintaining quality. In both cases, success requires balancing speed with disciplined execution.

Introduction: The Balancing Act

The global retailer's executive team stared at the holiday sales dashboard in disbelief. Their rushed AI recommendation engine, meant to boost fourth-quarter revenue, had instead triggered a 20% drop in conversions. The system, deployed without adequate testing, was suggesting niche products to mainstream shoppers (artisanal coffee grinders to instant coffee buyers, professional-grade camera gear to casual photographers).

In stark contrast, their competitor was celebrating. By taking a different approach - launching a focused pilot program that rigorously tested recommendations before scaling - they'd achieved a 15% revenue increase. Same technology, radically different outcomes. This tale of two retailers illustrates that quality business leadership, fueled by AI, requires both fast and smart moves. Customer expectations evolve overnight, and technologies are transforming faster than ever. I've repeatedly observed the most effective leaders master a delicate balance. They know precisely when to accelerate and when to apply the brakes, recognizing that speed without rigor leads to failure, while rigor without speed means missing crucial opportunities.

Key Takeaways:

- **For Organizations Beginning Their AI Journey:** Start with a small, well-defined pilot that can quickly demonstrate results, like testing your recommendation engine with a limited customer segment. Set clear checkpoints to measure both speed and accuracy. Be ready to adjust quickly based on customer response.

- **For Organizations Scaling AI:** Expand methodically using evidence from your pilot's success. Keep tight monitoring systems that can quickly detect and correct issues. Have a clear rollback plan ready if performance drops.

After all, rushing headlong into AI initiatives is dangerous. It leads to costly missteps: solutions that miss the mark, investments that yield low or no returns, and damaged trust that takes years to rebuild. The most successful AI leaders have learned to thread this needle, combining rapid innovation with disciplined execution. They maintain momentum while ensuring impact.

This art of balancing speed with rigor forms the second principle of Bold AI Leadership. In this chapter, I'll define what this balance looks like in practice, explore the common pitfalls that organizations face, and provide concrete steps to help you achieve results without sacrificing quality. I'll also share practical visualization tools to help you to master the needed balance. Because in today's landscape, success isn't measured by who sprints ahead fastest but by who builds and maintains a sustainable competitive advantage.

In this chapter, we'll explore how to achieve this balance, avoid common pitfalls, and implement actionable strategies for success.

Definition: Speed with Rigor in Bold AI Leadership

Today, speed isn't just a competitive advantage; it's a necessity. Businesses that hesitate risk losing market share, falling behind competitors, or becoming irrelevant. However, speed alone is not enough. Moving too quickly without structure or discipline leads to failed initiatives, wasted investments, and eroded trust.

Speed with rigor is the deliberate pursuit of rapid progress balanced with disciplined execution. It means launching AI initiatives with a sense of urgency but ensuring they are well-designed, thoughtfully implemented, and aligned with measurable outcomes. It's about adopting a sprinting mindset (fast, iterative, and adaptive) while maintaining the long-term focus needed to scale sustainably. This principle applies to every stage of AI implementation:

- **Ideation:** Quickly identifying opportunities for AI to add value but validating assumptions with data and stakeholder alignment before proceeding
- **Deployment:** Rapidly deploying pilots or Minimum Viable Experiences (MVEs) to gather feedback while ensuring rigorous testing and risk management
- **Scaling:** Expanding successful pilots to drive business-wide transformation without compromising on quality, security, or alignment with strategic goals

Think of it as driving a race car: you accelerate on the straightaways but apply the brakes around curves. Failing to adjust your pace at critical moments leads to a crash. The most effective AI leaders know when to push forward aggressively and when to slow down, refine, and course-correct.

Why It Matters

AI adoption is often described as a race, but crossing the finish line first isn't enough. You must stay in the race long enough to dominate your lane. Leaders who embody speed with rigor:

- **Reduce Risk of Failure:** By maintaining disciplined oversight, leaders avoid expensive mistakes and reputational damage.
- **Maximize Value Delivery:** Leaders prioritize projects that align with clear business outcomes, ensuring measurable impact.
- **Build Trust:** Leaders demonstrate reliability and competence, earning the confidence of stakeholders, employees, and customers.

Real-World Analogies

Imagine a global hotel chain deploying an AI-powered dynamic pricing system. A speed-only approach might involve rolling out the system across all properties without adequate testing, risking price fluctuations that alienate loyal customers and disrupt revenue streams. A rigor-only approach might involve spending years perfecting pricing algorithms while competitors seize market share with more adaptive strategies.

Speed with rigor means starting with a pilot program at select properties, where AI works alongside experienced revenue managers. The AI analyzes factors such as occupancy rates, local events, competitor pricing, booking lead times, guest demographics, and seasonal trends to suggest price adjustments. Human experts validate these suggestions, applying their contextual knowledge to fine-tune the system. By gathering real-time feedback from guests, market data, and frontline staff, they refine the model to balance competitiveness, profitability, and guest satisfaction. Once optimized, the human + AI partnership is scaled across the entire brand, ensuring consistent results and adaptability to market shifts.

This concept serves as the guiding light for leaders navigating AI's fast-paced and complex terrain. In the next section, we'll explore common pitfalls that arise when organizations fail to achieve this critical balance.

Key Takeaways:

- **For Organizations Beginning Their AI Journey:** Start by pairing AI with experienced human experts in a limited context. Use pilot programs to demonstrate value while building trust. Focus on gathering concrete feedback and measurable results.

- **For Organizations Scaling AI:** Look for opportunities to replicate successful human + AI partnerships across the organization. Maintain the balance between automation and human oversight as you scale. Use lessons from early adopters to improve implementation in new areas.

Pitfalls: The Risks of Prioritizing Speed or Rigor Over Balance

The path to successful AI adoption presents challenges, and the stakes are high. While speed is vital in today's market, rushing without rigor leads to costly failures. Conversely, excessive caution can paralyze progress and waste opportunities. Finding the right balance is crucial, yet organizations often encounter pitfalls that derail their efforts.

To help you navigate these challenges, I've categorized common pitfalls into three key areas: Vision Pitfalls, Execution Pitfalls, and Culture Pitfalls. Each category highlights the key risks that can hinder your AI journey and offers insights into prevention.

Vision Pitfalls

A clear vision is the compass for any AI initiative. Without it, even well-intentioned projects can go astray. These pitfalls highlight how a lack of strategic clarity can undermine AI efforts from the outset, leading to wasted resources and missed opportunities.

Lack of Clear Vision   AI initiatives lack direction without a clear alignment with strategic goals.

> **Example:** A manufacturer deploys predictive maintenance AI without defining how it reduces downtime or costs, leading to leadership skepticism.
> **Key Watch Point:** Establish quantifiable success metrics before launch (technical and business key performance indicators [KPIs]).

Misaligned Priorities   AI projects focus on technology over solving meaningful business problems.

> **Example:** A financial firm builds an AI chatbot that doesn't align with customer service goals, frustrating users and missing opportunities.
> **Key Watch Point:** Map each AI initiative to specific strategic objectives.

Undefined Problem   AI initiatives become distractions when they aren't rooted in solving real problems.

> **Example:** A retailer implements AI for inventory but ignores supplier delays (the true bottleneck), minimizing impact.
> **Key Watch Point:** Validate the core problem with stakeholders before investing in AI.

Vision Checkpoint

- Clearly define the problem.
- Establish measurable success metrics.
- Involve and validate with stakeholders.
- Align with the strategic roadmap.

Execution Pitfalls

Even the most promising AI strategies can falter without disciplined execution. These pitfalls highlight common missteps in implementing AI initiatives, emphasizing how flawed processes, inadequate testing, and a failure to scale effectively can undermine even the best-laid plans.

Overlooking Feedback   Treating AI as a one-time deployment ignores its need for continuous improvement.

> **Example:** A logistics company deploys route optimization AI but doesn't update it based on driver feedback, limiting effectiveness.
> **Key Watch Point:** Build feedback loops and establish regular model reviews.

Inadequate Testing   Rushing AI deployment without thorough testing leads to poor performance and lost trust.

> **Example:** A hotel chain's AI pricing alienates loyal customers by overcharging them.
> **Key Watch Point:** Create a comprehensive testing framework (including edge cases and failure modes).

Scaling Failures   Promising AI pilots stall without the infrastructure or buy-in needed for expansion.

> **Example:** A pharmaceutical company optimizes one production line with AI but can't scale due to data integration issues.
> **Key Watch Point:** Design pilots with scalability in mind (infrastructure, integration).

Execution Checkpoint

- Clear feedback mechanisms are established.
- Testing covers various scenarios.
- Infrastructure is ready for scale.
- Monitoring systems are in place.

Culture Pitfalls

AI adoption isn't solely about technology; it's fundamentally about people. These pitfalls highlight the critical role of organizational culture, demonstrating how resistance to change, lack of collaboration, and erosion of trust can undermine even the most technically sound AI initiatives.

Siloed Teams   Lack of collaboration between technical and business teams causes AI solutions to miss the mark.

> **Example:** A bank's data science team develops a fraud detection model without input from compliance, resulting in false positives.
> **Key Watch Point:** Establish cross-functional teams early and maintain stakeholder communication.

Employee Resistance   Fear of job displacement or skepticism about AI hinders adoption.

> **Example:** Logistics workers resist AI scheduling, viewing it as a threat instead of a helpful tool.
> **Key Watch Point:** Proactively address concerns through transparent communication and involvement.

Lack of Trust   Stakeholders are less likely to adopt AI solutions they don't understand or trust.

> **Example:** A healthcare provider's AI diagnostic tool is underutilized due to lack of physician training and trust.
>
> **Key Watch Point:** Invest in training and education to build understanding and confidence.

Culture Checkpoint

- Key stakeholders are involved in planning.
- Change management strategies are in place.
- Plans to build and maintain trust exist.
- You are prepared to address concerns and resistance.

Understanding these pitfalls is the first step to avoiding them. By aligning AI initiatives with strategic goals, implementing disciplined processes for testing and scaling, and fostering a culture of collaboration and trust, organizations can unlock AI's transformative potential and avoid common traps.

In the next section, we'll explore actionable steps to balance speed with rigor, enabling your organization to harness AI's transformative power while steering clear of these pitfalls.

Actionable Steps: Achieving Speed with Rigor

To master the balance of speed and rigor, leaders must combine rapid innovation with disciplined execution. This means adopting processes that ensure quick wins without sacrificing quality or sustainability. The following actionable steps provide a framework for achieving this balance, with each step including an operational efficiency example and a revenue-generating example, along with visualization tips to align stakeholders around measurable outcomes.

Step 1: Define the Job to Be Done

Focus Question: What is the core task or outcome we're trying to achieve?

Example 1: Optimize Customer Service Efficiency

- **Job to Be Done:** Reduce call center response times.

- **The Challenge:** Imagine Sarah, a loyal customer, calling your support line. She's met with an endless loop of hold music. Frustration mounts, and she's ready to take her business elsewhere. This is the current state: long wait times that erode customer satisfaction and drive away valuable customers.

- **The Solution:** Now, picture this: AI steps in to handle the routine inquiries. Sarah's simple questions are answered instantly by a helpful chatbot. Human agents, like David, are freed up to address the more complex issues, providing personalized support and building stronger customer relationships. This is the future state: AI and humans working together to create a seamless and efficient experience.

  - **AI Role:** Automate repetitive tasks, such as answering FAQs, and suggest potential solutions for common issues.

  - **Human Role:** Build relationships, address nuanced challenges, and handle escalations with empathy and creativity.

Example 2: Launch a Predictive Maintenance Revenue Stream

- **Job to Be Done:** Create a subscription-based predictive maintenance service for industrial clients.

- **The Challenge:** Picture a factory floor grinding to a halt. A critical machine has failed unexpectedly, halting production and costing the company thousands of dollars in lost revenue and emergency repairs. This is the current state: companies plagued by unplanned downtime, facing costly disruptions and productivity losses.

- **The Solution:** Now, imagine sensors on those machines feeding data to an AI, which detects subtle anomalies that a human eye would miss. The AI predicts the impending failure weeks in advance, allowing for scheduled maintenance and preventing the crisis. This proactive approach becomes a valuable subscription service, providing clients with peace of mind and maximizing their operational efficiency.

  - **AI Role:** Monitor equipment performance, analyze sensor data, and detect early warning signs of failure.

  - **Human Role:** Coordinate maintenance schedules, oversee customer relationships, and address unique client requirements.

Visualization Tip

Use a **side-by-side comparison** of the current and future workflows to visually illustrate the impact of AI. On one side, depict the bottlenecks and inefficiencies of the current state (e.g., long queues in customer service or frequent equipment failures). On the other side, highlight the streamlined processes of the future state, supported by measurable KPIs like:

- Reduced call response times
- Increased customer satisfaction scores
- Improved equipment uptime and new revenue streams

Why It's Useful

This visualization allows stakeholders to immediately grasp the value of the transformation by making the inefficiencies of the current state painfully clear. It also provides:

- **A Shared Understanding:** Aligns cross-functional teams around the same vision
- **A Compelling Narrative:** Makes the future state feel tangible and achievable
- **Actionable Clarity:** Clearly connects AI capabilities to measurable outcomes, inspiring confidence and buy-in from leadership and teams

By presenting both the pain points and opportunities visually, this approach lays the groundwork for a focused, outcome-driven AI initiative.

Step 2: Build Feedback Loops for Continuous Learning

Focus Question: How do we ensure the AI system evolves and improves over time?

Example 1: Streamline Retail Inventory Management

- **Job to Be Done:** Reduce overstock and stockouts by refining AI-driven inventory forecasting.
- **The Challenge:** Imagine a retail chain struggling with inventory. In one store, shelves are packed with unsold winter gear, while in another, customers are frustrated by empty spaces where popular summer items should be. The initial AI system, while helpful, misses these local nuances, leading to both wasted stock and lost sales.
- **The Solution:** Now, picture store managers actively providing feedback to the AI system. "We're seeing a surge in demand for beach towels due to

the unexpected heatwave," they report. This on-the-ground intelligence, combined with sales data and social media trends, allows the AI to adapt its forecasts, resulting in optimized inventory and happier customers.

- o **AI Role:** Analyze sales patterns, refine demand forecasts, and integrate real-time feedback into the models.
- o **Human Role:** Provide qualitative insights on localized trends (e.g., seasonal spikes, local events) and validate AI predictions against market realities.

Example 2: Enhance Fraud Detection Models for Financial Transactions

- **Job to Be Done:** Reduce false positives while identifying fraud with greater precision.
- **The Challenge:** Think of a busy customer service department flooded with calls from frustrated customers whose legitimate transactions have been flagged as fraudulent. The AI model, while designed to protect against fraud, is overly sensitive, creating unnecessary disruptions and eroding customer trust.
- **The Solution:** Now, imagine fraud investigators providing detailed, specific feedback to the AI system. "This was a large but legitimate purchase," they explain. "This pattern is a new tactic used by cybercriminals." This expert input refines the AI's understanding of fraudulent behavior, reducing false positives and allowing investigators to focus on genuine threats.
  - o **AI Role:** Monitor transaction patterns, adapt models based on investigator input, and detect emerging fraud trends.
  - o **Human Role:** Analyze flagged transactions, provide expert feedback on fraud patterns, and suggest refinements to improve the AI's accuracy.

Visualization Tip

Create a **feedback loop diagram** that visually maps how human insights and AI outputs reinforce each other. The diagram should include:

- **Input Sources:** Highlight data sources like sales data, store manager insights, fraud investigator feedback, and customer feedback.
- **AI Model Updates:** Show how these inputs refine AI algorithms and enhance model performance.
- **Results:** Include measurable KPIs such as improved forecast accuracy, reduced false positives, increased customer satisfaction, and enhanced operational efficiency.

Why It's Useful

This visualization helps stakeholders understand the dynamic and evolving nature of AI systems, emphasizing that AI performance improves over time with active collaboration. It provides:

- **Transparency:** Demonstrates how human feedback is integral to AI success, fostering trust and engagement
- **Progress Tracking:** Clearly shows the measurable benefits of iterative learning, such as accuracy gains, cost reductions, and improved customer experience
- **Informed Decision-Making:** Encourages teams to focus on continuously maintaining and optimizing AI systems rather than treating them as static, "set-it-and-forget-it" solutions

By reinforcing the symbiotic relationship between humans and AI, this visualization underscores the value of investing in continuous improvement and collaboration, ensuring AI remains agile, effective, and aligned with evolving business needs.

Step 3: Start with Minimum Viable Experiences (MVEs)

Focus Question: What is the smallest, most achievable step we can take to demonstrate value?

Example 1: Pilot AI-Driven Marketing Campaigns

- **Job to Be Done:** Test AI-generated ad copy to improve click-through rates (CTR).
- **The Challenge:** Imagine a marketing team, led by Stewart, spending hours crafting ad copy. Despite their best efforts, the results are inconsistent, and CTR are stubbornly low. This is the current state: manual copywriting that is time-consuming and yields underwhelming results.
- **The Solution:** Now, picture Stewart's team piloting an AI tool that generates and refines ad copy. They start with a small segment of customers, carefully tracking the results. The outcome? A 20% increase in click-through rates! This early success validates the AI's potential and secures buy-in for a wider rollout.
  - **AI Role:** Generate ad variations and optimize for target audiences.
  - **Human Role:** Curate AI-generated ads, select the most effective ones, and provide strategic direction.

Example 2: Introduce Smart Maintenance Alerts for Utility Providers

- **Job to Be Done:** Pilot an AI system for detecting and reporting equipment malfunctions.
- **The Challenge:** Think of a utility company, where maintenance crews rely on routine inspections. Equipment failures often go undetected until it's too late, leading to costly downtime and service disruptions. This is the current state: reactive maintenance that is inefficient and disruptive.
- **The Solution:** Now, imagine the company piloting an AI system that uses sensors to monitor equipment and predict malfunctions. In a pilot region, this system reduces downtime by 30%! This tangible result demonstrates the AI's value and justifies a broader implementation.
  - **AI Role:** Analyze equipment performance data and identify early warning signs.
  - **Human Role:** Validate alerts, coordinate maintenance responses, and ensure system reliability.

Visualization Tip

Create a **pilot success heatmap** to visually showcase the impact of your initial deployment. Include:

- **Performance Metrics:** Highlight key results like CTR increases for marketing campaigns or downtime reductions for maintenance pilots.
- **Regional or Segment Breakdown:** Show how the pilot performed across different regions, audiences, or product categories.
- **Scalability Insights:** Use the heatmap to emphasize areas where the pilot succeeded and opportunities for scaling the solution to maximize return on investment (ROI).

Why This Matters

A clear, visual representation of pilot results allows stakeholders to quickly grasp the tangible impact of AI initiatives. By showcasing measurable success in a specific context, the heatmap builds confidence in the AI's potential for broader adoption, aligning teams around the next steps for scaling the solution.

Step 4: Measure ROI with Clear Metrics

Focus Question: How will we prove the value of this initiative?

Example 1: Optimize Energy Usage for Manufacturing Plants

- **Job to Be Done:** Reduce energy costs by optimizing equipment scheduling.
- **The Challenge:** Picture a sprawling manufacturing plant, its machines humming at full power during peak hours. The energy bills are astronomical, eating into profits. This is the current state: inefficient energy consumption driven by suboptimal scheduling.
- **The Solution:** Now, imagine an AI system that analyzes energy usage patterns and dynamically schedules equipment operation for off-peak hours. The result? A significant 20% reduction in energy expenses, directly boosting the company's bottom line.
  - ○ **AI Role:** Monitor energy usage patterns and identify cost-saving opportunities.
  - ○ **Human Role:** Validate AI schedules and adjust based on production priorities.

Example 2: Monetize Data Insights for Retail Clients

- **Job to Be Done:** Generate a new revenue stream by selling anonymized customer data insights.
- **The Challenge:** Think of a retailer sitting on a goldmine of customer data but lacking the tools to effectively leverage it. Valuable insights remain locked away, while potential revenue streams go untapped. This is the current state: underutilized data and missed monetization opportunities.
- **The Solution:** Now, imagine an AI system that processes this data, revealing valuable customer behavior trends. The retailer can then offer subscription-based access to these anonymized insights, creating a new and profitable revenue stream.
  - ○ **AI Role:** Analyze customer behavior trends and deliver action-able insights.
  - ○ **Human Role:** Package insights into usable reports, market the data service, and maintain client relationships.

Visualization Tip

Design an **ROI dashboard** to clearly demonstrate the financial and operational impact of AI initiatives. Include:

- **Key Metrics Comparison:** Compare pre- and post-implementation results, such as energy cost reductions for manufacturing plants or revenue growth from data monetization initiatives.
- **Timeline of Results:** Show how the initiative progressed over time, highlighting milestones like pilot completion, full deployment, and initial ROI.
- **Customizable Views:** Enable stakeholders to drill down into specific areas (e.g., regions, product categories, or client segments) for a detailed understanding of results.

Why This Matters

An ROI dashboard provides a powerful, real-time visualization of business value creation. It builds trust by translating AI's impact into language that resonates with decision-makers: dollars saved, revenue generated, or efficiency gained. By aligning stakeholders around tangible outcomes, this tool not only validates the initiative's success but also secures buy-in for future AI investments.

By following these actionable steps, leaders can maintain a balance of speed and rigor, ensuring that AI efforts not only meet immediate objectives but also lay the groundwork for sustainable success. Each example demonstrates the power of combining human ingenuity with AI's capabilities, showcasing not just what's possible, but also how to achieve it.

Real-World Story: Zurich Insurance's AI Assurance Framework

Zurich Insurance Group provides a powerful example of how speed with rigor can drive transformational outcomes at scale while safeguarding trust.

- **Job to Be Done:** Streamline claims processing and accounts receivable management while ensuring compliance, fairness, and operational excellence across global markets.
- **Current State:** Imagine Zurich's employees bogged down in paperwork, manually reviewing countless claims and processing policies. This led

to bottlenecks, high administrative costs, and frustratingly slow service for their 55 million customers across 210 countries and territories. The pressure to improve efficiency and customer satisfaction was immense.

- **The Solution:** Zurich deployed an AI-powered claims automation system and accounts receivable solution. This allowed for faster processing, reduced errors, and freed up employees to focus on more complex, customer-centric tasks. Zurich also implemented its AI Assurance Framework to ensure fairness, reliability, inclusiveness, and security, building trust in the new system. Local teams provided feedback to refine AI recommendations and adapt solutions to regional contexts, ensuring the AI was both fast and accurate.

  - **AI's Role:** Analyze claims data to automate decision-making processes, reducing manual review times and identifying potential errors or inconsistencies.

  - **Human's Role:** Oversee AI outputs through the **AI Assurance Framework,** ensuring fairness, reliability, inclusiveness, and security. Local teams provided feedback to refine AI recommendations and adapt solutions to regional contexts.

- **Outcome:** Zurich's AI-powered claims automation delivered substantial improvements. Claim review times were slashed by a remarkable factor of 58, and eight hours were saved per policy review. These efficiencies directly contributed to a 21% year-over-year increase in operating profit, with business operating profit rising another 7% in the first half of 2024. Beyond the financial gains, this also enabled Zurich to provide faster, more personalized service to its 55 million customers and improved employee morale by reducing tedious tasks.

Visualization Tip

Create an **AI Assurance Impact Dashboard** to demonstrate Zurich's results.

- **Efficiency Gains:** Compare claim review times and labor savings before and after AI implementation.
- **Profitability Metrics:** Highlight year-over-year increases in operating profit tied to the AI initiative.
- **AI Governance Metrics:** Include compliance indicators, such as fairness audits, security checks, and model reliability scores, to underscore Zurich's rigorous approach.

Key Takeaways:

- **For Organizations Beginning Their AI Journey:** Focus on clear, measurable business outcomes like processing time and cost reduction. Build governance frameworks early to ensure trust and compliance. Start with well-defined use cases that can demonstrate quick wins.

- **For Organizations Scaling AI:** Implement structured feedback loops to continuously improve AI performance. Balance rapid deployment with rigorous oversight. Use success metrics from initial implementations to build support for broader adoption.

Why It Works

Zurich's iterative refinement of AI systems across 160 global use cases proves that speed without rigor is unsustainable. Their emphasis on rigorous governance through the **AI Assurance Framework** fostered stakeholder trust while significantly accelerating measurable business outcomes. Zurich's example underscores that balancing urgency with structured oversight is essential for long-term AI success.

Visualization Tool Example for Speed with Rigor

To illustrate how leaders can build trust through transparency, the AI Trust & Impact Navigator provides a comprehensive view of how AI governance, performance, and business impact align (see Figure 2.1). In brief, this tool integrates key trust indicators with performance metrics to ensure responsible AI deployment, enabling leaders to build sustainable trust, optimize performance, and drive accountability. See Appendix B for a breakdown of the AI Trust & Impact Navigator, including its key elements and implementation steps.

The AI Trust & Impact Navigator Helps Leaders:

- Monitor and demonstrate the alignment of AI governance, performance, and business impact

- Utilize data points such as Performance Metrics and Governance Metrics

- Leverage the tool's quad-view display layout, which shows Operational

Excellence (top left), Risk & Compliance (top right), Business Impact (bottom left), and Trust Indicators (bottom right), along with status indicators for comprehensive analysis

- Understand update frequency and sample metrics for effective monitoring

The tool is implemented through steps like Framework Setup, Integration, Visualization, and Continuous Improvement, addressing common pitfalls such as Governance Gaps, Performance Blind Spots, and Trust Erosion. Success is indicated by Governance Excellence, Operational Impact, and Trust Metrics.

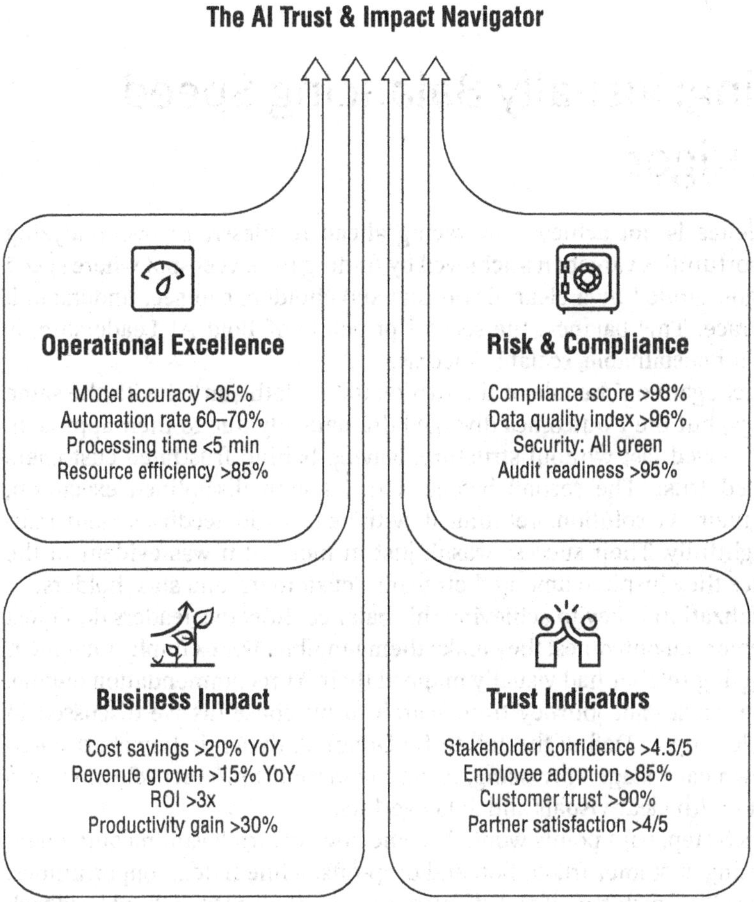

The AI Trust & Impact Navigator

Operational Excellence

Model accuracy >95%
Automation rate 60–70%
Processing time <5 min
Resource efficiency >85%

Risk & Compliance

Compliance score >98%
Data quality index >96%
Security: All green
Audit readiness >95%

Business Impact

Cost savings >20% YoY
Revenue growth >15% YoY
ROI >3x
Productivity gain >30%

Trust Indicators

Stakeholder confidence >4.5/5
Employee adoption >85%
Customer trust >90%
Partner satisfaction >4/5

FIGURE 2.1   AI Trust & Impact Navigator: Build trust, optimize performance, drive accountability. This visualization tool helps leaders move fast—with rigor. By connecting AI governance, performance, and business outcomes in a single view, the Navigator enables transparency, builds trust, and ensures sustainable impact.

From Insight to Action

The AI Trust & Impact Navigator helps leaders build sustainable trust, optimize performance, and drive accountability by providing a holistic view of trust and impact metrics. The AI Trust & Impact Navigator empowers leaders to move beyond compliance-focused governance to create truly sustainable AI initiatives. The purpose of this tool is to drive informed decisions that allow you to proactively manage both trust and performance for better outcomes, not just track data points.

Closing: Visually Balancing Speed with Rigor

AI excellence is not achieved by racing ahead recklessly or overanalyzing until opportunities vanish; it's achieved by finding the sweet spot where speed meets rigor, guided by a clear vision that stakeholders can see, understand, and embrace. This balance, the second principle of Bold AI Leadership, is essential for sustainable, scalable success.

Reflect again on the tale of the two retailers. Both started with the same technology, but their outcomes diverged dramatically due to their approach. The first moved fast without structure, leaving behind frustrated customers and eroded trust. The second balanced speed with disciplined execution, piloting their AI solution, refining it with real-world feedback, and scaling thoughtfully. Their success wasn't just in metrics; it was evident in the confidence they inspired among their teams, customers, and stakeholders.

Visualization is key to achieving this balance. Effective leaders don't just discuss potential outcomes; they make them tangible. For example, imagine if the struggling retailer had visually mapped their AI recommendation engine, tracing the customer journey from search to purchase (as we discussed in Actionable Step 1: Define the Job to Be Done). A dynamic flowchart could have shown each stage - browsing, recommendations, product selection, and checkout - with clear visuals and data overlays.

At each step, pain points would become obvious: irrelevant recommendations causing customer frustration and drop-offs, while hidden opportunities, like cross-selling or personalized offers (as in Actionable Step 2: Build Feedback Loops), would emerge. Layering on a future-state projection would illustrate AI-powered recommendations solving these issues, boosting click-through rates, and reducing cart abandonment. Overlaid KPIs, like increased conversions or higher average order values (as in Actionable Step 4: Measure ROI with Clear Metrics), would make the potential business impact compelling.

By creating clear demonstrations of AI's impact, leaders bridge the gap between possibility and reality. This Show Not Tell approach transforms skeptics into advocates and abstract ideas into actionable insights. For the retailer, such visualization would have revealed problems early, fostered stakeholder confidence, and optimized the AI before launch.

This act of seeing both current flaws and future potential anchors decision-making in clarity and alignment. It's a defining practice of Bold AI Leadership: balancing speed with rigor to drive purposeful, sustainable outcomes.

While this visual approach demands discipline, it accelerates, rather than hinders, progress. The most effective leaders use visualization to identify risks early, adapt quickly, and build momentum (aligning with Actionable Step 3: Start with Minimum Viable Experiences). They understand that in today's agile environment, the greatest risk isn't moving too fast or being too thorough; it's failing to move at all.

The second principle of Bold AI Leadership provides the framework for decisive action while maintaining the guardrails for success.

As you move forward, ask yourself: are we balancing speed with rigor, and are we effectively showing, not just telling, what success looks like? In the next chapter, we'll explore the third principle of Bold AI Leadership: simplicity. You'll discover how to make AI initiatives approachable and clear, ensuring their value resonates across every level of your organization.

Leadership in the AI era demands more than vision; it requires the ability to make that vision visible to others. Visually balancing speed with rigor equips you with the mindset and tools to transform ideas into action and action into lasting impact. The path is clear, and the tools are in your hands. Now it's time to show the way.

Your Turn: Bold AI Leadership in Speed with Rigor

AI success doesn't come from reckless speed or excessive caution; it comes from balancing agility with disciplined execution. Whether your organization is experimenting with AI for the first time or optimizing existing implementations, the key to long-term success is knowing how to move fast enough to stay competitive and structured enough to safely deliver lasting value.

This exercise will help you assess where your organization's approach to AI sits on the speed-to-rigor spectrum and where adjustments can improve both adoption and outcomes. For a simplified version of the below detailed approach, see Figure 2.2.

AI Project Readiness Checker

Use this simple tool to assess your readiness for an AI initiative

Understanding Your Starting Point

Have you identified a specific business challenge to address?
Example: Reducing customer response time, improving inventory forecasts

| Yes | Partially | No |

Do you have data related to this challenge?
Example: Customer service logs, sales history, process documentation

| Yes | Partially | No |

Have key stakeholders agreed this is a priority?
Example: Department heads, end users, IT team

| Yes | Partially | No |

Basic Safety & Quality Checks

Can you test the solution with a small group first?
Example: One department or team before full rollout

| Yes | Partially | No |

Do you have a way to measure success?
Example: Current vs. future response times, accuracy rates

| Yes | Partially | No |

Is there a clear process to gather user feedback?
Example: Regular check-ins, feedback forms, usage metrics

| Yes | Partially | No |

⑦ Use this checklist to guide your AI initiative planning. More "Yes" answers indicate better readiness. "Partially" or "No" answers highlight areas needing attention before proceeding.

FIGURE 2.2 AI Progress Readiness Checker.

Assess: Are You Prioritizing Both Speed and Rigor?

If New to AI:

- **Analyze Technology Decisions:** How are technology decisions typically made - quickly or cautiously?
- **Evaluate Initiative Progress:** Are initiatives often delayed in planning or rushed into implementation?
- **Determine Stakeholder Focus:** Do stakeholders prioritize short-term gains or long-term impact?
- **Identify Critical Use Cases:** Map two to three potential AI applications where both speed and quality control are essential.
- **Learn from Past Rollouts:** Review your last three technology rollouts to identify practices that effectively balanced speed and careful execution.
- **Design a Pilot Framework:** Create a pilot framework that incorporates rapid testing cycles and quality checkpoints.

If Already Using AI:

- **Evaluate AI Implementation:** How would you characterize your current AI implementation approach?
- **Analyze Project Flow:** Are AI projects frequently delayed or launched without sufficient testing?
- **Define Scaling Criteria:** Do you have clear criteria for determining when to scale vs. refine AI initiatives?
- **Measure Success Regularly:** How often do you measure the success of AI initiatives before expanding them?
- **Classify AI Projects:** Audit your AI portfolio and categorize projects as "too slow," "too fast," or "well-paced."
- **Document Impact Examples:** Provide specific examples where speed or caution has significantly affected AI outcomes.
- **Develop a Balanced Scorecard:** Create a scorecard to track both:
  - Speed metrics (e.g., deployment time, iteration frequency)
  - Quality indicators (e.g., accuracy rates, stakeholder satisfaction)

Reflect: Learning from Past Technology Efforts

- **For AI users:** Which AI projects have suffered from being launched too quickly without adequate safeguards? Which have been hindered by delays and indecision?

- **For AI Explorers:** Considering past technology deployments (e.g., automation, cloud, CRM), what strategies worked well, and what challenges arose?
- How does your leadership team weigh risk vs. reward in technology adoption? Does it tend to favor speed over thoroughness, or vice versa?
- Where has your organization effectively balanced speed with structure in the past, and how can those lessons be applied to AI?
- How effectively does your organization measure success, and are there clear milestones before scaling technology solutions?

Take Action: Fine-Tuning Your Approach

- **Visualize Your Path:** Create a simple visual map outlining your starting point and initial goals for AI implementation or refinement.
- **Establish Checkpoints:** Develop a progress dashboard to monitor key milestones and decision points:
  - Does the project address a genuine business need?
  - Are we conducting tests with actual users?
  - Do we have clear criteria for success?
  - Use a traffic light system (green = proceed, yellow = caution, red = stop and revise).
- **Define Go/No-Go Criteria:** Establish clear visual indicators for determining readiness to proceed to the next phase:
  - Basic success signals (e.g., user satisfaction, system reliability)
  - Potential risk factors (e.g., technical issues, regulatory concerns)
  - Resource availability (e.g., budget, personnel)
- **Prioritize Safety and Simplicity:** Implement foundational safeguards without creating overly complex processes.

Why This Matters

In today's business landscape, success with AI requires balancing three critical forces (as shown in Figure 2.3):

- **Competitive Pressure:** Move too slowly and watch competitors capture your market. Digital-native companies are already deploying AI to reshape customer expectations and industry standards.
  - **Too Fast:** Unsustainable advantage - rushing to deploy without proper foundation
  - **Too Slow:** Market irrelevance - losing competitive edge as others innovate
  - **Balanced:** Increased market share, improved customer satisfaction, industry leadership position

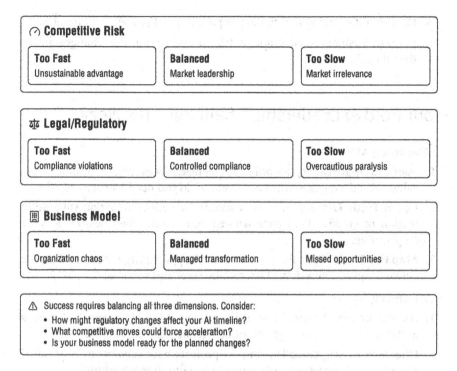

FIGURE 2.3   The three critical forces that need to be balanced.

- **Regulatory Reality**: Rush without proper controls, and risk serious legal and compliance issues. AI governance frameworks are evolving rapidly, with significant consequences for missteps.
  - **Too Fast:** Compliance violations - risking fines, penalties, and reputation damage
  - **Too Slow:** Overcautious paralysis - missing opportunities due to excessive fear
  - **Balanced:** Protected brand value, reduced risk exposure, stakeholder trust
- **Operational Readiness**: Your organization's ability to absorb and benefit from AI transformation determines success. The right pace matches your team's capacity for change.
  - **Too Fast:** Organization chaos - overwhelming teams and systems
  - **Too Slow:** Missed opportunities - failing to build necessary capabilities
  - **Balanced:** Enhanced productivity, optimized processes, improved decision-making

  Success requires balancing all three dimensions. Consider:
- What competitive pressures might necessitate accelerating your AI initiatives?

- How might evolving regulations impact your AI strategy and timeline?
- Is your business model adequately prepared for the changes introduced by AI?

Your Bold AI Leadership Challenge This Week

Not Using AI Yet:

1. **Spot the Opportunity:** Identify one business process where AI could create value. Would a quick experiment work, or do you need a structured pilot?

2. **Learn from History:** Review a recent technology adoption (like automation or cloud). What pace worked best? Apply these lessons to your AI planning.

3. **Map the Trade-Offs:** For your chosen AI opportunity, what's the balance between speed and safety? List specific risks and rewards.

AI Already in Use:

1. **Assess Recent Work:** Look at your latest AI deployment. Did testing and refinement get enough attention? What were the results?

2. **Check Your Rhythm:** Do your AI projects have regular review cycles? Are you catching issues early while maintaining momentum?

3. ***Show AI—Don't Tell It***: Choose an active AI project and create a simple visual representation of your speed-to-structure balance for stakeholder clarity.

Remember

Bold AI Leaders master the balancing act: speed without guardrails creates chaos and risk. Caution without momentum invites disruption and obsolescence. Success lies in embracing both every single day.

CHAPTER 3

Simplicity

Making AI Approachable, Accessible, and Understandable

At every stage of AI adoption, from initial exploration to advanced implementation, organizations face a common challenge: making AI approachable and understandable. The world is brimming with AI-powered potential, yet for many, it feels shrouded in an intimidating fog of jargon, algorithms, and incomprehensible technical details.

Introduction: The Role of Simplicity in Bold AI Leadership

This complexity fosters fear and mistrust, erecting barriers that slow adoption and stifle innovation. The discomfort is palpable, not just among the general public, but also in boardrooms, within teams, and even among technology leaders tasked with driving AI initiatives. Simplicity is the antidote to this paralysis. Bold AI Leaders know that to bridge the gap between possibility and reality, they must make AI approachable, accessible, and understandable. This doesn't mean oversimplifying or diluting its power; it means using clarity and plain language to shine a light on AI's potential, making it feel less like a mysterious black box and more clearly a tool that enhances human ingenuity.

Imagine two boardroom presentations on the same Wednesday morning. Both teams are pitching an AI solution to help pharmacists prevent dangerous drug interactions. The stakes: $10 million to revolutionize patient safety. The first presenter drowns the room in technical details. "Our neural network processes prescription histories using a multi-layer architecture..." Slides packed with code and database schemas flash by. The Head of Pharmacy Operations checks his phone. The Chief Safety Officer's eyes glaze over. When asked about real-world impact, the presenter gets tangled in technical specifications.

The second presenter walks to the center of the room and brings up a live display. "Meet George, a patient who just walked into our downtown pharmacy." The screen shows a pharmacist scanning a new prescription. Instantly, the AI highlights a dangerous interaction with George's blood pressure medication. A clear alert appears, showing the specific risks and suggesting three safer alternatives. The entire process takes eight seconds. The room watches as real-time data flows across the screen - Dangerous interactions prevented today: 247. Average detection time: 3.2 seconds. Patient safety score: 99.8%. Projected annual savings from avoided adverse events: $12.3 million.

"This isn't just a warning system," the presenter explains, expanding the view to show hundreds of pharmacies using the system simultaneously. "It's a safety revolution. Every green pulse is a patient protected from harm. Every blue signal is a pharmacist making faster, safer decisions." The Chief Medical Officer starts nodding. The CEO writes "PATIENT STORIES" in large letters. By the time the presenter shows how the system caught three life-threatening interactions just this morning, the decision is clear.

The difference? One presenter talked about AI features. The other showed how it saves lives. This contrast highlights a universal truth: simplicity is not just a presentation strategy, but a leadership imperative. By showing, not telling, how AI creates tangible value, leaders foster trust, inspire action, and drive alignment.

Key Takeaways:

- **For Organizations Beginning Their AI Journey:** Replace technical jargon with visual storytelling and real patient outcomes. Instead of explaining how the AI works, show its impact through simple, relatable scenarios like "George's story." Use clear metrics (like "247 interactions prevented today") that anyone can understand.

- **For Organizations Scaling AI:** Simplify complex AI systems into easily digestible demonstrations. Transform data-heavy presentations into visual narratives that connect directly to stakeholder priorities. Make AI's value visible through real-time, easy-to-understand visual communication tools.

This chapter explores how to achieve simplicity in AI leadership, overcome common barriers, and empower your organization to embrace AI's transformative potential.

Definition: Simplicity in Bold AI Leadership

Simplicity requires leaders to make AI's value visible, relatable, and actionable through clear demonstrations that resonate with people. It doesn't mean diluting AI's power but, instead, aiming to remove barriers - linguistic, technical, and cultural - that hinder understanding and adoption. Bold AI Leaders don't just describe AI's potential; they bring it to life, showing how it enhances human ingenuity to deliver meaningful outcomes.

At its core, simplicity means:

- **Showing Outcomes, Not Obscuring Complexity:** Bold AI Leaders use vivid visualizations and relatable scenarios to illustrate how AI amplifies human decisions, transforming complex data into clear actions.
- **Building Trust Through Transparency:** By simplifying language and processes, leaders reveal the reasoning behind AI's recommendations, demonstrating how human judgment validates and enhances these insights.
- **Empowering Users with Actionable Insights:** Leaders design AI outputs that complement human expertise, providing clear, intuitive guidance that inspires confidence and drives decisive action.

Imagine simplicity as a window into AI's potential: not a technical black box but a transparent, practical view of how AI works alongside humans to achieve meaningful results. Leaders who embrace simplicity prioritize Show Not Tell, turning AI from an abstract concept into a tangible experience that teams can see, relate to, and trust.

Seeing Simplicity in Action: Real-World Scenarios

In industries around the globe, the most successful AI implementations share a common thread: they make complex technology understandable and actionable through clear demonstrations of value. Here's how the human + AI partnership thrives when simplicity takes center stage:

In Operations and Logistics

- **Show the Why:** A warehouse worker views a heatmap of afternoon rush orders, clearly seeing why AI recommends restocking aisle 7 now. This insight turns algorithmic suggestions into actionable priorities, making AI's value tangible.

- **Demonstrate the Partnership**: A manufacturing supervisor watches an AI dashboard highlight equipment flagged for maintenance due to potential failure within 48 hours. Armed with AI insights and their on-the-ground expertise, they schedule repairs and prevent costly downtime.

In Healthcare and Service

- **Make Impact Visible**: A hospital administrator sees a live demonstration of AI flagging patients based on risk factors. Clear visuals link symptoms to alerts, and the prioritized list is shared with care teams, improving patient outcomes in real time.
- **Collaborative Decision-Making**: An airline gate agent uses AI to rebook passengers during a weather delay. The AI tool visualizes alternate travel routes, while the agent adds empathy and personal explanations, turning disruption into trust-building moments.

In Retail and Hospitality

- **Reveal Clear Trends**: A retail manager adjusts staffing after seeing an AI-generated forecast showing how weather and local events will affect customer foot traffic. Before-and-after visuals illustrate reduced wait times, linking AI insights to tangible benefits.
- **Visualize Inventory Decisions**: A restaurant owner compares past sales with AI-driven projections for weekend trends. The side-by-side visuals help them confidently optimize orders, reducing waste while meeting customer demand.

In Agriculture

- **Illuminate the Data**: A farm operator uses AI to map soil moisture levels, uncovering actionable patterns. They refine irrigation schedules by combining this insight with their knowledge of seasonal weather trends, conserving water and boosting yields.
- **Simplify Insights**: A fruit grower uses an AI heatmap to identify orchard blocks ready for harvest. This clear visual aligns labor and market demands, maximizing quality and profitability.
- **Predict and Prevent**: A vineyard manager receives pest alerts from AI, based on weather and historical data. Validating these insights with their expertise, they implement targeted prevention strategies, protecting crops efficiently.

Key Takeaways:

- **For Organizations Beginning Their AI Journey**: Transform complex data into visual tools that workers can instantly understand, like heatmaps for warehouse workers or color-coded alerts for healthcare teams. Focus on making AI outputs as simple to read as a traffic light or weather forecast.

- **For Organizations Scaling AI:** Create consistent visual languages across different departments, helping everyone from farm workers to airline staff quickly grasp AI insights. Replace technical explanations with intuitive displays that show clear next steps, like "restock now" or "check these plants first."

Practices for Showcasing Simplicity

Simplicity in AI leadership isn't achieved by chance. It requires deliberate actions and a commitment to clarity at every step. The following key practices are designed to help leaders bring simplicity to life, ensuring that AI becomes an accessible, actionable, and trusted tool. These strategies bridge the gap between complexity and understanding, making AI's value visible and relatable to everyone involved.

1. **Visualize the Why Behind AI Decisions**

   Show how AI derives insights and why they matter using intuitive tools.
   - Replace dense technical explanations with visual comparisons that highlight improvements.
   - Use live data visualizations to illustrate cause-and-effect relationships.
   - Provide dashboards that link AI outputs to relevant KPIs, enabling stakeholders to explore insights interactively.

2. **Make the Human Role Clear**

   Highlight the collaboration between humans + AI.
   - Map decision points where human expertise validates or enhances AI recommendations.
   - Share case studies where human involvement improved AI outputs.
   - Use workflow diagrams to demonstrate how AI augments, rather than replaces, human judgment.

3. **Demonstrate Real-Time Impact**

   Connect AI insights to outcomes that matter to stakeholders.
   - Present before-and-after visuals to showcase measurable results, such as increased efficiency or reduced costs.
   - Display live performance indicators that illustrate ongoing improvements.
   - Use scenarios that tie AI outputs directly to improved decision-making, building confidence in its value.

These practices foster trust, transparency, and collaboration, enabling teams to understand and act on AI insights. Simplicity accelerates AI adoption and ensures sustainable success.

Bringing Simplicity to Bold AI Leadership

Simplicity in AI leadership is about removing the mystery and revealing the value through clear visuals, relatable examples, and actionable insights. By focusing on Show Not Tell, leaders transform complexity into clarity and skepticism into trust.

When teams see AI's logic, trust its outputs, and understand its role as a partner to human expertise, they confidently act on its insights. This is the essence of Bold AI Leadership: illuminating AI's potential in ways that empower people to embrace and harness its transformative power.

Pitfalls: When Complexity Undermines Business Success with AI

While simplicity may sound intuitive, many organizations fall into traps that hinder AI adoption, breed mistrust, or fail to deliver results. These pitfalls arise when leaders fail to prioritize clarity, transparency, and accessibility in their AI initiatives. Below, we explore three categories of pitfalls - Vision, Execution, and Culture - that can derail even the most promising AI initiatives.

Vision Pitfalls

1. **Jargon Overload**
   - **What Happens:** Teams rely on overly technical language that alienates stakeholders, from C-suite leaders to frontline employees.
   - **Example:** A manufacturing AI team initially presented its predictive maintenance tool with dense slides of statistical terminology. Plant managers were confused and disengaged. After revising their approach to include a live demo showing the system predicting a 48-hour equipment failure, coupled with a plain-language explanation, the managers left with excitement rather than skepticism.
   - **Key Watch Point:** Use clear, industry-relevant language and visual demonstrations to highlight concrete business impact.

2. **Complex Solution Syndrome**
   - **What Happens:** Organizations build overly sophisticated AI solutions that overwhelm users and complicate simple tasks.
   - **Example:** A financial services firm developed an AI risk assessment tool with dozens of configurable parameters. However, users simply needed clear "approve/review/deny" recommendations. The extra features went unused, adding confusion instead of value.
   - **Key Watch Point:** Prioritize simple, effective solutions that address core business needs, starting with the minimum viable product (MVP).

3. **Failure to Show the Value**
   - **What Happens:** AI initiatives emphasize technical capabilities instead of demonstrating practical benefits.
   - **Example:** A retailer showcased its inventory AI's advanced algorithms but failed to explain how it reduced stockouts and increased sales. In contrast, their competitor led with metrics showing how the system boosted revenue by 15% and improved on-time delivery rates.
   - **Key Watch Point:** Lead with tangible outcomes (cost savings, efficiency gains, or revenue growth) backed by real data.

Execution Pitfalls

1. **Confusing Outputs**
   - **What Happens:** AI systems provide complex data without clear, actionable insights.
   - **Example:** A logistics AI generated detailed route optimization heatmaps but failed to provide simple "best route" recommendations that drivers could act on. In contrast, a competitor offered an intuitive dashboard showing the top three route options, along with potential time and fuel savings, making the AI indispensable.
   - **Key Watch Point:** Ensure AI outputs guide clear decisions or actions, emphasizing usability.

2. **Overwhelming Users with Features**
   - **What Happens:** Solutions become cluttered with unnecessary features that obscure core functionality.
   - **Example:** A hospital's patient risk assessment tool included advanced population health analytics, but nurses struggled to quickly identify high-risk patients. After simplifying the interface to a color-coded priority list, adoption soared by 60%.
   - **Key Watch Point:** Start with essential features that solve immediate problems (MVP), then expand based on user needs.

3. **Lack of Feedback Integration**
   - **What Happens:** Teams deploy AI solutions without mechanisms to learn from user experience.
   - **Example:** A utility company launched an AI energy optimization system but didn't allow facility managers to report when recommendations didn't align with real-world conditions. The system's credibility suffered. When a feedback loop was introduced, user insights improved the AI's accuracy by 30%.
   - **Key Watch Point:** Build feedback loops into your deployment process and act on user input to refine the system.

Culture Pitfalls

1. **Mistrust of AI Systems**
   - **What Happens:** Employees and customers mistrust AI due to a lack of transparency or poor communication about its purpose and benefits.
   - **Example:** A sales team ignored AI-generated lead scores because they didn't understand how the scores were calculated or why they mattered. A follow-up training session demonstrated the AI's logic using real examples, leading to a 40% increase in adoption.
   - **Key Watch Point:** Build trust by clearly explaining how AI works, its limitations, and where human judgment plays a critical role.

2. **Siloed Development**
   - **What Happens:** Technical teams build AI solutions in isolation from business users.
   - **Example:** An insurance company's AI claims processing tool failed, because developers hadn't consulted adjusters about their workflows. After forming a cross-functional team, the system was redesigned and adoption increased.
   - **Key Watch Point:** Establish cross-functional teams early, ensuring solutions align with real-world workflows and objectives. Diverse perspectives strengthen outcomes.

3. **Resistance to Simplification**
   - **What Happens:** Organizations resist simplification, believing sophisticated solutions are inherently better.
   - **Example:** A data science team opposed simplifying an algorithm's interface, fearing it would undermine their credibility. When they finally adopted a user-friendly design, adoption increased, and they earned broader recognition for delivering practical value.
   - **Key Watch Point:** Measure success by business impact and user adoption, not technical complexity.

Pitfall Checkpoint

Before launching your AI initiative, ensure you can answer the following questions:

- Is our solution focused on solving specific business problems?
- Have we made the value proposition clear to all stakeholders?
- Are our AI outputs actionable and easy to understand?
- Do we have mechanisms to gather and act on user feedback?
- Have we involved end users in the design process?
- Is our training focused on practical application rather than technical details?

Success with AI requires balancing sophisticated capabilities with simple, intuitive delivery. By avoiding these pitfalls, leaders can build AI solutions that people trust, understand, and use effectively to drive better outcomes.

Actionable Steps: Simplicity in Action

Simplicity is not just a guiding principle; it's a strategic tool that enables Bold AI Leaders to bridge the gap between complexity and understanding. By showing its value rather than merely telling stakeholders about its potential, simplicity transforms AI from an abstract concept into a relatable, actionable force.

The following actionable steps are designed to help you embody simplicity in your AI initiatives. By prioritizing clear communication, intuitive design, and the human + AI partnership, you'll inspire trust, drive adoption, and achieve sustainable success. Each step includes operational and revenue-focused examples, along with visualization tips to bring AI's transformative impact to life.

Step 1: Speak the Stakeholder's Language

Focus Question: How do we present AI in a way that resonates with users?

Example 1: Improve Operational Understanding

- **Job to Be Done:** Simplify energy usage reporting and optimize energy consumption for manufacturing teams.
- **The Challenge:** Imagine a team of factory floor managers, staring at dense reports filled with complex energy metrics. They see historical data but lack insights into future energy usage patterns and how to proactively optimize consumption. This is the current state: valuable data going underutilized, leading to reactive energy management and higher costs.

- **The Solution:** Now, picture those same managers using a simple dashboard powered by AI. The AI predicts energy spikes, identifies inefficiencies, and provides optimized schedules for machinery. Key metrics are translated into practical terms: "dollars saved," "hours optimized," "potential downtime avoided." The AI's prescriptive recommendations empower the team to make informed decisions and proactively improve efficiency.

  - **AI Role:** Predict energy usage patterns based on various factors (e.g., production schedules, weather forecasts, equipment performance). Identify cost-saving opportunities through optimized scheduling and resource allocation. Generate prescriptive recommendations for energy reduction.

  - **Human Role:** Validate AI recommendations, considering real-time operational constraints. Integrate AI-driven schedules into the overall production plan. Provide feedback to refine the AI's predictions and recommendations.

Example 2: Enhance Revenue-Generating Insights

- **Job to Be Done:** Empower sales teams with actionable customer insights.
- **The Challenge:** Think of a sales team drowning in customer data - segmentation reports, purchase histories, demographic information. The AI provides this data but lacks clear guidance on how to turn it into sales. This leads to missed opportunities and inefficient sales efforts.
- **The Solution:** Now, imagine the AI generating a simplified report: "Top Five Upsell Opportunities," with clear recommendations for each. Sales teams can focus on high-potential leads, personalize their pitches, and close more deals.

  - **AI Role:** Analyze customer behavior to identify profitable segments and predict upsell opportunities.

  - **Human Role:** Craft tailored pitches based on AI insights, building relationships and closing deals.

Visualization Tip

Use journey simulations or interactive ROI heatmaps to translate AI's complexity into relatable narratives. Simulate a customer's journey enhanced by AI recommendations or use heatmaps to highlight high-performing regions or segments, enabling stakeholders to see AI insights in action.

Human Role Highlighted in Visualizations: Sales teams interact with the simulation to refine strategies, ensuring recommendations align with real-world experience.

Step 2: Prioritize User-Friendly Design

Focus Question: How do we ensure AI solutions are intuitive and accessible?

Example 1: Streamline Operational Tools

- **Job to Be Done:** Introduce AI-powered patient triage to intelligently automate prioritization in a hospital setting.
- **The Challenge:** Imagine a chaotic emergency room where nurses are overwhelmed with incoming patients. They struggle to quickly assess and prioritize cases using *manual and subjective* methods, leading to delays and potential risks.
- **The Solution:** Now, picture an AI system that instantly analyzes patient data (vitals, symptoms, medical history) to objectively flag high-risk cases with a simple traffic light system (red = immediate attention, yellow = urgent, green = routine). This intelligent automation allows nurses to focus on providing care, knowing the AI is helping them prioritize effectively.
  - **AI Role:** Intelligently analyze patient data (vitals, symptoms, medical history) to predict risk levels. Automatically flag high-risk cases based on objective criteria.
  - **Human Role:** Use professional judgment to validate AI recommendations, considering nuanced factors. Provide personalized care and interventions based on the AI-informed prioritization.

Example 2: Improve Customer Experience for Revenue Growth

- **Job to Be Done:** Increase customer trust in e-commerce recommendations through personalized explanations.
- **The Challenge:** Think of online shoppers scrolling through product pages, bombarded with generic recommendations. They're skeptical, wondering if the suggestions are truly relevant or just sales tactics. This lack of transparency hinders trust and reduces purchase rates.
- **The Solution:** Now, imagine a "Why We Recommended This" button powered by AI. It provides personalized explanations for each product suggestion, highlighting relevant features based on the customer's *individual* browsing history and preferences. This *intelligent personalization* builds trust and encourages purchases.
  - **AI Role:** Intelligently analyze browsing history, purchase patterns, and product features. Generate personalized explanations for product recommendations using natural language processing.
  - **Human Role:** Validate the AI's logic and refine explanations for specific demographics or marketing campaigns. Monitor customer feedback and adjust the AI's personalization strategies.

Visualization Tip

Create AI-powered explainer videos or interactive storyboards to show the intelligent logic behind AI's recommendations in a user-friendly way. These tools demonstrate how AI intelligently simplifies workflows while empowering users to trust and adopt its outputs.

Human Role Highlighted in Visualizations: Staff or customers interact with the explainer tools, asking questions or adding context, emphasizing the collaborative nature of intelligent decision-making.

Step 3: Clarify Results with Contextual Data

Focus Question: How do we ensure AI outputs are actionable and trusted?

Example 1: Provide Actionable Insights for Operations

- **Job to Be Done:** Optimize energy savings in utility companies by providing context-aware recommendations.

- **The Challenge:** Imagine energy analysts receiving AI alerts about high consumption, but the recommendations are vague: "Reduce energy usage." They lack the specific context needed to take action, leading to frustration and inaction.

- **The Solution:** Now, picture an AI system that provides context-aware recommendations: "Shift operations to 7 p.m. for off-peak savings," or "Reduce pressure in pipeline A by 10%." The AI automatically considers factors like current demand, equipment load, and pricing to generate optimized actions, ensuring immediate implementation and maximum savings.

  - **AI Role:** Contextually analyze usage patterns, pricing, and operational constraints. Generate optimized, action-oriented recommendations with clear next steps.

  - **Human Role:** Implement AI recommendations, considering real-time operational needs and safety protocols. Provide feedback to the AI to refine its contextual understanding and recommendations.

Example 2: Align AI Outputs with Revenue Goals

- **Job to Be Done:** Reduce customer churn in a subscription service by providing context-rich retention strategies.

- **The Challenge:** Think of customer success teams receiving churn-risk scores from an AI, but lacking guidance on how to effectively retain those customers. This leads to generic, ineffective retention efforts and continued churn.

- **The Solution:** Now, imagine the AI providing context-rich retention strategies, such as "Offer a 20% discount on the premium plan" for price-sensitive customers or "Provide personalized onboarding for new features" for engagement-focused customers. The AI automatically segments customers and optimizes retention actions based on individual needs and behavior.
  - **AI Role:** Contextually analyze customer data (usage, demographics, feedback) to identify churn predictors. Generate optimized, personalized retention strategies with specific recommended actions.
  - **Human Role:** Design and execute the AI-recommended retention strategies, adding a personal touch and addressing unique customer concerns. Monitor the effectiveness of the strategies and provide feedback to the AI.

Visualization Tip

Use **augmented reality (AR) overlays** or **before-and-after comparisons** to illustrate the impact of AI-driven contextualization. For example, AR overlays could highlight specific energy usage improvements directly on utility equipment, showing operators exactly where to make adjustments.

Human Role Highlighted in Visualizations: Operators use AR overlays to cross-check AI outputs with physical conditions, ensuring alignment with real-world needs and safety.

Step 4: Demonstrate Value Through Visual Storytelling

Focus Question: How do we show AI's potential in a way that inspires confidence?

Example 1: Show Operational Success in Logistics

- **Job to Be Done:** Reduce delivery times intelligently using AI-powered route optimization.
- **The Challenge:** Imagine truck drivers receiving confusing or inefficient route suggestions from a basic navigation system. They're skeptical of technology, relying on their own experience, leading to inconsistent delivery times and increased fuel costs.
- **The Solution:** Now, picture an AI system that intelligently generates real-time heatmaps, visualizing proactively optimized routes that

account for traffic, weather, and delivery priorities. This intelligent automation reduces delivery times by 20% and increases driver confidence in the AI's capabilities.

- o **AI Role:** Intelligently and continuously analyze traffic, weather, delivery patterns, and vehicle data. Proactively optimize routes in real-time, considering various factors.

- o **Human Role:** Validate AI-generated routes, adapting to unexpected on-the-ground challenges (e.g., road closures). Provide feedback to the AI to improve its route optimization.

Example 2: Inspire Confidence in Retail

- • **Job to Be Done:** Intelligently increase sales through proactively optimized personalized recommendations.

- • **The Challenge:** Store managers are hesitant to trust basic sales reports or simple recommendation lists. They need to see clear evidence that AI can accurately predict customer behavior and drive sales.

- • **The Solution:** Now, imagine an AI system that proactively simulates customer journeys, visualizing how personalized and timely recommendations influence purchase decisions and intelligently drive conversion rates. This proactive approach builds confidence in the AI's ability to boost revenue.

  - o **AI Role:** Intelligently analyze customer purchase patterns, browsing behavior, and demographic data. Proactively optimize personalized recommendations and timing to maximize sales.

  - o **Human Role:** Oversee AI implementation, incorporating staff feedback and sales strategies to refine recommendations. Monitor the AI's impact on sales and customer behavior.

Visualization Tip

Build **digital twins** or **immersive 3D data landscapes** to showcase the operational or revenue outcomes of AI implementations. For instance, a retail chain could use a digital twin of a store to simulate foot traffic patterns and inventory flows proactively optimized by AI.

    Human Role Highlighted in Visualizations: Store managers interact with the digital twin, testing proactively optimized scenarios and providing feedback to further refine AI recommendations.

Why These Steps Work

Simplicity, when paired with clear demonstrations and a human-centered approach, ensures that AI insights resonate with stakeholders, fostering trust and alignment:

- **Trust and Engagement:** Intuitive visualizations and simple explanations build trust and align teams around shared objectives.
- **Empowered Decisions:** Clear, actionable outputs enable users to make informed decisions with confidence and speed.
- **Human + AI Synergy:** A focus on collaboration ensures AI augments, rather than replaces, human expertise, creating robust and adaptable solutions.

When leaders prioritize simplicity, they transform AI from an intimidating technology into an approachable, trusted ally, driving adoption, fostering alignment, and achieving sustainable success.

Real-World Story: Valley Medical Center

Valley Medical Center in Renton, Washington, faced a significant challenge: their process for managing patient care decisions wasn't meeting federal guidelines and placed a heavy burden on staff. Determining the correct level of care for patients (whether they needed full inpatient care, observation, or could be discharged) was a complex balancing act. Providing care at a higher level than necessary risked financial reimbursement denials, while offering care at a lower level could compromise patient outcomes and fail to meet regulatory standards.

To address this, Valley Medical Center implemented Dragonfly, an AI-powered utilization management tool. Dragonfly uses a Care Level Score (CLS), a scale from 0 to 157, to assess how well a patient's current care status aligns with their medical needs and regulatory requirements. For example, a high CLS indicates that the patient's care level is appropriate, while a lower score signals that adjustments may be needed.

This system streamlined a previously cumbersome process. With Dragonfly, nurses could rely on AI to analyze patient data and generate actionable recommendations. This allowed them to focus on their clinical expertise, ensuring patients received the right level of care that maintained compliance and optimized financial reimbursement.

AI and Human Partnership in Action

Before Dragonfly, Valley Medical Center struggled with time-consuming patient situation reviews and inconsistent case management. With Dragonfly, AI took on the burden of analyzing patient data, providing actionable recommendations, and streamlining decisions:

- **AI's Role:** Analyze patient data, generate CLS recommendations, and highlight priority cases for review.
- **Human Expertise:** Nurses validated and refined AI recommendations, applying their clinical judgment to ensure patient-centric decisions.

This collaboration resulted in measurable improvements:

- A 66.7% increase in case review volume, raising completion rates from 60 to 100%
- A 25% reduction in extended stay observation rates, from 36.2 to 27.3%
- The right-sizing of observation rates, increasing them from 4 to 13%, bringing them in line with local and federal benchmarks

Moreover, the system's shared-view feature streamlined communication between providers and payers, with partner organizations like Humana reporting 15–17 minutes saved per case review.

Simplicity in Action

Valley Medical Center's success stemmed from the simplicity of the Dragonfly system. Rather than overwhelming users with complex interfaces or jargon, the tool provided actionable insights in the form of a clear CLS metric and a streamlined workflow:

- **Clarity Through Metrics:** The CLS metric distilled complex patient data into a single, easily understandable number, empowering nurses to make rapid, informed decisions.
- **Ease of Use:** Dragonfly's intuitive interface minimized the learning curve, promoting rapid adoption and efficient use across the organization.

By combining AI's analytical power with human expertise, Valley Medical Center achieved operational efficiency without sacrificing the quality of patient care.

Outcomes of Bold AI Leadership

Valley Medical Center's implementation of Dragonfly exemplifies Bold AI Leadership, demonstrating how simplicity and human + AI collaboration drive real-world impact:

- **Empowering Human Expertise:** AI provided data-driven recommendations, while nurses applied their professional judgment to ensure decisions were patient-centered.
- **Building Trust Through Transparency:** The CLS metric and user-friendly workflows demystified AI outputs, making them accessible to frontline staff and leadership alike.
- **Delivering Measurable Value:** The right-sizing of observation rates, reduction in extended stays, increased case review volume, and time savings highlight how simplicity translates into quantifiable results.

Key Metrics of Success

- **Case Review Volume:** Increased from 60 to 100% (a 66.7% improvement)
- **Extended Stay Observations:** Reduced from 36.2 to 27.3% (a 25% improvement)
- **Observation Rate Alignment:** Right-sized from 4 to 13%, aligning with benchmarks
- **Time Savings:** 15–17 minutes saved per case review for payer-provider collaboration

By embracing simplicity and prioritizing the human + AI partnership, Valley Medical Center transformed its utilization management process. This real-world example highlights how Bold AI Leadership simplifies complex systems, builds trust, and delivers lasting value for both organizations and the patients they serve.

Key Takeaways:

- **For Organizations Beginning Their AI Journey:** Distill complex medical decisions into simple, actionable metrics like the Care Level Score. Make AI approachable through straightforward visual indicators, avoiding technical algorithms. Demonstrate how AI simplifies daily workflows, not complicating them.

- **For Organizations Scaling AI**: Convert complex AI insights into clear, actionable recommendations that frontline staff can easily understand and trust. Create simple feedback loops that allow users to validate and improve AI suggestions (user interface and user experience are key here!). Use straightforward visuals to demonstrate impact across departments.

Visualization Tool Example for Simplicity

To illustrate how leaders can showcase the collaborative power of humans working collaboratively with AI, the Human + AI Decision Map visually demonstrates their partnership in decision-making (see Figure 3.1). In brief, this tool reveals how AI supports human expertise rather than replacing it, fostering understanding and trust in AI tools. See Appendix C for a detailed breakdown of the Human + AI Decision Map, including its key elements and implementation steps.

Human + AI Decision Map

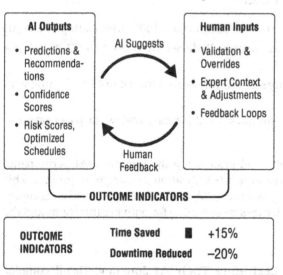

FIGURE 3.1 Human + AI Decision Map: Smarter decisions through collaboration. This visual shows how AI-generated insights and human expertise work in tandem.

The Human + AI Decision Map Helps Leaders:

- Visually demonstrate how AI recommendations and human input work together
- Utilize data points such as AI Outputs and Human Inputs
- Leverage the collaborative workflow layout and outcome indicators
- Understand visualization style and sample metrics for effective communication

The tool is implemented through steps like Data Integration, Mapping the Workflow, Visual Design, and Iterative Refinement, addressing common pitfalls such as Overloading Users with Details, Neglecting the Human Role, and Lack of Real-World Context. Success is indicated by Trust in AI Outputs, Improved Decision Outcomes, and Stakeholder Confidence.

From Insight to Action

The **Human + AI Decision Map** drives better decisions by clearly showing how humans and AI collaborate. By visualizing this interplay of human expertise and AI insights, it builds unshakeable trust and empowers teams to move from analysis paralysis to confident action. The key is to transform complex data into actionable guidance, not just present information.

Closing: Simplicity Drives Success

Communication clarity (not technical complexity) is your most powerful tool in AI leadership. As you guide your organization forward, your ability to strip away technical jargon and reveal AI's true value will set you apart. You've likely sat through meetings where experts tried to impress with complex terms, only to watch trust and enthusiasm fade. Your strength lies in doing the opposite: making the complex clear and the abstract tangible.

When you make AI approachable and its benefits visible to your stakeholders, you'll watch skepticism transform into trust, and resistance bloom into enthusiasm. Your success won't hinge on having the most sophisticated AI environment; it will come from making AI's benefits clear and actionable for everyone in your organization.

As you take your next steps, embrace Show Not Tell. Your visual demonstrations of value will speak louder than any technical explanation. When you speak your stakeholders' language and show how AI enhances their expertise rather than replaces it, you'll build the momentum needed for lasting change.

Your journey to AI excellence begins with a simple question: Can you explain your vision so clearly that everyone, from the boardroom to the break room, can see their role in it?

Your Turn: Bold AI Leadership in Simplicity

AI's potential is immense, but if people can't understand its value, they won't trust it (or use it). Simplicity is critical and is broader than just communication; it's a strategic leadership approach that drives AI adoption, engagement, and impact. AI that is difficult to understand, wrapped in technical jargon, or lacks a clear real-world application will struggle to gain traction. Whether your organization is just starting to explore AI or already leveraging it in key workflows, now is the time to assess how clearly your AI initiatives communicate value. Bold AI Leaders don't wait for understanding to happen organically; they shape it through clear visualizations and relatable examples.

This exercise will help you identify areas where complexity is slowing progress and where a clearer, more visual approach can drive better engagement, understanding, and adoption.

Assess: Where Are You on the Simplicity Journey?

If New to AI:

- **Analyze Reactions to Technical Discussions:** Are stakeholders engaged or overwhelmed by technical details?
- **Evaluate Conversation Focus:** Do discussions center on business impact or technical specifications?
- **Identify Resistance Sources:** Where do you see resistance to new technology due to lack of understanding?
- **Map AI Opportunities:** Describe two to three key business challenges where AI could help, using plain language.
- **Visualize AI Solutions:** Create simple visual explanations of how AI can address these challenges.
- **Design a Jargon-Free Framework:** Develop a presentation framework for introducing AI initiatives without technical jargon.

If Already Using AI:

Evaluate your current AI communication approach:

- **Evaluate AI Communication:** How effectively are AI benefits communicated to end users?

- **Identify Underutilized Solutions:** Where are AI solutions underutilized due to complexity?
- **Analyze User Struggles:** Where do teams struggle to understand how and when to apply AI tools?
  - **Audit Documentation and Training:** Review existing AI documentation and training for clarity.
  - **Document Success Stories:** Provide examples where simpler explanations increased adoption.
  - **Create an Engagement Visualization:** Develop a visual to track:
    - Usage metrics (active users, frequency of use)
    - Understanding indicators (training completion, help desk requests)

Reflect: Clarity, Confidence, Connection

- **Assess Audience Understanding:** Think about a recent AI presentation or discussion. Did everyone leave with a clear understanding of how AI could help them?
- **Analyze Simplicity Techniques:** When was the last time you used a visual, a metaphor, or a story to explain an AI concept? What was the response?
- **Identify Simplicity's Impact:** Where have AI initiatives in your organization gained the most traction? What role did simplicity play in that success?
- **Reflect on Vulnerability:** When was the last time you admitted not knowing something about AI? What was the impact on your credibility and relationships?
- **Compare Success Factors:** How do your most successful AI initiatives differ from the less successful ones? What role did communication clarity play in that difference?

Take Action: Simplify, Show, Engage

- **Simplify Existing Materials:** Choose an AI concept, report, or presentation and simplify its language and visuals.
- **Tailor Communication:** Identify three stakeholder groups (executives, employees, customers) and define the clearest way to communicate AI's impact to each.
- **Prioritize Demonstrations:** Instead of describing AI, show its value through visual storytelling, live demos, or user testimonials.
- **Challenge Yourself:** Try explaining an AI concept without using any AI-related jargon. Can you make it so clear that a non-technical colleague immediately understands the value?

Why This Matters

The organizations that thrive with AI aren't necessarily the ones with the most advanced technology; they are the ones that make AI's benefits visible and relatable for everyone involved. AI success requires purposeful avoidance of unnecessary complexity. It requires clarity and trust to gain adoption. The Bold AI Leaders who excel don't just talk about AI; they show its impact in ways that everyone can understand.

Your Bold AI Leadership Challenge This Week

Not Using AI Yet:

- **Analyze Success Stories**: Find an AI success story from your industry and analyze its communication style.
- **Observe Internal Discussions**: How is AI discussed in your organization? As a complex threat or a helpful tool?
- **Identify Simplification Opportunities**: Choose a process where AI could simplify tasks and improve outcomes.
- **Practice Clear Explanations**: Explain an AI concept to a non-technical colleague and assess their comprehension.

AI Already in Use:

- **Observe User Interaction:** Shadow three users of an AI tool and observe how they interact with it. Do they find it intuitive and useful, or do they struggle with complexity?
- **Document Simplification Impact**: Document one example where simplifying the explanation of an AI-driven process helped drive better engagement or adoption.
- **Evaluate Insight Presentation**: Review how AI-generated insights are presented in your organization. Are they clear, timely, and easy to act on, or do they require unnecessary interpretation?

Remember

Simplicity is a leadership superpower. AI adoption relies on trust and understanding, not technical complexity. Adoption happens when people see AI's value, trust it, and feel confident using it. This process of building trust through simplicity naturally flows into establishing collaborative human + AI partnerships, the focus of our next chapter.

CHAPTER 4

Human-Centricity

Unlocking Potential Through Human + AI Partnerships

Organizations at every point on the AI journey, from those planning their first initiative to those expanding mature programs, face a critical challenge: putting people at the center of AI strategy. Success depends not on technology alone but on creating meaningful partnerships between human capabilities and AI systems.

Introduction: The Heart of Bold AI Leadership

Picture two global advisory firms, both embracing AI to transform how they develop their most precious resource: their people.

- At Heritage Advisory, an ambitious AI initiative turns their renowned apprenticeship model upside down. Senior partners find themselves competing with an AI that claims to "democratize expertise." First-year analysts, overwhelmed by endless AI-generated insights, lose the art of critical thinking. During a make-or-break client presentation, a team confidently presents AI-generated recommendations, only to freeze when the CEO asks, "But what do you think?" Within a year, they lose three major accounts and their legendary training program sees applications drop by half.

- At Catalyst Partners, they're writing a different story. Their approach starts with a profound insight: AI shouldn't replace judgment but rather create space for more of it. Their platform acts as a master curator of collective wisdom, connecting analysts with mentors and surfacing relevant experiences. Senior partners have deeper coaching conversations, freed from routine analysis. During client meetings, teams display a powerful combination of data-driven insights and nuanced understanding that their competitors can't match.

The technology was similar. The difference? Heritage tried to automate wisdom; Catalyst amplified it. One diminished their people; the other elevated them.

Key Takeaways:

- **For Organizations Beginning Their AI Journey:** Start by mapping how AI can amplify your team's strengths. If your senior analysts excel at client relationships, use AI to handle data analysis so they can double their client face time. Create clear before/after comparisons showing how AI increases meaningful human interaction.

- **For Organizations Scaling AI:** Regularly assess your automation/augmentation balance, aiming to automate routine work while amplifying human capabilities in high-value areas. Take Catalyst's approach: using AI to handle basic analysis so senior partners can focus on deeper coaching conversations. Track and celebrate metrics like "coaching hours per week" and "time spent on strategic client discussions" to show how AI creates space for expertise to shine. Build feedback loops where human insight continues to improve AI recommendations.

This Principle Transcends Consulting:

- At ABC Medical Center, AI augments clinical judgment, surfacing case histories and research that empower doctors to focus on patient care and nuanced decisions.

- At Learning Academy, AI handles routine tasks like grading papers and draft lesson plans, freeing teachers to personalize mentoring and engage meaningfully with students.

What consistently makes the difference? **Human-centricity**.

Why Human-Centricity Matters

We're experiencing a world where technology doesn't just make us more efficient; it makes us more human. Where AI doesn't replace the spark of creativity in a designer's eye, the reassuring touch of a nurse's hand, or the wisdom in a mentor's words. Instead, it amplifies these uniquely human qualities, creating space for more moments of genuine connection, breakthrough insights, and transformative decisions.

When organizations get this right, the impact is profound. Those that embrace true Human + AI partnerships don't just see better numbers; they witness the transformation of their people. Teams become more innovative, customers feel more understood, and employees find deeper meaning in their work.

AI Alone Isn't Enough

AI can process massive datasets and identify patterns with incredible speed and accuracy, but it lacks the creativity, empathy, and judgment that define human decision-making. Pair AI with human ingenuity, and the results are transformative.

Human + AI: A Superior Formula

Human-centric AI leverages the strengths of both people and technology. AI handles repetitive tasks, analyzes data, and provides evidence-based recommendations. Humans bring context, creativity, and critical thinking to make the final call. This collaboration drives better decisions, greater efficiency, and improved experiences for employees and customers alike.

The Bold AI Leadership Connection

Bold AI Leaders understand that human-centricity is a business imperative and not just a "nice-to-have." Organizations that embrace Human + AI partnerships outperform their competitors, generating higher revenue, enhancing employee engagement, and delivering superior customer satisfaction.

In this chapter, we'll explore how Bold AI Leaders:

- **Empower Users:** Design intuitive, inclusive AI systems
- **Build Trust:** Prioritize transparency, fairness, and explainability
- **Drive Impact:** Align AI with human needs to deliver measurable results

Let's begin by defining what it means to be truly human-centric and why this approach is essential for Bold AI Leadership.

Definition

Human-centricity is the philosophy and practice of designing AI systems to complement human strengths, amplify human potential, and respect human judgment. At its core, human-centricity ensures that technology serves people, not the other way around. It prioritizes collaboration between humans and AI, where each contributes unique strengths to achieve better outcomes.

Bold AI Leaders recognize that the most transformative AI solutions emerge not when AI operates in isolation, but when it works as a partner to human ingenuity. This partnership allows AI to handle tasks like data analysis, repetitive workflows, and pattern recognition while leaving room for humans to focus on creativity, critical thinking, and nuanced decision-making.

My Guiding Principles for Human-Centric AI

To align AI technology with human needs and aspirations, I've curated a set of guiding principles. These principles emphasize empowering users, fostering trust, and driving impactful results, all while ensuring tangible business value.

1. **Augment, Don't Replace: The Power of Partnership**

   Think of AI as your team's brilliant research assistant, not its replacement. The goal is to supercharge human capabilities, not substitute them. When implemented thoughtfully, AI handles routine tasks and initial analyses, freeing professionals to focus on complex decision-making, strategic thinking, and meaningful human interactions. The result is enhanced performance and satisfaction across the board.

2. **Empower Through Accessibility: Breaking Down Barriers**

   Great AI is like a well-designed smartphone - powerful yet intuitive. By replacing technical jargon with plain language and incorporating interactive learning elements, AI systems become accessible to users of all skill levels. When everyone can harness AI's potential, innovation thrives across the organization.

3. **Build Trust Through Transparency: Opening the Black Box**

   Effective AI systems don't just make recommendations; they explain them. When users can trace insights back to source data, understanding not just what the AI suggests but why, skepticism transforms into confidence. This transparency drives adoption and ensures meaningful use of AI tools.

4. **Prioritize End Users' Needs: Starting with Why**

The best AI solutions begin by understanding the "job to be done": the real problem users are trying to solve. Rather than starting with technology capabilities, successful implementations focus on user challenges, aspirations, and desired outcomes. By aligning AI capabilities with these core jobs to be done, solutions naturally enhance human capabilities rather than just automating tasks. This approach ensures AI creates meaningful impact, freeing users to focus on higher-value work while effectively handling routine operations that support their primary objectives. Organizations that excel at this don't just layer AI onto existing processes; they fundamentally reimagine how work gets done!

5. **Iterate and Learn: Growing Together**

Like any great partnership, Human + AI excellence requires continuous dialogue. Successful organizations treat their AI systems like team members who need ongoing coaching. Regular feedback, performance monitoring, and continuous adjustments ensure AI solutions evolve alongside workforce needs, staying relevant and effective. AI is not "set it and forget it"; it's a living system that requires ongoing attention, refinement, and adaptation to deliver sustained value.

6. **Create Value for All: The Ripple Effect**

True human-centric AI creates wins across the board. Well-designed systems empower better decision-making, reduce workplace stress, and enhance experiences for everyone involved. When implemented thoughtfully, AI initiatives drive both quantitative improvements and qualitative benefits that resonate throughout the organization.

These principles, derived from my extensive professional experience and academic research, are crucial for fostering successful Human + AI partnerships. They provide a framework for AI initiatives that are both technically sound and organizationally effective.

The Foundation: Data Quality and Governance

Picture building a beautiful house on sand. No matter how perfect the design, it won't stand. The same principle applies to human-centric AI. Before any of our six guiding principles for human-centric AI can truly deliver value, we need solid ground to build upon.

When Catalyst Partners transformed their mentorship program, their success wasn't simply due to clever AI design; it started with years of meticulously documented case studies, carefully preserved client insights, and rigorous data governance. Their data wasn't just clean; it was rich with human context and consistently updated.

Think of data quality as the soil from which human-centric AI grows:

- Fresh data keeps solutions relevant and aligned with current business realities.
- Careful bias monitoring ensures fairness and equitable outcomes for all users.
- Strong governance protects both privacy and trust through transparent policies.

Without this foundation, even the most thoughtfully designed AI systems can produce misleading or outdated results. With it, human-centric AI flourishes, delivering reliable insights that users can confidently act upon.

While data quality and governance might not be the most exciting part of AI leadership, they're absolutely essential. They're the invisible force multiplier that turns good human-centric AI into great human-centric AI.

These principles represent more than best practices. They are essential elements of Bold AI Leadership. Organizations that embrace these guiding principles deliver AI solutions that transcend technical requirements to foster trust, empower teams, and generate lasting value. This foundation enables effective Human + AI partnerships that unlock the full potential of both, creating a future where technology augments, rather than diminishes, human capabilities.

Pitfalls: When Human-Centric AI Falls Short

Even the most well-intentioned AI initiatives can go sideways, undermining trust and value instead of enhancing human capabilities. These missteps lead to mistrust, underutilization, or even harm, eroding the very foundation of Human + AI partnerships. Bold AI Leaders must be vigilant in recognizing and addressing these pitfalls to ensure their initiatives truly serve human needs and deliver lasting value.

Here, I explore three categories of pitfalls - Vision, Execution, and Culture - that can derail even the most promising AI initiatives.

Vision Pitfalls: Missing the Forest for the Trees

1. The Automation Obsession

The Trap: Chasing cost savings through automation while missing opportunities to amplify human potential

The Warning Sign: When conversations focus more on replacing than enhancing

The Fix: Starting with the "why" - the job to be done - and aligning AI initiatives with human-centric business value creation

2. The Data Deficit

The Trap: Building on shaky data foundations, leading to biased or unreliable outputs

The Warning Sign: When AI outputs reflect historical biases or produce inconsistent results

The Fix: Investing in data quality, diversity, and governance before scaling AI solutions

3. The Ivory Tower Syndrome

The Trap: Designing solutions without real user input

The Warning Sign: When end users say "This isn't what we need"

The Fix: Making users your co-creators, not just consumers

Execution Pitfalls: Where Good Ideas Go to Die

1. The Black Box Blunder

The Trap: Deploying AI systems that can't explain their decisions

The Warning Sign: When users reject AI recommendations due to lack of trust

The Fix: Building explainability into your AI from day one

2. The "Set and Forget" Fallacy

The Trap: Treating AI as a one-time implementation rather than a living system

The Warning Sign: When system performance gradually declines

The Fix: Implementing robust feedback loops and regular refinement cycles

3. **The Expert Echo Chamber**

The Trap: Creating tools only technical experts can use

The Warning Sign: When adoption is limited to power users

The Fix: Designing for inclusivity from the ground up

Culture Pitfalls: When People and Tech Collide

1. **The Fear Factor**

The Trap: Teams viewing AI as a threat rather than an ally

The Warning Sign: When resistance and workarounds become the norm

The Fix: Championing AI as an enhancer of human potential, not a replacement

2. **The Solo Flight**

The Trap: Developing AI solutions in technical isolation

The Warning Sign: When solutions solve the wrong problems

The Fix: Building cross-functional teams that blend technical and business expertise

3. **The Feature Frenzy**

The Trap: Prioritizing technical sophistication over practical value

The Warning Sign: When complex features go unused

The Fix: Focusing relentlessly on solving real business problems

Remember

The most dangerous pitfalls often come disguised as best practices. Stay vigilant, keep your users at the center, and never stop questioning assumptions. That's what Bold AI Leadership is all about.

Consider this compelling example: "Best Practice: Standardize AI tools across the organization for consistency and efficiency."

Sounds reasonable, right? But here's how this "best practice" became a pitfall for a global consulting firm:

They implemented a standardized AI writing assistant across all departments, believing consistency would improve efficiency. The tool was highly rated and worked excellently for client proposals and reports. However, their creative team found it stifled their unique voice, their legal team needed more specialized compliance features, and their research team required different capabilities entirely.

By rigidly following the "best practice" of standardization, they actually reduced effectiveness. The Bold AI Leadership solution? They shifted to a flexible, modular approach where teams could customize their AI tools while maintaining core integration standards. This meant the creative team could preserve their distinctive style, legal could add compliance checks, and researchers could access specialized features, all while keeping the benefits of organizational consistency where it mattered.

The Lesson: What looks like a solid best practice can become a trap if we don't constantly question how it serves our users' actual needs. **Pitfall Checkpoint**

Before launching your AI initiative, ask:

- Are we aligning AI with broader business goals and human-centric principles?
- Have we established robust data practices to ensure fairness, accuracy, and relevance?
- Are end users involved in the design process to ensure usability and alignment with their needs?
- Have we prioritized transparency and explainability to build trust?
- Do we have feedback mechanisms in place to adapt and improve over time?

By proactively addressing these pitfalls, organizations can avoid common missteps and lay the groundwork for successful Human + AI partnerships that empower people and deliver measurable business value.

This structured approach to recognizing and mitigating risks ensures your AI initiatives remain human-centric, impactful, and aligned with the principles of Bold AI Leadership.

Actionable Steps: Bring Human-Centric AI to Life

Bold AI Leaders don't just implement AI; they design solutions that enhance human capabilities and create measurable value. The actionable steps that they take focus on showing, not just telling, how Human + AI partnerships will transform their organizations. By grounding each step in human-centric principles, we align AI initiatives with real-world needs, making the value of AI clear and compelling.

Each step includes battle-tested examples and ready-to-implement strategies that turn Human + AI partnerships from concept to reality.

Step 1: Make Users Your Co-Creators

The Rule: If they don't help build it, they won't use it.

Focus Question: How do we ensure AI solutions meet the needs of those who use them?

Example 1: Empower Frontline Employees

- **Scenario:** In a hospital setting, AI streamlines patient triage by prioritizing high-risk cases. However, initial adoption is slow because nurses feel excluded from the system's design.

- **Show Not Tell Solution:** Engage nurses early in development. Co-create workflows that reflect their expertise, and run **"Day in the Life" interactive workshops** to demonstrate how AI supports, not replaces, their decisions.

Example 2: Build Customer Confidence

- **Scenario:** An e-commerce platform's AI recommends products but lacks transparency, making customers skeptical.

- **Show Not Tell Solution:** Introduce a **"Why We Recommended This" feature** that explains recommendations in simple, relatable terms. Use customer testimonials to show how the feature improves their shopping experience.

Key Practice: Design with empathy. Involve end users in prototyping and testing and demonstrate the AI's value through **live scenarios** or **real-time feedback loops**.

Step 2: Build Trust Through Show and Tell

The Rule: Transparency isn't a feature; it's the foundation.

Focus Question: How do we ensure AI systems are trusted and understood?

Example 1: Enhance Operational Decisions

- **Scenario:** AI monitors manufacturing processes and flags equipment for maintenance. Teams hesitate to act on its recommendations due to unclear reasoning.

- **Show Not Tell Solution:** Pair AI outputs with **visual decision trees**, showing why specific actions are needed. Use case studies to illustrate successful interventions.

   Example 2: Drive Strategic Alignment

- **Scenario:** A board of directors resists AI adoption, concerned about bias in decision-making.

- **Show Not Tell Solution:** Present a **bias audit visualization** that highlights fairness metrics and explains how bias is mitigated, fostering trust and confidence in the system.

Key Practice: Use **visual storytelling tools** to make AI decisions transparent and relatable. Highlight how human oversight enhances fairness and accountability.

Step 3: Amplify Don't Replace

The Rule: AI should make humans better at being human.

Focus Question: How do we design AI to augment, not replace, human capabilities?

Example 1: Empower Knowledge Workers

- **Scenario:** A consulting firm uses AI to generate client insights, but junior consultants feel their roles are diminished.

- **Show Not Tell Solution:** Position AI as a research assistant, surfacing key data and saving time. Demonstrate its role in enabling consultants to focus on crafting creative, strategic solutions through **live "with and without AI" project demonstrations**.

Example 2: Improve Employee Engagement

- **Scenario:** Employees resist AI automation, fearing job displacement.

- **Show Not Tell Solution:** Run **interactive training sessions** where employees use AI to automate repetitive tasks, freeing up time for meaningful work. Show examples of improved workflows and measurable productivity gains.

Key Practice: Regularly demonstrate how AI complements human expertise with **side-by-side comparisons** of tasks completed with and without AI support.

Step 4: Make It Living, Make It Learn

The Rule: Static AI is dead AI.

Focus Question: How do we ensure AI systems evolve with user needs?

Example 1: Continuous Learning in Retail

- **Scenario:** AI predicts customer demand, but seasonal changes lead to inaccuracies.
- **Show Not Tell Solution:** Introduce weekly **AI Learning Reports** that highlight specific adjustments made to the AI based on real-world sales patterns. For instance, one week's report could show how user feedback helped the AI recognize an unexpected surge in winter apparel demand, leading to better inventory alignment. These reports keep stakeholders informed and engaged, showing tangible progress in the AI's learning journey.

Example 2: Foster Collaborative Refinement

- **Scenario:** A team deploys AI for lead scoring but finds discrepancies between scores and sales outcomes.
- **Show Not Tell Solution:** Use **AI Learning Reports** to highlight how sales teams' feedback has refined scoring logic. For example, a report might feature a specific instance where a low-scoring lead converted to a sale, prompting the AI to adjust its weighting of certain criteria. By sharing these evolving insights, teams see their role in shaping smarter, more accurate AI systems.

  Key Practice: Treat AI as a living system.

- Implement **weekly AI Learning Reports** to showcase how feedback loops drive continuous improvement. These reports can include:
  - Real-world examples of where user input corrected AI errors.
  - Updates on model adjustments and how they've improved performance.
  - Metrics showing the impact of refinements, such as increased accuracy or reduced errors.
- Share these reports across teams to demonstrate the collaborative evolution of the system.

Step 5: Spread the Wealth

The Rule: If everyone doesn't win, then nobody wins.

Focus Question: How do we align AI initiatives with organizational and societal goals?

Example 1: Improve Customer Experiences

- **Scenario:** A subscription service uses AI to personalize offerings but lacks metrics to track impact.

- **Show Not Tell Solution:** Visualize the **customer journey** before and after AI implementation, showing improvements in satisfaction and retention metrics.

Example 2: Enhance Team Collaboration

- **Scenario:** AI improves individual productivity but fails to support team workflows.
- **Show Not Tell Solution:** Use **collaborative decision maps** to show how AI insights benefit group strategies, highlighting how business value creation ripples across departments.

Key Practice: Align AI projects with clear metrics that reflect both business and human outcomes. Use **interactive ROI models** to communicate the broader impact of AI on customers, employees, and organizational goals.

Why These Steps Work

Human-Centric AI + Show Not Tell = Results

By emphasizing actionable, visible demonstrations, these steps transform AI from an abstract concept into a trusted partner. Teams see AI's potential firsthand, fostering trust, engagement, and adoption.

- **Trust and Clarity:** Transparent, relatable tools build confidence in AI systems.
- **Empowered Teams:** AI amplifies human capabilities, ensuring users feel supported, not sidelined.
- **Tangible Impact:** Clear metrics and real-world examples show how AI delivers measurable value.

By anchoring your AI initiatives in human-centric principles and ensuring they are seen and experienced, you'll drive adoption, inspire action, and create enduring business success.

Execution Accelerators

1. **Quick Wins First**
   - Launch 30-day pilot programs.
   - Focus on high-visibility, low-complexity wins.
   - Document and showcase early successes.
2. **Measure What Matters**

   Before launching any AI initiative, establish:
   - Human impact metrics (time saved, satisfaction scores)

- Business impact metrics (ROI, efficiency gains)
- Learning metrics (system accuracy, adoption rates)

3. **Tell Success Stories**
   - Create "Before & After AI" case studies.
   - Share user testimonials.
   - Visualize improvement metrics.

Making It Stick: Your 90-Day Launch Plan

Days 1–30: Foundation
- Form user advisory group.
- Map current pain points.
- Select pilot project.

Days 31–60: Implementation
- Launch pilot with heavy user involvement.
- Collect daily feedback.
- Make rapid adjustments.

Days 61–90: Scale
- Document wins and lessons.
- Train champions in other departments.
- Plan expansion based on user demand.

Remember

Speed beats perfection: Start small, show results, and then scale what works. Your first human-centric AI solution doesn't need to be perfect; it needs to be real.

Power Tip

Create an "AI Win Wall" where teams can post their success stories and learning moments. Make progress visible and celebration constant.

The Bottom Line

Human-centric AI requires a full-spectrum commitment, from boardroom vision to frontline implementation. Success happens when leaders champion the strategy and teams shape the execution. Every level of the organization plays a vital role: executives set the course, managers build the bridges, and users provide the insights that make AI solutions truly transformative.

This goes beyond simple implementation. We're creating an environment where AI amplifies capabilities across every level of the organization, from executive leadership to customer service teams. When strategic vision aligns with practical expertise, AI delivers breakthrough value.

Real-World Story: Falkonry Changes the Stainless Industry

One of the stories that captured my attention during my doctoral research originated in the heart of the U.S.-heavy industry, where a leading stainless steel manufacturer faced a pressing question: how could they modernize operations with AI while preserving the human expertise that built them into an industry leader? Enter Falkonry, an AI services firm led by CEO Nikunj Mehta. Guided by human-centric principles, Falkonry's strategy seamlessly integrated AI into the organization, amplifying human expertise rather than replacing it.

The Challenge: Leveraging AI Without Undermining Expertise

Operating in a highly specialized environment, the steel producer sought to use AI for predictive maintenance and process optimization. However, their journey to success was paved with challenges:

- **Data Complexity:** Industrial data was unstructured, often containing flaws that only surfaced during analysis.
- **Data Value Decay:** As Nikunj Mehta put it, "Data is like coffee, not oil." Its value diminishes rapidly, requiring immediate action for meaningful insights.
- **Workforce Skepticism:** Employees worried AI would disrupt established workflows or misinterpret critical nuances.
- **Proving Value:** Executives demanded clear, measurable ROI to justify investment and sustain support.

The Solution: A Collaborative, Agile, and Transparent Approach

Falkonry tackled these challenges using a Show Not Tell strategy, ensuring that AI's value was evident to everyone involved.

Step 1: Engaging Subject-Matter Experts (SMEs) One of Falkonry's pivotal strategies was involving SMEs from the client organization to play an active role in shaping the AI. This approach focused on leveraging the deep expertise of those who understood the data and its real-world applications best.

What Is Data Labeling? Data labeling involves annotating datasets to help AI systems recognize patterns and make predictions. For example, in manufacturing, labeling might include identifying operational data that indicates normal equipment behavior vs. signs of potential failure. Traditionally, this task is outsourced to external vendors or specialized firms, which can be costly, time-consuming, and detached from the unique nuances of the organization's operations.

Falkonry's Human-Centric Alternative Falkonry turned this model on its head by empowering internal teams to contribute their domain expertise directly:

- **Reducing Costs:** Instead of paying for external labeling services, internal teams annotated data based on their familiarity with equipment, processes, and workflows.

- **Enhancing Relevance:** Internal SMEs provided immediate, context-rich feedback, ensuring that the AI system learned from real-world, nuanced examples rather than generic or out-of-context datasets.

- **Building Trust:** By incorporating SME insights into the AI's learning process, Falkonry demonstrated that human expertise was vital. SMEs saw their knowledge reflected in AI outputs, fostering a sense of ownership and confidence in the system.

Falkonry also addressed a common concern: would this approach add more to the SMEs' already busy workloads? They showed how iterative feedback cycles could be seamlessly integrated into existing workflows. Instead of lengthy and disruptive processes, SMEs provided input in short, manageable bursts, ensuring both efficiency and effectiveness.

Iterative Feedback in Action Rather than simply telling SMEs how their input mattered, Falkonry demonstrated it through iterative feedback cycles:

- **Visible Refinements:** As SMEs labeled data and corrected AI outputs, they saw tangible improvements in accuracy and relevance. For example, if a machine vibration reading was mislabeled as a minor fluctuation, the SME's correction would immediately adjust the model's future interpretations.

- **Real-Time Results:** Weekly AI Progress Reports highlighted how SME feedback improved AI predictions, creating a transparent feedback loop where users could see tangible refinements and better understand the system's evolving capabilities.

By placing SMEs at the heart of the process, Falkonry didn't just build better AI; they built stronger relationships between humans and machines. This approach showcased the power of human-centric AI in action, proving that human expertise is indispensable in crafting effective, impactful solutions.

Step 2: Agile, Iterative Rollout   Falkonry avoided overpromising or overwhelming the organization by adopting a phased, iterative approach:

- **Weekly AI Learning Reports:** Transparent updates detailed how user feedback improved AI predictions, turning skepticism into trust.
- **Real-Time Adjustments:** Maintenance teams' inputs were incorporated immediately, showcasing the system's adaptability.
- **Tuna Fish, Not Whales:** Falkonry prioritized smaller, high-probability for success projects to build momentum and refine workflows before scaling.

Pro Tip: Many AI project failures stem from poor project selection, where AI isn't the optimal solution. Choose projects wisely!

By demonstrating progress in real time, Falkonry avoided overwhelming stakeholders with abstract promises and instead highlighted tangible improvements.

Step 3: A Portfolio Approach to Additive Success   Falkonry strategically built a portfolio of interconnected AI initiatives to maximize impact and maintain momentum:

- **Start with the Right Projects:** The team focused on adjacent or low-hanging fruit projects - initiatives that were more likely to succeed due to clear goals, accessible data, and engaged stakeholders. This ensured early wins that demonstrated AI's potential.
- **Efficiency Through Continuity:** By leveraging shared data, workflows, and lessons learned, each project benefited from the successes and insights of its predecessors. This approach minimized redundancy and accelerated implementation timelines.
- **Paving the Way for Broader Adoption:** Each successful initiative served as a proof point, showing stakeholders how AI could drive meaningful change across the organization. These early wins built trust, enthusiasm, and a foundation for scaling AI across more complex and ambitious areas.

Pro Tip: Use a visualization tool to map the additive impact of these adjacent efforts. For example, a **cumulative impact chart or heatmap** could illustrate how incremental improvements from each project contribute to overall organizational success. By visually connecting the dots between individual initiatives, leaders can show stakeholders the broader value and potential of scaling AI efforts. This fosters alignment and keeps momentum strong.

Step 4: Communicating Value Across Levels Nikunj emphasized that data without action is like a "rose spotlight" - beautiful but ultimately useless. To make AI's impact undeniable:

- **Executive Engagement:** Falkonry helped project champions craft compelling narratives that highlighted ROI and operational benefits.
- **Employee Buy-In:** Real-world examples of how AI streamlined workflows reassured frontline workers and demonstrated that their expertise remained vital.

Falkonry's transparent communication ensured all stakeholders understood how AI amplified (not disrupted) their contributions.

The Results: Tangible Impact and Cultural Transformation
Falkonry's partnership with the steel producer delivered transformative results:

- **Reduced Downtime:** Predictive maintenance minimized equipment failures, boosting productivity.
- **Maximized Data Value:** Acting promptly on fresh data unlocked actionable insights.
- **Engaged Workforce:** SMEs who contributed to AI development became its strongest advocates.
- **Clear ROI:** Measurable outcomes solidified executive support, driving ongoing investment in AI.

By showing how AI improved specific outcomes rather than simply telling stakeholders about its capabilities, Falkonry shifted organizational culture. Employees now view AI as a partner in success, and executives have seen it deliver measurable business value.

Lessons in Bold AI Leadership

Falkonry's success exemplifies how human-centric AI initiatives can thrive through actionable strategies that focus on visibility, collaboration, and iterative improvement. Their approach aligns with the Show Not Tell approach by making AI's value clear and relatable at every step:

- **Act on Data Quickly:** Like coffee, data loses its value quickly if not used promptly. Falkonry ensured real-time application of data insights, turning them into actionable decisions before they became outdated. Through regular updates, teams could see immediate results, reinforcing the importance of timely action.

- **Engage SMEs Deeply:** Falkonry didn't just tell SMEs they were crucial; they showed them, integrating their feedback into AI's learning process and visibly reflecting their contributions in the system's improved outputs. This visible impact built trust and fostered ownership.

- **Start Small, Scale Strategically:** Rather than overpromising grand AI transformations, Falkonry demonstrated success through smaller, adjacent projects. These projects, chosen carefully for their high likelihood of success, visibly showcased AI's incremental value, building momentum for larger efforts.

- **Communicate Value Clearly:** Weekly AI Progress Reports visually illustrated how user feedback shaped and refined the AI system, reinforcing transparency and trust. Additionally, Falkonry worked with champions to craft narratives that brought results to life, ensuring both frontline teams and executives understood the tangible benefits of AI initiatives.

This story demonstrates how Falkonry effectively used a Show Not Tell approach to transform potential challenges into scaled success. By amplifying human ingenuity and clearly showcasing the value of AI at every step, they exemplified the essence of Bold AI Leadership.

Key Takeaways:

- **For Organizations Beginning Their AI Journey:** Make your SMEs central to AI implementation. Have them guide AI development through "show and tell" sessions where they demonstrate their decision-making process. Create regular touchpoints where experts can see how their input shapes the AI's understanding, building trust through direct involvement.

- **For Organizations Scaling AI:** Transform SMEs into AI champions by showing how their expertise makes the system better. Use weekly AI Progress Reports to highlight how expert feedback improved predictions and prevented errors. Create opportunities for experts to mentor others in effective human + AI collaboration.

Visualization Tool Example for Human-Centricity

To illustrate how AI initiatives enhance human potential, the Human Impact Visualization provides a clear and engaging representation of AI's effects on employees and organizational outcomes. (See Figure 4.1.) In brief, this tool highlights the tangible benefits of human + AI collaboration, fostering trust and alignment among stakeholders. See Appendix D for a detailed breakdown of the Human Impact Visualization, including its key elements and implementation steps.

HUMAN IMPACT OF AI:
AMPLIFYING PEOPLE, DRIVING PERFORMANCE

EMPLOYEE BENEFITS

12 hrs/week saved via automation

ENGAGEMENT METRICS

85% Adoption of AI tools

90% Feel confident using AI

ORGANIZATIONAL OUTCOMES

35% Fewer manual errors

40% Faster decision-making

REAL-WORLD IMPACT

Progress arcs & before/after visuals

Employee quotes & team-level insights

FIGURE 4.1   Human impact of AI visualization: This visual highlights how AI empowers employees and accelerates outcomes. From saving time and reducing errors to boosting adoption and confidence, the data tells a clear story: AI enhances human potential.

The Human Impact Visualization Helps Leaders:

- Visually communicate the tangible effects of AI on employee roles, team dynamics, and organizational performance
- Utilize data points such as Employee Benefits, Engagement Metrics, and Organizational Outcomes

- Leverage formats like Outcome Representation and Interactive Layers
- Understand Impact Highlights and Sample Metrics for effective communication

The tool is implemented through steps like Define Key Metrics, Aggregate and Process Data, Design the Visualization, and Iterate Based on Feedback, addressing the common pitfalls of Overcomplicating Data, Neglecting Personal Stories, and Infrequent Updates. Success is indicated by Higher Engagement, Improved Productivity, and Leadership Confidence.

From Insight to Action: The Human Impact Visualization (Figure 4.1) serves as a storytelling device that brings the benefits of AI to life. By combining data-driven insights with personal narratives and intuitive visuals, this approach ensures stakeholders at all levels understand and appreciate the transformative power of human + AI collaboration. The goal is to drive a fundamental shift in how people experience and engage with AI, not just share data.

Closing: Human-Centricity Is the Future of Bold AI Leadership

A consultant walks confidently into a client meeting, armed not only with AI-driven insights but also the wisdom gained from years of hands-on experience. Across the table, the client doesn't see just another presentation; they see a partnership where data meets human intuition, precision meets empathy, and technology amplifies expertise.

This is the world of human-centric AI - a world where technology doesn't overshadow people but elevates them. It's where AI systems adapt to users, not the other way around. It's where human creativity, judgment, and empathy remain at the core, supported by AI's ability to process vast amounts of information with speed and accuracy.

Throughout this chapter, we've explored what happens when organizations embrace the human-centric approach. From the transformational success of Falkonry in the steel manufacturing industry to the six principles that form the foundation of effective Human + AI partnerships, the takeaway is undeniable: when people and technology work together, they achieve extraordinary results.

Consider the lessons learned along the way. We've seen how placing SMEs at the heart of AI projects leads to better, faster outcomes while building trust and ownership. We've explored the power of starting small with adjacent projects, creating momentum and showing, not just telling, how AI drives value.

And we've highlighted the importance of keeping data fresh and actionable, like brewing coffee that's meant to be enjoyed hot and fresh.

Human-centricity offers a practical roadmap for leaders who want to create real, measurable impact. For those who want to design AI solutions that reflect the needs of the people they serve. For those who seek to build trust through transparency. And maintain unwavering focus on creating outcomes that matter.

The future of AI lives where Human + AI partnerships thrive. Bold AI Leaders understand this. They know that when technology supports people, it doesn't just make organizations more efficient; it makes them more human. Let's continue this journey, building a future where Human + AI partnerships redefine what's possible!

Your Turn: Bold AI Leadership in Human-Centricity

Human-centric AI isn't a low-value, academic concept; it's a practice that must be embedded into daily operations, strategy, and leadership. Whether your organization is just starting to explore AI or already leveraging it in key workflows, now is the time to assess how well AI and human expertise are working together. The following questions and challenges will help you evaluate where you stand, reflect on past experiences, and take tangible steps to ensure AI is enhancing (not replacing) your team's impact.

Bold AI Leaders don't wait for AI adoption to happen organically; they shape it with intention, ensuring that technology serves people so that businesses can achieve their full potential.

Assess: Where Are You on the Human + AI Journey?

If New to AI:
- How comfortable is your team with the prospect of AI adoption - excited or concerned?
- Where do you see opportunities for AI to enhance (not replace) human expertise?
- What lessons from past technology rollouts could guide human-centric AI implementation?
- Map two to three workflows where AI could amplify your team's capabilities.
- Create a human impact assessment framework for evaluating AI initiatives.
- Design pilot programs that emphasize human + AI collaboration.

If Already Using AI:

Evaluate your current human + AI integration:

- How well do human expertise and AI capabilities complement each other?
- Are AI tools integrated effectively into existing workflows?
- Where do teams feel enhanced or constrained by AI tools?
  - Audit existing AI implementations for human-centricity.
  - Document specific examples where human + AI collaboration improved outcomes.
  - Create a human impact visualization tracking
    - Engagement metrics (user satisfaction, collaboration instances)
    - Value indicators (time saved, quality improvements)

Reflect: Recognize AI's Role in Your Organization

- If you're actively using AI, where has it provided the most tangible benefit? Improving decision-making, enhancing creativity, or increasing efficiency? Where has it fallen short?
- What concerns or excitement does your leadership team have about AI?
- Think about past technology rollouts (such as CRM, automation, or cloud adoption) in your organization. What worked well? What challenges arose? How can these insights inform your AI adoption approach?
- If you or your team has been hesitant to embrace AI-powered tools, was it because:
  - It lacked transparency?
  - The insights weren't timely or actionable?
  - The technology wasn't aligned with user needs?
  - There wasn't a clear plan for integrating AI into existing workflows?

Take Action: Making AI Work for Humans

- If you're already using AI, review a recent AI-generated insight or recommendation:
  - Was it clear, relevant, and useful?
  - Did it arrive in time to be useful, or was it outdated by the time it was applied?
  - How could the system improve its timing, clarity, or contextual relevance?

- If you're considering AI adoption, identify a key business challenge where AI could enhance, rather than replace, human expertise.
  - How can you make the impact of AI more visible to your team through clear, real-world demonstrations?
  - Where can you use visual storytelling to show AI's value to stakeholders so that they understand its impact?

Why This Matters

AI's true power is in amplifying human potential. Whether streamlining workflows, accelerating innovation, enhancing creativity, or improving customer experiences, AI delivers the most value when it works in sync with people. But for AI to be a force multiplier, it must be timely, relevant, and seamlessly integrated into how work actually gets done. The organizations that get this right don't just implement AI; they build dynamic Human + AI partnerships that evolve, adapt, and create lasting impact.

Your Bold AI Leadership Challenge This Week

Not Using AI Yet:

- Shadow three team members in different roles - creative, operational, and strategic - to identify where AI could provide meaningful support.
- Identify a situation where AI could assist with productivity, customer engagement, or innovation without replacing human skills.
- Pinpoint one workflow where timing is critical (e.g., forecasting, customer outreach, or supply chain adjustments) and explore how AI could deliver fresher, more actionable insights.
- Review past technology rollouts in your organization. What lessons can be applied to make AI adoption smoother?

AI Already in Use:

- Shadow three users of your AI system and observe how they interact with AI-generated insights, recommendations, or creative assistance.
- Document and share one instance where human expertise significantly improved or refined an AI-generated result. This will help demonstrate the value of Human + AI collaboration.
- Evaluate whether your AI insights remain fresh and relevant or if they need to be updated more frequently to maximize their value (outdated insights can hinder decision-making and reduce effectiveness).

Remember

The goal isn't to perfect AI itself; it's to ensure AI empowers your people to drive the best business outcomes.

What's Next

Business success, powered by any technology, requires that we build and sustain momentum. Without a system for building and reinforcing progress, even the most promising project will stall. This is even more true for AI initiatives.

In the next chapter, we'll introduce the **AI Performance Flywheel**, a proven system for turning AI potential into sustained business value. This model provides a structured way to build trust, execute effectively, scale AI across your organization, and empower continuous innovation.

Remember

What's Next

CHAPTER 5

The AI Performance Flywheel

Turning AI Potential Into Business Results

The gap between AI's promise and actual business results isn't primarily technical; it's human. In the previous chapters, we explored why Bold AI Leadership matters and how to build the foundation for AI-driven business evolution. But having the right mindset and principles isn't enough. Leaders also need a structured system to turn AI potential into measurable business performance.

Sarah's Challenge: When AI Stalls Before It Delivers

Sarah Chen, COO of Central States Insurance Group (CSIG), was facing a pivotal moment. She leaned forward at the long mahogany conference table, scanning the faces of their board members. She knew AI could help. Claims processing was slow, risk assessment inconsistent, and customer satisfaction was slipping. Meanwhile, competitors were starting to leverage AI to gain an edge. But as she made her case for AI-driven transformation, she could feel hesitation in the room. One executive finally spoke up: "Where's the proof?"

It was the same challenge many leaders face: not a lack of technology, but a lack of trust and momentum.

With $2 billion in annual premiums and 2,000 employees across five states, CSIG was not a tech company; it was a traditional insurer with traditional problems.

Sarah knew AI could help, but she didn't know where to start. Her company had no formal AI strategy, just scattered discussions about automation and analytics. She had data, a vision, and a sense that AI could create efficiencies, but she needed a structured way to determine where to begin and how to gain traction.

Yet despite these advantages, AI wasn't delivering measurable business results.

- The board wanted proof before investing further.
- Managers resisted AI-powered changes, worried about disrupting workflows.
- Employees feared automation, seeing AI as a threat rather than an enabler.

Sarah's frustration grew. The technology was sound, but without trust, progress kept stalling before AI had a chance to create value.

She knew AI had the potential to transform claims processing, but potential wasn't enough. She needed trust. Without it, every conversation with leadership stalled at the same point: "How do we know this will work?" To move forward, she needed more than belief; she needed to prove that AI could deliver real results without disrupting the business.

Sarah realized AI wouldn't succeed through isolated wins alone. She needed a repeatable system, one that could build trust, drive execution, and sustain progress long enough for AI to prove its value. Instead of treating AI adoption as a single project, she needed to create a cycle of continuous reinforcement. That's when she discovered my AI Performance Flywheel - a system designed to turn AI potential into business results, not just once, but repeatedly (see Figure 5.1).

Why AI Fails Without Momentum

Sarah's experience isn't unique. Across industries, leaders face two major challenges with AI adoption:

- Some start strong but stall - an AI pilot succeeds, but momentum fades before it scales.
- Others never start at all - AI feels promising, but uncertainty around risks, ROI, or execution prevents action.

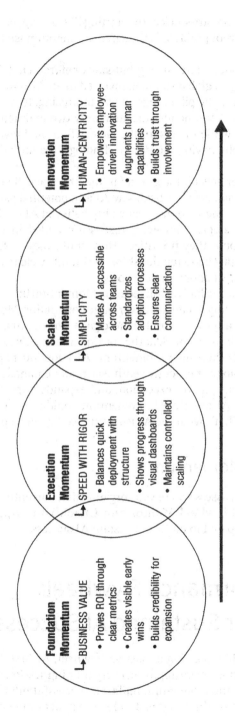

FIGURE 5.1 The AI Performance Flywheel: A four-phase system for sustained AI success. Each phase activates a key Bold AI Leadership principle (shown in caps) and builds on previous momentum. The overlapping structure illustrates how phases reinforce each other, creating compound effects that accelerate AI-driven business results.

Whether organizations are stuck at the starting line or trapped in proof-of-concept purgatory, the root problem is the same: momentum isn't automatic. It has to be built.

For some, AI adoption starts strong but stalls before delivering impact. Midwest Manufacturing, a global supplier, invested in an AI-powered predictive maintenance system. The pilot program was promising. It reduced equipment downtime by 45%. Yet nine months later, only two maintenance teams were using the system, while the rest of the factory floor had reverted to traditional methods. Despite having the right technology, the initiative failed to gain traction.

For others, AI never gets off the ground in the first place. Sterling Financial, a midsize wealth management firm, saw AI as a potential game changer for client portfolio recommendations. Leadership believed AI could help personalize investment strategies, but every discussion ended in uncertainty: Which AI use case should they prioritize? How could they ensure compliance? Would AI disrupt client relationships? Without a clear strategy, no decision was made, and AI adoption never began.

Midwest Manufacturing had early Execution Momentum but failed to scale their success, while Sterling Financial never built Foundation Momentum in the first place. Without a system to bridge these gaps, both companies stalled.

Whether organizations are stuck at the starting line or stalled after initial success, the problem is the same: momentum. AI adoption requires more than just strong technology or executive enthusiasm; it demands a structured approach that builds trust, drives execution, and expands impact over time. Sarah realized that for AI to succeed, momentum couldn't be accidental; it had to be engineered. That's what the AI Performance Flywheel provides.

Assess Your AI Momentum

Before moving forward, assess where your organization currently stands. Use the **AI Performance Flywheel Momentum Checklist** in Appendix E to determine if you're prepared to build and sustain AI success.

The AI Performance Flywheel: A System for Sustained AI Success

Think of AI adoption like pushing a massive flywheel. At first, the effort is exhausting. Every meeting, every approval, every training session feels like an uphill battle. But then, the momentum builds: a successful pilot proves AI's value. Teams start trusting the insights. Leadership shifts from skepticism to demand. Like a real flywheel, each successful AI implementation makes the next turn easier, driving compounding results. The AI Performance Flywheel is designed to engineer this momentum, ensuring AI adoption is not a one-time project but an ongoing business capability.

Traditional AI roadmaps treat adoption as a linear project, often leading to stalled momentum. The Flywheel ensures AI success compounds over time, turning it into an ongoing business capability.

The Flywheel consists of four interconnected phases:

1. **Foundation Momentum**: Converting skepticism into trust through concrete results
2. **Execution Momentum**: Scaling initial wins into operational improvements
3. **Scale Momentum**: Turning departmental successes into enterprise-wide change
4. **Innovation Momentum**: Creating competitive sustainability

Each phase reinforces the next, creating a self-sustaining cycle of AI-driven business transformation.

How Sarah Applied the AI Performance Flywheel

When Sarah took the reins of her company's AI journey, she knew that scattered efforts wouldn't lead to scaled, tangible business results. Building momentum would be key, stacking early AI wins like LEGO blocks to create a foundation that could scale. The AI Performance Flywheel gave her a repeatable system for assembling those blocks. Rather than deploying AI in disconnected pockets or chasing the latest tools, Sarah followed a structured path to build trust, scale with precision, and embed innovation into the company's culture. Her story shows how thoughtful execution transforms AI from a hyped shiny object into a strategic growth engine.

Foundation Momentum: Building Trust and Credibility

Every AI transformation needs a foothold. For Sarah, that point was claims processing: an area where AI could deliver immediate value while minimizing disruption. AI had potential across multiple areas of the business, but without a structured way to identify the best entry point, momentum would stall before it even began. The Flywheel helped her focus on a high-impact, low-risk initiative that would build trust and create early success.

Instead of launching AI without a clear direction, Sarah took a strategic approach. She started by identifying one area where AI could create immediate value. After reviewing company pain points, she focused on claims processing: an area where AI could improve efficiency while minimizing disruption.

- She launched a targeted AI pilot in one department.
- ROI visualizations clearly demonstrated efficiency gains.
- She engaged employees in AI training, ensuring they saw AI as an assistant, not a replacement.

Within three months, the pilot reduced manual claim reviews by 25%.

This success wasn't just technical; it was psychological. Employees began to see AI as a tool for making their work easier, not a threat to their jobs.

Foundation Momentum Checklist:

- **Pick the Right First Move:** Focus on a problem that's visible, urgent, and AI-ready (e.g., claims processing, fraud detection).
- **Make Success Unignorable:** Use visualization tools (before/after dashboards, cost-saving heatmaps) to showcase AI's early wins.
- **Win Over the Skeptics:** Upskill employees not just on AI tools but on how AI makes their jobs easier (not replaces them).

Execution Momentum: Strengthening AI into Operational Success

Early trust was critical, but trust alone wouldn't scale AI. Sarah now faced a new challenge: expanding AI from a controlled pilot to full-scale operations without disrupting the business. Moving from a test environment to daily workflows brought new complexities that needed careful navigation.

At first, expansion into the full claims department looked like a seamless transition. Processing times continued improving, AI-assisted workflows reduced backlog, and employee adoption remained steady. But then, an unexpected bottleneck emerged.

Challenge: AI Wasn't Learning Fast Enough
Claims adjusters reported that AI recommendations were accurate but repetitive. The system was struggling to adapt to new claim patterns as fast as human teams could. The root cause? The AI model had been trained on historical claims data, but emerging fraud tactics and new policy rules weren't reflected in real time.

Sarah knew that for AI to deliver lasting value, it needed continuous learning mechanisms, not just a one-time training set.

Solution: Building Feedback Loops for Smarter AI   Sarah's team worked with IT to establish a continuous AI refinement process:

- **Live Model Updates:** Instead of retraining AI quarterly, they introduced biweekly data refreshes to ensure AI models reflected evolving fraud tactics and policy changes.
- **Adjuster-Informed AI Tuning:** Claims teams could now flag AI recommendations as "useful" or "incorrect" directly in their workflow, feeding real-world feedback into the system.
- **Human-AI Collaboration Metrics:** Instead of just tracking speed, they measured AI's ability to assist adjusters in complex cases, refining accuracy based on real-world usage patterns.

By making AI a dynamic learning system, not just a fixed model, Sarah ensured it kept pace with the real-world complexities of claims processing.

Momentum Shift: AI Was No Longer Just Fast. It Was Getting Smarter

- AI accuracy improved significantly after incorporating adjuster feedback.
- Claims teams trusted AI more as they saw their inputs refining the system.
- The board, seeing AI's ability to continuously improve, approved funding for expansion into other departments.

Execution Momentum Checklist

- Scale AI within the initial department before expanding further.
- Provide data-driven feedback loops for continuous improvement.
- Ensure leadership champions AI adoption at every level.

Scale Momentum: Expanding AI Impact Without Losing Focus

With trust in AI growing and measurable results in claims processing, other departments saw the opportunity to leverage AI for their own challenges, creating a pull effect, and they wanted in. But Sarah knew that scaling AI wasn't just about expanding its reach; it required careful alignment across teams, processes, and objectives to maintain momentum.

To scale successfully, CSIG needed to address three key roadblocks:

- **Adapting AI Training for Underwriters**

   Underwriters approached AI differently than claims teams. While adjusters relied on AI for structured decision support, underwriters needed predictive modeling, and many resisted AI-driven recommendations, fearing a lack of transparency in risk assessments.

Sarah's Solution: Interactive AI Risk Workshops

Instead of generic AI training, her team developed scenario-based workshops where underwriters could test AI-driven risk models in real-time, adjust inputs, and see how the system arrived at its recommendations. By making AI an interactive, explainable tool, trust in AI-driven underwriting grew.

- **Ensuring AI Compliance in Fraud Detection**

Expanding AI into fraud detection required close collaboration with legal and regulatory teams. Fraud detection AI needed to provide traceable decision-making before regulators would allow full automation.

Sarah's Solution: Pre-Approved AI Audit Trails

CSIG's compliance leaders worked with Sarah's team to ensure fraud detection AI produced detailed audit trails, meeting regulatory standards before rollout. This prevented delays, rework, and resistance from legal teams.

- **Breaking Down AI Silos Across Departments**

With AI now in multiple areas, departments weren't sharing insights, limiting AI's potential. Risk assessments in underwriting didn't feed into fraud detection models, and claims processing insights weren't being used for pricing improvements.

Sarah's Solution: A Centralized AI Insights Dashboard

To connect AI insights across teams, Sarah's team developed a company-wide AI hub, allowing claims, underwriting, and fraud teams to see shared insights in real time. This prevented AI from operating in silos and created cross-functional collaboration.

How Sarah Maintained Momentum During Scale
Rather than pushing AI into departments haphazardly, Sarah established an AI Expansion Task Force: a cross-functional team of claims leaders, underwriters, compliance officers, and IT specialists. Their job was to identify roadblocks and resolve them before they slowed AI's momentum.

- **Training and Trust:** Underwriters received AI-driven risk modeling training, while adjusters gained explainability tools to enhance decision-making confidence.

- **Compliance Alignment:** The task force worked with legal and risk teams to ensure fraud detection AI met regulatory standards before rollout.

- **Data Standardization:** The team implemented a centralized AI dashboard, connecting insights across departments to prevent data silos and align decision-making.

These structured efforts ensured AI didn't just expand; it became integrated, standardized, and strategically aligned across CSIG.

Momentum Shift: From Departmental AI to Enterprise AI

A year earlier, AI was an isolated experiment in claims processing. Now, it was a core business capability used across multiple functions.

- AI-powered underwriting reduced risk assessment time.
- Fraud detection AI improved accuracy while maintaining compliance.
- AI projects expanded from one to eight, spanning multiple departments.

Most importantly, Sarah wasn't the one pushing AI forward anymore. Department heads were asking for AI to improve their teams. AI had moved from isolated pilots to a company-wide transformation engine.

- Scale Momentum Checklist Expand AI capabilities into adjacent departments.
- Standardize AI workflows for repeatable, scalable implementation.
- Use visualization tools to showcase company-wide AI impact.

Innovation Momentum: Driving Continuous Advantage

AI wasn't just transforming workflows; it was now shaping strategy. Teams began proactively identifying new AI use cases. Claims processors suggested ways AI could improve customer communication. Underwriters proposed new risk assessment models. Even departments initially skeptical of AI were now asking "What else can we transform?"

The shift was clear: AI had evolved from a top-down initiative into a bottom-up force for innovation. Employees who once viewed AI with suspicion were now its biggest champions, seeing it as a tool to enhance their expertise rather than replace it. What started in claims processing had become a company-wide engine for continuous improvement.

Despite the growing momentum, Sarah recognized that unstructured AI adoption carried risks. To ensure AI remained human-centric while harnessing employee enthusiasm, she worked with leadership to create formal innovation channels:

- The **AI Advisory Council:** A cross-functional group of frontline employees, managers, and AI specialists who identified new AI opportunities based on daily challenges. This shifted AI from an executive-driven initiative to one where employees directly shaped its evolution.

- **AI Experimentation Sprints:** Each quarter, teams could propose and test AI-driven improvements without requiring extensive approval processes. Some of CSIG's most successful AI applications, like personalized fraud risk alerts and automated compliance tracking, emerged from these structured innovation periods.

- To ensure AI innovation remained both agile and responsible, CSIG established lightweight AI governance principles, ensuring that new AI experiments aligned with business strategy, compliance requirements, and ethical guidelines.

- **Human + AI Partnership:** Leadership codified this approach in all AI roadmaps, ensuring AI systems enhanced rather than replaced human expertise. Every AI initiative required clear plans for human oversight, employee upskilling, and transparent decision pathways.

Momentum Shift: AI as a Culture of Innovation

A year earlier, AI was a top-down initiative. Now, it was embedded into how teams worked, learned, and innovated.

- New AI use cases emerged organically from employees, not just leadership.
- AI became a tool for augmenting expertise, not replacing human roles.
- The company's AI roadmap became an iterative, employee-driven process.

AI was no longer just a business capability; it was part of the company's culture.

- Innovation Momentum Checklist   Establish an AI Advisory Council to encourage employee-driven AI adoption.
- Dedicate structured time for AI experimentation to fuel bottom-up innovation.
- Embed Human + AI augmentation principles in AI adoption roadmaps.

Closing: The AI Performance Flywheel Builds Momentum That Drives Results

Sarah doesn't need to convince anyone anymore. AI is working, and everyone knows it. The proof isn't in a deck; it's in the daily workflows, the faster decisions, the higher profits, and the teams asking "What can we do next?"

This is the power of momentum-driven AI. It's not built on flashy pilots or one-off successes. It's built like Sarah built it: with intention. Each initiative stacking like a LEGO block, each success reinforcing the next, until AI isn't an experiment; it's embedded in how the business runs, scales, and innovates.

Across this chapter, we followed Sarah's journey through the four phases of the AI Performance Flywheel. We saw how trust was built through low-risk, high-ROI use cases. We watched operational success spark demand across departments. We learned how smart governance and cross-functional collaboration transformed growth into sustainable scale. And we witnessed the shift when innovation stopped being top-down and started emerging organically from teams empowered by AI.

Consider the lessons we've picked up along the way. Momentum isn't luck; it's engineered. It's built by making AI visible, showing value early, inviting feedback, and keeping humans at the center. It's protected by structure and culture, and fueled by repeatable wins that earn confidence and unlock creativity.

The AI Performance Flywheel isn't just a framework; it's a force. Sarah's journey shows that AI momentum isn't magic; it's method. It's how bold leaders turn AI promises into business performance. Not once, but again and again.

Looking Ahead to Part 2: The Five AI Success Pillars

Momentum alone isn't enough. Without the right foundation, even AI with the potential to create significant business value can stall or fail to scale. Consider how Sarah's claims processing initiative could have faltered: without strong Data practices, the AI might have made unreliable predictions; without Customer-Centricity, the solution might have ignored crucial user needs; without Collaborative Teams, the insights might have stayed trapped in departmental silos. Sarah's success required building and sustaining momentum with a clear strategic framework. That framework is built on my research-backed five critical pillars: Business Value Creation, Customer-Centricity, Collaborative Teams, Cultural Shifts (Embracing Iterative Learning), and Data as a Strategic Asset. These pillars provide stability and direction that ensure AI adoption isn't just a short-term win but a long-term competitive advantage.

The AI Performance Flywheel is the engine that drives momentum, but the Five AI Success Pillars keep it on course (see Figure 5.2). In Part 2, we'll explore how each pillar reinforces the Flywheel, creating a structured, repeatable system for turning AI's potential into sustained business impact.

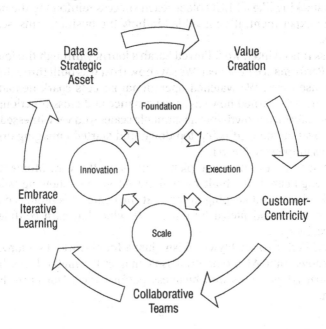

FIGURE 5.2 **How the Five AI Success Pillars reinforce the AI Performance Flywheel:** *The Five AI Success Pillars provide the structural foundation that sustains AI momentum across the Flywheel. Business Value Creation drives Foundation Momentum by proving early ROI and building credibility for AI investments. Customer-Centricity fuels Execution Momentum by ensuring AI solutions align with user needs, making adoption smoother and more impactful. Collaborative Teams enable Scale Momentum by breaking down silos and standardizing AI integration across departments. Cultural Shifts (Embracing Iterative Learning) reinforces Scale Momentum by helping teams embrace AI-driven workflows, fostering a cultural shift towards a fail fast and pivot norm, and embedding AI into daily operations. Data as a Strategic Asset supports all phases by ensuring AI is built on high-quality, well-governed, and accessible data. Together, the AI Performance Flywheel and the Five AI Success Pillars create a structured, repeatable system for turning AI's potential into sustained business results.*

Key Takeaways from Part 1: How the Flywheel and Five AI Success Pillars Work Together

AI success depends on starting strong, scaling effectively, and sustaining results. The AI Performance Flywheel provides a structured, repeatable system to prevent AI from stalling at any phase. Whether you're launching your first AI initiative or expanding AI's impact across your enterprise, ask yourself: Where is our AI initiative in the Flywheel? And what's the next step to build or sustain momentum? AI doesn't typically fail due to technology limitations—it fails when organizations lack a system to turn AI potential into sustained business value.

The AI Performance Flywheel operationalizes the Bold AI Leadership principles, transforming Business Value, Speed with Rigor, Simplicity, and Human-Centricity into an iterative, self-sustaining system.

- **Each Flywheel phase operationalizes Bold AI Leadership principles:**
  - **Foundation Momentum** brings **Business Value** from concept to reality by proving AI's ROI through measurable early wins.
  - **Execution Momentum** applies **Speed with Rigor** to move AI from pilot to operations, ensuring rapid deployment without sacrificing quality.
  - **Scale Momentum** relies on **Simplicity** to streamline AI adoption across teams, making solutions accessible and repeatable.
  - **Innovation Momentum** sustains AI by embedding **Human-Centricity** into strategy, keeping AI aligned with employee needs, business goals, and long-term adaptability.

The Five AI Success Pillars fuel the Flywheel, ensuring AI initiatives stay focused on high-impact, strategic priorities.

The takeaway? AI success hinges on business alignment, not just tech.

In Part 2, we'll explore how each of these pillars strengthens AI momentum and scales transformation, providing the foundation for AI-driven business success.

PART 2

Strategic Priorities (The Five AI Success Pillars)

Part 2 introduces the second layer of the Bold AI Leadership Model: strategic AI priorities. To effectively implement the bold mindset outlined in Part 1, leaders need clear strategic priorities. In this part of the book, I present my five research-backed pillars - Business Value Creation, Customer-Centricity, Collaborative Teams, Cultural Shifts, and Data as a Strategic Asset - to guide leaders in implementing AI that drives business value. Using these priorities ensures that AI initiatives remain aligned with organizational goals while fostering trust, engaging stakeholders, and creating measurable outcomes.

Of all the complexities involved in AI efforts, how do I know that these specific five pillars are so critical? In my 2023 doctoral research, I studied 46 enterprises successfully using AI across a variety of industries, and from this work, these pillars emerged. I brought my decades of technology and leadership experience into this research and then applied academic rigor to surface these success pillars. This is my unique lens: I bridge the gap between pragmatic field experience and academic precision. It's through this combination that I'm able to clarify the secret sauce pillars that provide a structured framework for building sustainable, results-driven AI strategies.

In the following chapters, we'll explore each pillar in detail, discovering practical examples and visualization tools to effectively demonstrate ROI, foster collaboration, build trust, and drive innovation. This part will equip you with a structured and adaptable foundation for integrating AI into your organizations sustainably and iteratively, ensuring results that scale over time.

PART 2

Strategic Priorities (The Five AI Success Pillars)

CHAPTER 6

Business Value Creation

The Bedrock of AI Success

Success with AI starts with a laser focus on Business Value Creation, the first of my five AI success pillars. This chapter equips you with the insights and frameworks you need to ensure your AI initiatives deliver tangible business outcomes. You'll discover how to identify, measure, and amplify the value of AI across your organization, turning promising technologies into powerful drivers of profitability and growth.

The Cost of Getting AI Value Wrong

In 2019, a multinational retailer launched a highly anticipated AI-powered demand forecasting system. The promise? AI would optimize inventory levels, reduce waste, and improve margins across its global supply chain. However, within months, the system's failure to deliver on this promise became evident, as unexpected stock shortages and overages caused chaos throughout the supply chain. The core problem? The company had failed to align AI implementation with core business needs, mistakenly assuming that the sophistication of the technology alone would drive value. Consequently, the system lacked clear business impact metrics, leading to a $100M+ inventory miscalculation, a costly but crucial lesson in why AI success is fundamentally dependent on creating business value, not simply deploying advanced algorithms.

Contrast that with Intel, which adopted a value-first approach to AI. Instead of implementing AI for AI's sake, Intel maintained a laser focus on solving a clearly defined real business problem: optimizing spare parts inventory management. By rigorously aligning AI initiatives with measurable goals and demonstrating tangible results, Intel achieved remarkable success, saving $600M in just two years.

The takeaway? AI doesn't typically fail because of technological limitations; it fails when organizations neglect to connect AI initiatives to the creation of real and measurable business value.

Definition and Relevance: Why Leaders Should Care

Business Value Creation means ensuring that every AI initiative is fundamentally linked to a clearly defined and strategically important business goal. These goals typically fall into one of three key categories:

- **Operational Efficiency:** Streamlining processes, reducing costs, and automating routine tasks to optimize resource allocation
- **Revenue Growth:** Developing innovative business models, expanding into new markets, and creating new products or services
- **Enhanced Customer Experiences:** Personalizing interactions, creating seamless and frictionless experiences, and increasing customer satisfaction and loyalty

A commitment to Business Value Creation is not simply advantageous; it is fundamental to achieving AI success. McKinsey found that companies that scale AI well get up to three times more ROI than those that don't, mainly because they prioritize real business value over complex tech.

Organizations that fail to anchor their AI efforts in Business Value Creation expose themselves to several significant risks:

- **"Toy AI" Syndrome:** Investing in "shiny" or trendy AI projects that lack a clear path to generating measurable business impact
- **No Clear ROI:** Implementing AI without defining and tracking key performance indicators (KPIs) to demonstrate a positive return on investment
- **Wasted Resources:** Initiating AI projects that fail to scale beyond the pilot stage, resulting in a loss of both time and money

This chapter provides the insights and tools to address these challenges. By the end of this discussion, you'll have a clear understanding of:

- How to effectively measure AI's business impact
- The critical factors in determining when to scale an AI initiative and when to pivot
- Proven frameworks for ensuring that AI projects are strategically aligned with overarching business objectives

Common Pitfalls – What Goes Wrong and Warning Signs

Neglecting to prioritize business value in AI initiatives leads to significant problems. The following are common pitfalls and the warning signs that indicate your project may be at risk:

The High Cost of Ignoring Business Value

Organizations pursuing AI often encounter pitfalls that derail their efforts and prevent them from achieving a positive return on investment. These mistakes, if unaddressed, can lead to wasted resources, eroded trust, and missed opportunities.

Pitfall #1: "Toy AI" Syndrome

- **Mistake:** Deploying AI for the sake of appearing innovative, without clearly defining how it will generate tangible business value. This often results in projects that are technically impressive but strategically useless.

- **Example:** A synthetic media company gained significant attention for its viral deepfake videos of celebrities but failed to develop a sustainable business model to monetize this technology, ultimately leading to the company's collapse. The pursuit of novelty overshadowed the need for profitability.

- **Warning Sign:** Your AI project generates excitement in demos but lacks a clear and measurable path to improving key business metrics like revenue, efficiency, or customer satisfaction.

Pitfall #2: Misaligned AI Strategy

- **Mistake:** Developing AI initiatives that are disconnected from the company's core strategic objectives. This leads to solutions that don't address critical business challenges or contribute to overall growth.

- **Example:** An insurance firm invested in an AI-powered chatbot to improve customer service, but the chatbot was not integrated with their existing claims processing systems. This lack of integration frustrated customers and failed to produce meaningful gains in efficiency.

- **Warning Sign:** Your AI system operates in isolation from essential business processes, failing to impact strategic goals and potentially creating friction for users.

Pitfall #3: No Clear Metrics for ROI

- **Mistake:** Implementing AI projects without defining specific, measurable, achievable, relevant, and time-bound (SMART) success criteria. This makes it impossible to accurately assess the initiative's effectiveness and demonstrate its value.

- **Example:** A manufacturing company used AI to predict equipment failures, but they did not track reductions in downtime or maintenance costs. This made it difficult for executives to determine if the AI was a worthwhile investment.

- **Warning Sign:** You are unable to clearly and confidently articulate how your AI project is improving the company's bottom line or contributing to strategic objectives.

Actionable Framework: How to Ensure AI Creates Real Business Value

AI becomes a true driver of business success when leaders implement a structured approach. The following framework provides a step-by-step guide to achieving measurable impact from your AI initiatives:

Step 1: Define the Job to Be Done

- **Ask:** What is the specific business problem or opportunity that AI can address?

- **Quick Win:** Identify and document the top three business challenges that AI could help your organization solve. Remember, a clear problem definition is essential for developing an effective AI solution.

Step 2: Align AI with Strategic Goals

- **Why?** AI initiatives must directly support the organization's overarching strategic objectives to ensure long-term relevance and impact.

- **Quick Win:** Explicitly connect every AI project to at least one specific C-level strategic goal.

- **Example:** To illustrate this, consider Zurich Insurance's implementation of an AI-driven claims system, which reduced processing time from weeks to less than 24 hours, directly aligning with their customer-first strategy.

Step 3: Start with Minimum Viable Experiences (MVEs)

- **Why?** Small, focused pilot projects allow you to validate AI's value and build momentum before scaling.
- **Quick Win:** Launch a two-week AI pilot in a single department to generate initial data and demonstrate early impact.
- **Example:** For instance, ING Wholesale Banking automated repetitive tasks, freeing teams to focus on customer needs, which boosted satisfaction and revenue.

Step 4: Measure ROI with Clear KPIs

- **Why?** Establishing clear KPIs is crucial for quantifying AI's impact and justifying further investment.
- **Quick Win:** Define at least one clear financial metric (e.g., cost savings, revenue increase, efficiency gain) to track the pilot's success.
- **Example:** Intel's AI-driven supply chain optimization provides a compelling example, reducing inventory needs by 30% and saving $600M— a directly measurable financial impact.

Step 5: Continuously Iterate and Scale What Works

- **Why?** AI systems require ongoing monitoring, evaluation, and refinement to maintain their effectiveness and adapt to evolving business needs.
- **Quick Win:** Implement a system of quarterly AI impact reviews to track progress, identify areas for improvement, and adjust strategies as needed.
- **Example:** Rolls-Royce's use of AI to clean up messy operational data demonstrates this, leading to more accurate and reliable AI models over time.

Measuring AI's Business Impact: Show the Value, Prove the ROI

After implementing AI, one fundamental question remains: is it truly delivering value to the business? Many organizations struggle to answer this, and as a result, promising AI projects stall, budgets get cut, and a damaging disconnect forms between AI teams and business leaders. To avoid this, we need a clear framework for measuring AI's impact—a system that translates AI outcomes into tangible business results.

AI Value Metrics: What Should You Measure?

AI's influence manifests in three key areas, each requiring distinct metrics:

1. **Efficiency Gains:** Can AI streamline operations, reduce costs, and boost productivity?
   - **Example Metrics:** Track operational cost reductions, time saved per task through automation, and overall automation rates.
   - **Real-World Example:** JPMorgan Chase's AI-powered document processing slashed contract review time by an impressive 360,000 hours annually, freeing up significant employee capacity.
2. **Customer Experience Improvements:** Does AI enhance customer satisfaction, engagement, and loyalty?
   - **Example Metrics:** Monitor Net Promoter Score (NPS), customer satisfaction (CSAT) ratings, and customer engagement levels.
   - **Real-World Example:** Sephora's AI chatbots contributed to an 11% increase in online conversion rates, demonstrating AI's power to drive sales through improved customer interaction.
3. **Revenue Growth & New Business Models:** Can AI unlock new revenue streams and transform business models?
   - **Example Metrics:** Measure revenue generated from AI-driven products or services, the number of AI-generated leads, and upsell/cross-sell success rates.
   - **Real-World Example:** Amazon's recommendation engine is responsible for a staggering 35% of their total revenue, showcasing AI's potential to become a core revenue driver.

The AI Value Measurement Framework: A Three-Step Guide

To ensure AI initiatives are rigorously evaluated and their impact is maximized, implement this three-step framework:

- **Step 1: Define Predefined Business Goals:**
  - Before launching any AI project, clearly articulate what success looks like in measurable terms.
  - **Example:** "Reduce manual claims processing time by 50% within six months."

- **Step 2: Establish Baseline Metrics Before AI Deployment:**
  - ○ Gather data on your current performance *before* implementing AI to provide a benchmark for comparison.
  - ○ **Example:** Track customer churn rates for a specific product or service before and after AI-powered personalization is introduced.
- **Step 3: Create a Continuous AI ROI Dashboard:**
  - ○ Develop a dynamic dashboard to monitor AI's ongoing impact in real-time, allowing for adjustments and optimization.
  - ○ **Example:** UPS uses real-time dashboards to track the impact of AI-driven route optimization on fuel consumption and delivery times.

Why Measurement Matters: The Key to Scaling AI Success

Many organizations struggle to scale AI beyond pilot projects because they fail to rigorously measure and demonstrate its value. Without clear metrics, AI initiatives are often perceived as costly experiments rather than strategic investments. By prioritizing measurement - establishing clear KPIs and consistently tracking AI's financial and operational impact - leaders can build stakeholder confidence, secure funding for expansion, and unlock AI's full potential to drive sustainable business growth.

Case Study and Lessons Learned – Real-World Applications

To illustrate the importance of Business Value Creation, consider these real-world examples:

Intel: Strategic AI Drives Substantial ROI

- **Challenge:** Intel faced significant costs associated with inefficient management of spare parts inventory.
- **Solution:** They implemented AI-driven optimization to predict demand and streamline inventory processes.
- **Results:** This strategic application of AI led to a 30% reduction in inventory levels and generated substantial cost savings of $600 million over two years, demonstrating a clear ROI.

The Technology-First Trap

- **Challenge:** A startup developed advanced AI video manipulation technology, focusing primarily on technical capabilities.
- **Mistake:** The team prioritized pushing technical boundaries without first validating market demand or establishing a clear revenue model.
- **Outcome:** Despite impressive demos and media attention, the company struggled to convert technical achievements into sustainable business value.

Key Takeaway: These cases highlight a critical lesson: AI initiatives must be driven by clear business objectives and deliver measurable value. Otherwise, they risk becoming costly distractions that fail to justify their investment.

Chapter Checklist and Next Steps

Before moving forward, ensure you've addressed these key considerations for Business Value Creation:

- **Strategic Alignment:** Does this AI project directly solve a real, high-impact business problem and support our overarching strategic goals?
- **Measurable Outcomes:** Have we defined clear and quantifiable ROI metrics (e.g., cost savings, revenue increase, efficiency gains) to track the project's success?
- **Iterative Implementation:** Are we committed to testing AI in small, measurable pilots and scaling only what delivers proven value?

By answering these questions affirmatively, you'll establish a solid foundation for your AI initiatives.

Next Chapter Preview: Prioritizing the Customer Experience

While Business Value Creation provides the bedrock for AI success, it's crucial to remember that technology serves a larger purpose: enhancing the human experience. In the next chapter, we'll shift our focus to Customer-Centricity, exploring how AI can be leveraged to anticipate customer needs, personalize interactions, and foster long-term loyalty.

Final Thoughts

Business Value isn't merely one component of AI success; it's the very foundation upon which all other achievements are built. If AI isn't delivering clear, measurable results, it shifts from being a valuable asset to a costly experiment.

CHAPTER 7

Customer-Centricity

Prioritizing Customer Needs for Business Impact

While many enterprises deploy AI primarily for automation and cost reduction, true business impact arises from leveraging AI to transform customer experiences. Practical experience and research consistently demonstrates that organizations prioritizing customer needs through AI achieve significantly stronger outcomes in satisfaction, loyalty, and revenue growth. This chapter explores how to strategically harness AI for deep customer engagement and operational excellence, moving beyond mere efficiency to build lasting customer relationships.

The Cost of Ignoring Customer Needs

In 2021, a major airline invested millions in an AI-powered chatbot designed to handle customer service inquiries. The goal? Reduce call center costs and streamline support. But within months, customer frustration skyrocketed. The AI couldn't handle complex issues, often looping passengers through irrelevant responses instead of connecting them to a human agent. Social media complaints flooded in, and the airline's customer satisfaction scores plummeted by 20%, forcing them to roll back the AI and reinvest in human support.

Now, contrast this with Starbucks, which took a customer-first approach to AI. Instead of focusing purely on cost reduction, Starbucks used AI-driven personalization to enhance the customer experience. Their Deep Brew AI platform customizes recommendations, manages inventory based on purchasing trends, and ensures customers receive personalized offers through the Starbucks app. The result? Higher engagement, increased loyalty, and a direct boost in revenue.

The takeaway? AI succeeds when it enhances customer experiences—not when it frustrates them.

Definition and Relevance: Why Customer-Centric AI Matters

At its core, Customer-Centric AI is about ensuring that AI is designed to enhance customer interactions, personalize experiences, and build long-term relationships, not just automate processes. AI should help businesses anticipate customer needs, reduce friction, and create seamless interactions.

Key Questions This Chapter Answers:

- How can AI create better customer experiences instead of just cutting costs?
- What are the biggest mistakes companies make when implementing customer AI?
- How can businesses measure the impact of AI-driven customer experiences?

Why Customer-Centric AI Is Critical to Business Success

According to a PwC study, 73% of customers say experience drives their purchase decisions, yet 60% of AI projects fail because they don't align with customer needs. The companies that win with AI use it to serve customers first, automate second.

Without a customer-centric approach, companies risk:

- Frustrating customers with rigid AI interactions
- Failing to personalize experiences, leading to disengagement
- Losing customer trust by prioritizing efficiency over experience

Common Pitfalls: What Goes Wrong and Warning Signs

To maximize AI's potential for enhancing customer relationships, it's crucial to understand the common challenges. This section provides a practical guide to the pitfalls that can derail AI initiatives, along with clear warning signs to help you stay on track.

Pitfall #1: AI That Frustrates Instead of Helps

- **Mistake:** Deploying AI to reduce costs rather than improve customer interactions.

- **Example:** The airline chatbot failure - customers got stuck in endless loops instead of getting real help.
- **Warning Sign:** If customers complain more after AI implementation than before, it's not adding value.

Pitfall #2: Lack of Personalization

- **Mistake:** AI delivers generic, one-size-fits-all recommendations.
- **Example:** A retail website launched AI-powered product recommendations, but instead of personalized suggestions, customers saw random items, leading to lower engagement instead of higher sales.
- **Warning Sign:** AI outputs feel irrelevant or disconnected from customer needs.

Pitfall #3: Focusing on AI Efficiency Over Customer Experience

- **Mistake:** AI is implemented to cut costs instead of improving service.
- **Example:** A bank introduced an AI-powered loan application system but failed to explain decisions, making customers feel uncertain and leading to higher drop-off rates.
- **Warning Sign:** If customer churn increases after AI adoption, the system may not be addressing real concerns.

The Future of AI-Powered Customer Experience

AI is rapidly reshaping how businesses interact with customers, evolving beyond simple chatbots and recommendation engines into deeply personalized, proactive, and predictive engagement tools. As organizations look ahead, several AI-driven trends will define the next era of customer experience.

- **Hyper-Personalization: AI-Driven One-to-One Customer Experiences**

    Customers increasingly expect AI to anticipate their needs and understand their preferences, often before they even articulate them. This goes beyond basic segmentation; AI is now capable of true personalization, where recommendations are based on real-time interactions, intent signals, and context-aware insights. For example, Spotify's AI-powered Discover Weekly analyzes individual listening patterns, context, and sentiment to deliver highly tailored music recommendations. This level of personalization leads to higher engagement rates, improved conversions and retention, and stronger brand loyalty as customers feel understood and valued.

- **AI-Powered Empathy: Emotional Intelligence in Customer Service**

  Traditional AI chatbots often frustrate customers with their inability to understand and respond to human emotions. The future of AI-powered customer service lies in emotion-aware AI, which can detect customer frustration, urgency, and other emotions from text, voice, and even facial expressions, and then adjust its tone and response accordingly. KLM's AI customer service system, for instance, uses sentiment analysis to identify frustrated customers in real-time and prioritize them for human escalation. This leads to higher customer satisfaction (CSAT) scores and reduces customer churn by demonstrating that the company values and understands their emotional needs.

- **Proactive AI: Anticipating Customer Needs Before They Arise**

  Rather than reacting to customer issues, AI is shifting toward proactive customer engagement, helping customers solve problems before they even know they exist. AI can now predict issues and send proactive recommendations before a customer encounters a problem. Tesla's AI-powered diagnostics, for example, notify car owners of potential mechanical issues before they fail, minimizing service disruptions and maximizing customer convenience. This proactive approach not only reduces support costs but also builds trust and strengthens the customer-brand relationship.

- **Multimodal AI: The Future of Frictionless Customer Interactions**

  Customers no longer interact with businesses through a single channel. AI is evolving to create seamless, multimodal experiences across voice, text, video, and augmented reality (AR). AI can now synchronize experiences across multiple platforms, ensuring continuous, personalized engagement. Google's AI Assistant, for instance, can transition from a voice conversation to text-based interactions, adjusting in real-time to the user's needs and preferences. This integration of AI across multiple touchpoints reduces friction in customer interactions and expands accessibility, allowing customers to interact in their preferred format.

Why This Matters: Future-Proofing AI-Powered Customer Experience

The companies that will win in the AI-powered future are those that focus not just on automation but on personalization, empathy, and proactive engagement. As AI capabilities grow, businesses must:

- **Invest in AI-Powered Hyper-Personalization:** Moving beyond static customer segmentation to create truly individualized experiences
- **Embed AI Empathy Models:** Ensuring AI systems detect and respond to human emotions with sensitivity and understanding
- **Transition from Reactive to Proactive AI:** Anticipating and resolving customer problems before they escalate, demonstrating a commitment to customer care
- **Embrace Multimodal AI:** Ensuring seamless and consistent interactions across all customer touchpoints, creating a unified and frictionless experience

Companies that master these next-gen AI trends will set new customer experience standards, making AI a true competitive advantage.

Actionable Framework: How to Build Customer-Centric AI

To effectively harness AI for customer benefit and avoid potential pitfalls, a structured approach is essential. The following five-step framework guides the strategic creation of Customer-Centric AI, ensuring that AI implementation strengthens and enhances customer relationships and drives positive outcomes:

Step 1: Map the Customer Journey Before Adding AI

- **Why?** AI implementation should enhance the customer's existing journey, not disrupt it or introduce new points of friction.
- **Example:** Disney's AI-powered Genie+ service helps guests optimize their park visits based on real-time wait times, seamlessly integrating with their existing park experience.
- **Quick Win:** Identify the three to five key customer pain points that AI could potentially alleviate or resolve.

Step 2: Personalize, Don't Generalize

- **Why?** Customers expect AI to understand their individual preferences, behaviors, and needs, providing relevant and tailored experiences.

- **Example:** Netflix's AI-powered recommendation system analyzes individual watch history to personalize suggestions, maximizing engagement and minimizing churn.

- **Quick Win:** Move beyond broad customer categories and implement dynamic customer segmentation to deliver more personalized interactions.

Step 3: Give Customers Control Over AI Interactions

- **Why?** Transparency and choice are essential for building trust. Customers should have the option to interact with a human representative when needed.

- **Example:** American Express's AI-powered fraud detection system allows customers to review and approve or dispute flagged transactions, empowering them in the decision-making process.

- **Quick Win:** Implement a clear AI opt-out or escalation path, ensuring customers can easily access human support when they prefer it.

Step 4: Use AI to Enhance, Not Replace, Human Interaction

- **Why?** AI should be seen as a tool to augment and empower human agents, not as a replacement for their empathy, creativity, and problem-solving skills.

- **Example:** The Ritz-Carlton's AI-powered customer service system gathers and provides hotel staff with detailed guest preferences, enabling them to deliver highly personalized and memorable service.

- **Quick Win:** Focus on using AI to surface relevant insights and information for employees, allowing them to provide more efficient and effective customer service.

Step 5: Measure Success with Customer Experience KPIs

- **Why?** The success of AI initiatives must be evaluated based on their impact on customer experience metrics, not just internal efficiency gains.

- **Example:** Sephora tracks key metrics like Net Promoter Score (NPS) scores, repeat purchase rates, and chatbot resolution times to gauge the effectiveness of their AI-driven customer experience strategies.

- **Quick Win:** Begin tracking essential customer experience metrics, such as CSAT and NPS, both before and after AI implementation to accurately measure the change.

Case Study and Lessons Learned: Real-World Applications

The difference between AI that delights and AI that disappoints often lies in how deeply organizations understand their customers' needs. Through two contrasting case studies, we examine how customer-centric AI implementation can either strengthen or strain customer relationships. These real-world examples illuminate the critical choices organizations face when deploying AI solutions and their lasting impact on customer loyalty.

Success Story: Starbucks – AI-Driven Personalization Wins Customer Loyalty

- **Challenge:** Starbucks needed to increase mobile engagement and repeat purchases.
- **Solution:** AI-powered Deep Brew system analyzes customer orders and customizes offers in the Starbucks app.
- **Results:** Increased customer retention, order frequency, and revenue per user.

Lesson Learned: The Airline Chatbot Disaster

- **Challenge:** The airline wanted to reduce call center costs with an AI chatbot.
- **Mistake:** The chatbot was not trained on complex customer queries, leading to frustration and brand damage.
- **Outcome:** Customer complaints spiked, and the company was forced to reinvest in human support.

Key Takeaways:

- **Customer Experience First, Technology Second**
  - Success requires designing AI solutions around genuine customer needs rather than purely technical capabilities.
  - The human element remains crucial. AI should enhance, not replace, meaningful customer interactions.
- **Strategic Implementation Matters**
  - Thorough testing and gradual rollout help prevent customer frustration.
  - Continuous learning and adaptation based on customer feedback is essential.
  - Always maintain human oversight and backup systems.

- **Measure What Matters**
  - Track both operational metrics (cost savings, efficiency) and customer experience metrics (satisfaction, retention).
  - Monitor the long-term impact on brand perception and customer loyalty.
  - Be prepared to adjust or pivot based on customer response.
- **Balance Innovation with Reliability**
  - While pushing technological boundaries, maintain focus on consistent, reliable service.
  - Create seamless transitions between AI and human support.
  - Ensure AI solutions actually solve customer problems rather than creating new ones.

Remember: The most successful AI implementations enhance the customer journey while improving operational efficiency, never sacrificing one for the other.

Chapter Checklist and Next Steps

Before moving forward, it's crucial to rigorously assess whether your AI initiatives truly prioritize customer needs. This checklist serves as your practical guide for customer-centric AI implementation, helping you validate the customer focus of your strategy and ensure that your AI creates genuine and lasting value. Use these points to evaluate current projects and guide your organization's future AI development. Remember that successful AI deployment isn't a one-time event, but a continuous journey of refinement based on ongoing customer feedback and evolving needs.

Customer-Centric AI Checklist:

Value and Impact

- ☐ **Customer Validation:** Have we validated this customer need through direct feedback and robust data analysis?
- ☐ **Root Cause Focus:** Does our AI solution address the fundamental root cause of the customer need, rather than merely treating the symptoms?
- ☐ **Meaningful Improvement:** Will this solution demonstrably and meaningfully improve our customers' overall experience?

Implementation and Design

☐ **Intuitive Interface:** Is the AI interface designed to be intuitive and accessible to all our customers, regardless of their technical proficiency?

☐ **Exception Handling:** Have we established clear and efficient paths for exception handling and seamless human escalation when necessary?

☐ **Diverse Needs:** Does our AI solution effectively accommodate the diverse preferences and needs of our customer base?

Measurement and Improvement

☐ **Baseline Metrics:** Have we established clear and measurable baseline metrics for customer satisfaction to track the impact of AI implementation?

☐ **Comprehensive Feedback:** Are we capturing both quantitative and qualitative customer feedback to gain a holistic understanding of their experience?

☐ **Continuous Learning:** Do we have robust mechanisms in place to continuously learn from customer interactions and refine our AI systems accordingly?

Ethics and Trust

☐ **Transparency:** Are we transparent and upfront with our customers about how AI is being used in their interactions with our company?

☐ **Bias Mitigation:** Have we taken proactive steps to address and mitigate potential bias in our AI systems and algorithms?

☐ **Data Protection:** Are we rigorously protecting customer privacy and ensuring the security of their data?

Next Chapter Preview: Collaborative Teams

The success of your AI initiatives depends on more than algorithms; it thrives on the power of collaborative teams. The next chapter reveals how you can build and lead high-performing AI teams that effectively blend technical excellence with strategic insight. This collaboration is key to transforming promising technologies into enterprise-wide value. You'll discover proven approaches for bridging the gap between technical expertise and business outcomes, ensuring your AI initiatives deliver meaningful results across your organization.

Final Thoughts

AI that puts people first can transform your customer relationships. While automation drives efficiency, exceptional customer experiences build lasting loyalty. Your AI strategy should enhance every interaction, making customers feel individually understood and valued, not trapped in digital workflows or treated like numbers in a database.

When you design AI systems that respect individual needs and deliver genuinely personal experiences, you create more than satisfied customers; you build trusted relationships that drive sustainable growth.

CHAPTER 8

Collaborative Teams

Developing Modern Skills and R&D Mindsets

A I's transformative potential is unlocked not by technical prowess alone but by strategic collaboration. Organizations that prioritize cross-functional teamwork consistently achieve superior AI outcomes, driving adoption, alignment, and measurable business impact. This chapter explores how to build and manage synergistic AI teams, moving beyond siloed development to harness diverse expertise and create solutions that address real-world challenges. Through practical insights and real-world examples, we examine how fostering robust feedback loops and establishing clear communication channels transforms AI initiatives into drivers of operational excellence.

The AI Team Challenge

AI's true potential is unlocked by fostering robust collaboration. While many organizations focus on individual technical skills, the path to exceptional AI results lies in building synergistic teams that bridge the gap between innovation and practical application.

Research across numerous AI deployments reveals a compelling truth: organizations that cultivate cross-functional AI teams achieve significantly stronger outcomes in adoption, alignment, and impact. This finding emerged consistently in examining successful AI initiatives. Enterprises that deeply integrate diverse expertise and effectively respond to real-world needs through collaborative AI create measurable business impact that goes far beyond isolated technical feats.

The data consistently shows that, whether through enhanced project alignment, reduced implementation friction, or proactive problem-solving, collaborative AI is the engine behind sustained enterprise value.

Consider this: in the strategic discussions I've observed, decision-makers frequently prioritize individual technical capabilities and siloed projects as the primary drivers of AI initiatives. However, organizations that truly excel take a different approach. They reframe the conversation, positioning collaborative teamwork as the catalyst for AI success.

John Deere provides a compelling example. By integrating farmers, agronomists, and AI engineers, they developed AI solutions that directly addressed agricultural challenges. The results proved powerful: higher adoption rates, greater efficiency, and increased revenue. Their success demonstrates how strategic team collaboration can simultaneously enhance AI effectiveness and strengthen business performance.

This chapter examines three critical elements of collaborative AI teams:

- The strategic value of prioritizing cross-functional collaboration
- Common pitfalls in building and managing AI teams
- Proven strategies that foster synergistic AI development

You'll discover how to leverage diverse expertise, establish clear communication channels, and create proactive feedback loops to build exceptional AI teams. One central question guides our exploration: how can you harness collaborative teamwork to deepen AI impact while driving operational excellence?

The Cost of Isolated AI Development

In 2022, a global bank invested heavily in an AI-driven fraud detection system, built in isolation by data scientists. The goal? Reduce fraud rates and streamline investigations. But within months, the system flagged excessive false positives, frustrating customers and overwhelming human investigators. Social media complaints flooded in, and the bank's operational efficiency plummeted, forcing them to retrain the AI and reinvest in cross-functional collaboration.

Now, contrast this with John Deere, which took a collaborative approach to AI. Instead of focusing purely on technical development, John Deere integrated farmers, agronomists, AI engineers, and supply chain experts. Their AI-driven precision agriculture solutions directly addressed real-world agricultural challenges. The result? Higher crop yields, increased farmer adoption, and a direct boost in revenue.

The takeaway? AI succeeds when it's built through collaboration, not when it's developed in isolation.

Definition and Relevance: Why AI Teams Need to Be Collaborative

In many organizations, AI development is siloed. Data scientists work separately from business leaders, engineers don't engage with frontline employees, and compliance teams are brought in too late.

Key Questions This Chapter Answers:

- Why do cross-functional AI teams outperform siloed teams?
- How can organizations bridge the gap between technical and business teams?
- What skills and mindsets do modern AI teams need to succeed?

Why Collaborative AI Teams Are Critical to Business Success

According to Harvard Business Review, companies that build cross-functional AI teams are 60% more likely to scale AI successfully compared to those that operate in silos.

Without collaboration, companies risk:

- Misaligned AI solutions that don't solve real business problems
- Lack of adoption because end users aren't involved in development
- Regulatory and ethical risks from failing to include compliance teams early

Common Pitfalls: What Goes Wrong and Warning Signs

While the potential of collaborative AI is undeniable, many organizations stumble over predictable roadblocks. Recognizing and avoiding these common pitfalls is crucial for transforming AI aspirations into tangible results. This section surfaces the critical mistakes that often derail AI initiatives, from isolated team efforts and leadership misalignments to strategic disconnects between technology and business objectives. By examining real-world examples and identifying key warning signs, I aim to equip you with the foresight needed to navigate these challenges and build a foundation for successful AI implementation.

Pitfall #1: AI Teams Work in Isolation

- **Mistake:** Data scientists build AI models without input from business or operations teams.
- **Example:** The bank's fraud detection AI failed because it wasn't trained on real-world fraud analyst workflows.
- **Warning Sign:** Your AI model works technically but isn't impacting business outcomes.

Pitfall #2: Business Leaders Lack AI Fluency

- **Mistake:** Executives don't understand AI's capabilities or limitations, leading to unrealistic expectations.
- **Example:** A CEO demanded an AI chatbot that could replace human sales reps, but without the right training data, it failed to generate relevant leads.
- **Warning Sign:** Leadership treats AI like magic instead of a tool requiring structured implementation.

Pitfall #3: No Alignment Between IT and Business Strategy

- **Mistake:** AI projects don't align with company goals, leading to wasted investment.
- **Example:** A retailer built an AI-powered inventory system, but supply chain teams weren't involved, leading to poor warehouse integration.
- **Warning Sign:** AI is not tied to KPIs that matter to executives.

The Future of AI Teams: Evolving Roles and Organizational Models

The traditional IT-driven approach to AI, where data scientists and engineers operate in isolation, is ill-suited for today's enterprise landscape. As AI becomes a core, enterprise-wide capability, organizations must redesign AI teams to be multidisciplinary, collaborative units that bridge technology, business, and strategy. In response, companies are moving away from siloed teams and adopting new organizational models that better align AI efforts with strategic goals.

AI Team Structures: Design for Purpose

As AI becomes a strategic enterprise capability, how organizations structure their AI teams plays a critical role in long-term success. Companies are moving beyond one-size-fits-all models and embracing flexible team

structures that align with their stage of AI maturity, governance needs, and business complexity.

Organizational Models That Work:

- **Centralized AI Teams:** AI development and management are handled by a dedicated AI Center of Excellence (CoE) that supports the entire organization.
  - *Best for companies early in their AI journey, ensuring strong governance, consistency, and knowledge sharing*
- **Federated AI Teams:** AI expertise is embedded across business units, enabling AI to be tailored to specific functions and industry needs.
  - *Best for mature AI organizations that require domain-specific applications and greater local ownership*
- **Hybrid AI Teams:** Combines centralized oversight with decentralized execution, balancing strategic alignment with operational flexibility.
  - *Best for scaling AI across complex enterprises while maintaining consistency and accountability*

By adopting these flexible structures, organizations enable faster AI deployment, tighter alignment with business objectives, and more scalable, impactful outcomes.

Expanding AI Team Roles: Beyond Tech Talent

Building upon the foundation of effective team structures, the roles within AI teams are also undergoing a significant transformation. As AI team structures evolve, so do the roles required for success. Gone are the days when AI initiatives were managed solely by data scientists and engineers. Today, success depends on a diverse mix of roles that bridge technical execution with business strategy, ethics, and change management.

New AI-Driven Roles and Responsibilities:

- **AI Ethicist:** Ensures AI is developed responsibly, fairly, and transparently, mitigating risks related to bias, compliance, and public trust
- **AI Translator:** Bridges communication between technical teams and business leaders, aligning initiatives with strategic goals
- **AI Product Owner:** Manages AI tools like products, focusing on usability, scalability, and end-user impact
- **AI Change Manager:** Drives workforce adoption by reducing resistance and building trust through communication and engagement

Incorporating these roles accelerates time-to-value while laying the groundwork for responsible, sustainable, and inclusive AI deployment.

These team members ensure that AI projects resonate with users, align with strategic priorities, and operate with integrity from the start.

Team DNA for AI Success

Every effective AI team member, regardless of role, should embody curiosity, continuous learning, and willingness to collaborate across disciplines. These human qualities are more predictive of AI project success than technical credentials.

Do You Need a Chief AI Officer? Rethinking AI Leadership

As I help organizations reshape their AI teams, I often get the same question: "Do we need a Chief AI Officer?"

My answer? It depends, but not in the way you might think. I don't believe every organization needs to create a new C-suite title to lead AI. What you *do* need is a clearly defined, empowered AI leadership function that drives strategy, ensures value alignment, and keeps ethics front and center. Your goal should be to structure your leadership to most effectively drive business impact.

What I Recommend: Character Traits Trump Technical Skills

Rather than defaulting to the addition of a Chief AI Officer role, I recommend appointing a dedicated AI Strategy Analyst: a permanent role designed to sit at the intersection of business strategy, emerging technology, and ethical oversight.

> *"Leadership needs to be permanent and is often best aligned under the AI Strategy Analyst. . . . This role can be filled by an external partner, but it's preferable to make this the permanent leader of the team."*
> *-From my article, "Building an Effective AI Team"*

This person doesn't just track AI trends; they translate insights into action, guide ad hoc AI teams, and make sure every initiative ties back to measurable business value. In short, they serve as the strategic compass for your AI function.

I also consider competitive intelligence - through environmental scanning, market analysis, and strategic positioning - to be core responsibilities. Your AI leader should continually monitor how the competitive landscape is shifting and help position your organization to seize AI-driven advantage.

Don't Wait for Unicorns!

Many firms delay AI progress while searching for a "perfect" hire - someone with deep AI knowledge, domain fluency, leadership skill, and regulatory savvy. That person rarely exists. Instead, invest in smart trusted internal leaders with the right mindset and supplement their growth with targeted external support.

Where Should This Role Report?

I recommend positioning this role under the Chief Strategy Officer (CSO), or in some organizations, a forward-thinking CIO or CTO. This structure ensures that AI efforts are driven by business goals, not buried in IT or confined to experimental teams.

> *"I recommend establishing an AI function that reports to the Chief Strategy Officer, or in organizations with forward-thinking technology leaders, to the CIO. . . This ensures the team is focused on value creation rather than just technical output."*
> *-From my article, "Building an Effective AI Team"*

What If You Don't Want a Chief AI Officer?

That's totally fine. In fact, there are several alternative titles I've found to be incredibly effective, especially for organizations that want flexibility and function without the baggage of new executive hierarchy.

Here are titles that you could consider:

- AI Strategy Analyst *(my preferred choice)*
- AI Technology Scout
- AI Innovation Analyst
- AI Industry Analyst
- AI Intelligence Specialist
- AI Emerging Technology Specialist
- AI Environmental Scanning Specialist
- AI Competitive Intelligence Analyst
- AI Technology Trends Analyst
- AI Technology Intelligence Analyst

Each of these roles can lead strategic AI initiatives without requiring a C-suite title and still carry the authority needed to drive meaningful change.

My Bottom Line

Whether or not your organization appoints a Chief AI Officer, you must define who owns AI strategy and business value creation. That leadership role should focus on:

- Translating AI opportunities into measurable business value
- Guiding ethical and compliant implementation
- Driving cross-functional collaboration
- Ensuring alignment with strategic enterprise goals
- Monitoring the competitive landscape and positioning the organization for AI-driven advantage

AI leadership isn't optional; it's foundational. The title doesn't matter as much as the influence, clarity, and strategic direction this role brings to the table. The right leader, empowered with the right authority and recognized by peers as a credible thought leader, can make the difference between scattered experiments and sustained transformation.

Who You Hire Matters: The Mindset of Strategic AI Leadership

Beyond defining the structure of AI leadership, the character of the leader themselves is also a key component. Once you've defined who will lead your AI efforts, whether it's a Chief AI Officer, AI Strategy Analyst, or another title, it's just as important to consider *what kind of person* you place in that role. In my work with senior executives and boards, I've seen time and again that the right attitude and mindset often outweigh even the most impressive résumés.

Let's be honest: hiring the perfect AI leader - the one who understands deep learning models, business strategy, regulatory risk, and change management - isn't just difficult; it's expensive. Most organizations can't afford to wait for (or pay for) a unicorn. And the good news is, you don't have to.

What matters more is finding someone who can grow into the role - a strategic thinker who's open to learning, skilled at connecting across functions, and unafraid of complexity. You can train on tools, but you can't train curiosity, humility, or adaptability.

That's why I encourage companies to invest in internal talent with the right mindset - people who know the business, are respected by peers, and are ready to champion AI through collaboration, not command. These individuals may not have a background in data science or machine learning, and that's okay. What they need is a foundation of trust and the ability to lead cross-functional conversations about how AI can deliver value.

To accelerate their success, partnering with an external AI expert or firm can be beneficial. Your internal leader brings organizational knowledge and influence, while the external advisor provides technical fluency, exposure to evolving best practices, and the ability to guide initial decisions. *In my experience, this hybrid approach—growing internal talent while supplementing with external expertise—creates the strongest foundation for sustainable, scalable AI leadership.*

Strategic AI leaders operate in an environment of rapid change, constant ambiguity, and high stakes. That means the person in the role must be more than technically capable; they must be curious, adaptable, and collaborative.

The Essential Traits of High-Impact AI Leaders

Here are the qualities I consistently look for (and develop) in individuals leading strategic AI initiatives. These are the traits that matter far more than technical credentials or job titles:

- **Growth Mindset**

   They're energized by change and see every challenge as a chance to learn. AI is an evolving space; they evolve with it. *AI strategy is not just a job; it's a mindset. I'd rather train someone with the right instincts than hire someone with the perfect résumé but the wrong mindset.*

- **Strategic Curiosity**

   They constantly connect the dots across teams, technologies, and market shifts. They ask smart questions like, *"Where can AI create the most value?"* and *"What trends are our competitors betting on?"*

- **Empathy and Communication**

   They listen across the organization and translate between technical and business stakeholders. Trust is their currency.

- **Comfort with Ambiguity**

   They don't freeze when there's no playbook. They bring structure to uncertainty and help others move forward with confidence.

- **Bias for Action**

   They don't just theorize, pontificate, and "hand wave"; they build. They are comfortable with progress, not perfection.

- **Courage**

   They challenge assumptions, speak truth to power, and make hard calls when others hesitate. Whether it's questioning legacy processes, calling out ethical concerns, or leading change through resistance, they lead with clarity and conviction, even when it's uncomfortable.

"I've worked with brilliant technologists who couldn't move AI past a prototype, and I've worked with curious, cross-functional, courageous thinkers who led full-scale AI transformation. The difference was mindset, not technical mastery."

When selecting someone for an AI strategy role, prioritize these traits. You can train on tools, but you can't train someone to be strategically curious, open to feedback, trusted by colleagues, or fearless in the face of change. Those traits are what truly differentiate high-impact AI leaders and enable the cross-functional collaboration that is vital to AI success.

Red Flag: Governance Without Action Is a Sign of Fear, Not Strategy When I walk into an organization and all they want to talk about is

AI governance, but no one is actively building, piloting, or learning, I know they don't have courageous (Bold) AI leadership.

Courageous leaders don't hide behind policies; they lead through experimentation, learning, and action. Governance is critical, but it can't be the only conversation. If your AI team spends 90% of its time defining frameworks and writing policies and 0% creating value, you've got a leadership gap.

Cross-Functional Collaboration: The Foundation of AI Success

Complementing these evolving team structures and specialized roles, cross-functional collaboration has become essential for delivering business value with AI. In parallel with new roles and team structures, cross-functional collaboration has become essential for delivering business value with AI. Effective AI initiatives now require the collective expertise of business leaders, domain experts, frontline users, and technical teams, all working together to ensure that solutions solve real-world problems and drive measurable outcomes.

Cross-Functional AI Collaboration: A New Standard for Execution:

- **Business Strategists:** Ensure AI initiatives directly support growth, efficiency, and customer-centric goals.
- **Domain Experts:** Provide specialized knowledge to guide relevant, high-impact AI applications in functions like supply chain, finance, or marketing.
- **End Users:** Share frontline insights to shape AI tools that are intuitive, effective, and widely adopted.
- **Data Scientists and Engineers:** Build models and solutions in collaboration with business stakeholders to ensure technical work drives strategic value.

A strong example of this model comes from Unilever, where an AI-powered demand forecasting team included supply chain managers, economists, and data scientists. This blend of expertise led to higher forecasting accuracy and better adoption, demonstrating how cross-functional collaboration enhances both performance and impact.

By embedding collaboration into AI execution, organizations position AI as a strategic enabler, not just a technical initiative. This approach ensures that AI projects are scalable, user-focused, and built to solve the right problems from day one.

Why This Matters: Structuring AI Teams for the Future

AI isn't just a technical function anymore; it's an enterprise-wide capability that requires cross-functional expertise, new leadership roles, and modernized team structures. To future-proof AI teams, organizations must:

- Choose the right AI team model (centralized, federated, or hybrid).
- Hire for new AI-driven roles beyond data scientists.
- Ensure AI teams work cross-functionally with business strategists and end users.

Companies that structure AI teams for collaboration will drive faster adoption, greater alignment, and higher business impact, making AI a true competitive advantage.

Actionable Framework: How to Build a Collaborative AI Team

To transform AI potential into tangible business results, organizations must adopt a structured approach to team building, moving beyond technical silos to foster collaborative excellence. Here's a pragmatic framework for constructing high-impact AI teams:

Step 1: Build a Cross-Functional AI Team from Day One

- **Why?** AI teams must include technical, business, and end-user stakeholders.
- **Example:** Spotify brings together data scientists, music curators, and marketers to refine AI-driven recommendations.
- **Quick Win:** Identify and bring in one non-technical team (sales, operations, HR) to an AI meeting this week.

Step 2: Establish an AI Translator Role

- **Why?** Many AI failures occur because business teams and AI engineers don't speak the same language.
- **Example:** JPMorgan created an AI strategy analyst role to bridge the gap between data science and business goals.
- **Quick Win:** Assign an AI Translator - someone with technical + business fluency - to AI projects.

Step 3: Train Business Leaders on AI Fundamentals

- **Why?** Business leaders don't need to code, but they must understand AI capabilities, risks, and ethics.
- **Example:** Microsoft's AI Business School trains executives to align AI with business strategy.
- **Quick Win:** Host a one-hour AI crash course for non-technical leaders.

Step 4: Align AI with Business Goals Using OKRs

- **Why?** AI must tie directly to measurable business impact.
- **Example:** Google uses Objectives and Key Results (OKRs) to measure AI success, focusing on customer satisfaction, revenue growth, or operational efficiency.
- **Quick Win:** Set one OKR for an AI project that ties AI impact to a business metric.

Step 5: Create an AI Feedback Loop

- **Why?** AI models must evolve based on real-world user input.
- **Example:** Rolls-Royce collects feedback from aircraft engineers to refine AI-powered predictive maintenance.
- **Quick Win:** Implement monthly AI reviews where business + technical teams assess results together.

Case Study and Lessons Learned: Real-World Applications

Real-world case studies offer powerful insight into what makes AI initiatives succeed (or fail). These examples highlight the critical role of cross-functional collaboration in ensuring AI solutions are practical, effective, and aligned with user needs.

Success Story: John Deere – AI Success Through Cross-Functional Collaboration

- **Challenge:** John Deere wanted to use AI to improve precision agriculture, but AI engineers had no farming experience.
- **Solution:** They built a collaborative team of farmers, agronomists, data scientists, and supply chain experts.
- **Results:** AI-driven smart tractors and sensors that help farmers maximize crop yields and reduce costs.

Lesson Learned: The Banking AI Disaster

- **Challenge:** The bank's fraud detection AI didn't involve fraud analysts, leading to too many false positives.
- **Mistake:** AI was developed in isolation from real-world user needs.
- **Outcome:** The bank had to retrain its AI, delaying implementation by six months.

Key Takeaways: Why Cross-Functional Collaboration Is Essential

- **AI must be grounded in real-world expertise.**

    Successful AI initiatives require input from those who deeply understand the context where the technology will be applied. At John Deere, AI only succeeded when engineers worked alongside farmers and agronomists. Without this frontline insight, solutions risk being irrelevant or impractical.

- **Collaboration prevents costly mistakes.**

    When AI systems are built in silos (like in the banking case), critical perspectives are missed. Involving fraud analysts from the beginning could have helped the bank avoid a six-month delay caused by retraining an ineffective model. Cross-functional collaboration helps flag potential issues early and reduces rework.

- **Cross-functional teams accelerate adoption and trust.**

    When business users, domain experts, and technical teams co-create AI solutions, there is greater trust in the outcomes. This leads to smoother implementation, faster user adoption, and stronger long-term engagement.

- **Siloed AI is risky AI.**

    Whether it's underperforming models, stakeholder resistance, or ethical blind spots, working in isolation increases the likelihood of failure. Cross-functional collaboration creates checks and balances that help align AI efforts with real business needs and outcomes.

- **Diverse teams drive innovation.**

    Bringing together different perspectives - technical, operational, strategic - sparks creativity and innovation. Solutions are more likely to be scalable, sustainable, and impactful when shaped by varied viewpoints.

Chapter Checklist and Next Steps

Use this checklist to assess whether your organization is structured to build and sustain effective, high-impact AI teams.

☐ **Strategic AI Leadership:**

- o Have you defined a clear AI leadership function (such as an AI Strategy Analyst) to guide strategic AI initiatives, monitor the competitive landscape, and position the organization for long-term advantage?

- o Are we balancing governance with courageous action? If all our AI energy is spent on policy without progress, we may have a leadership gap.

☐ **Team Structure and Composition:**
- Have you selected the right team model (centralized, federated, or hybrid) based on your organization's size, maturity, and goals?
- Is your AI team cross-functional, with representation from data science, business strategy, domain experts, and end users?

☐ **Specialized AI Roles:**
- Do you have specialized AI roles in place (such as an AI Ethicist, AI Translator, AI Product Owner, or AI Change Manager) to ensure ethical, effective, and scalable outcomes?

☐ **AI Fluency and Alignment:**
- Are your business leaders trained in AI fundamentals, so they can make informed decisions and set realistic expectations?
- Is each AI initiative aligned with a measurable business goal (e.g., through OKRs or KPIs)?

☐ **Collaboration and Feedback:**
- Have you established a feedback loop where technical and business teams regularly review AI performance and iterate based on real-world data?
- Are AI projects co-created with frontline users to ensure usability, adoption, and real-world relevance?
- Is collaboration part of your AI culture, not just a one-off strategy?

Next Chapter Preview: Cultural Shifts for AI Adoption

Technology alone won't drive transformation. Culture is the true multiplier. In the next chapter, we'll explore how to build the kind of culture that supports everything you've just learned, where collaboration, learning, and risk-taking aren't one-time events, but the way AI-enabled organizations operate every day.

Final Thoughts

AI succeeds when smart tech meets smart teamwork - diverse, collaborative teams solving problems that matter. Organizations that embrace cross-functional teaming don't just implement AI; they operationalize intelligence that drives trust, innovation, and lasting business value. By designing thoughtful team structures, redefining critical roles, establishing AI leadership, and embedding communication and feedback loops into every project, you're not just building AI; you're building a modern, resilient, and high-performing organization.

CHAPTER 9

Building a Cultural Where AI Can Thrive

In my research and with my clients, I found that successful AI adoption doesn't require a complete cultural overhaul; it requires a mindset that welcomes curiosity, accepts ambiguity, and learns from failure. AI thrives in environments that embrace experimentation, not perfection. In this chapter, I'll show you what that looks like in practice.

Why Experimentation, Trust, and Curiosity Matter More Than Perfection

When I observe organizations grappling with AI implementation, I consistently see culture challenges. As a matter of fact, I frequently state that "I will not spend one minute convincing you that you need AI." Organizations with a resistant culture, and leaders disinterested in addressing that problem, are not where I spend my time. We often focus on the sophistication of algorithms and the power of computing, but the real key to AI success lies in building a culture where AI can thrive. In my experience, it's less about implementing AI tools and more about cultivating a mindset where learning equals ROI, employees embrace AI, trust its insights, and continuously learn to work alongside it.

I've witnessed this firsthand. Take the cautionary tale of a Fortune 500 retailer. They poured resources into a cutting-edge AI-driven demand forecasting system, expecting it to revolutionize their inventory management. The technology was there, but the rollout flopped. Why? Store managers, entrenched in years of experience, resisted the AI's recommendations, clinging to their intuition and established practices. The result? Inefficient stock levels, lost sales, and a significant hit to their bottom line. The core issue, as I see it, wasn't the AI's accuracy; it was the absence of a culture that supported its adoption. They lacked the failure-absorbent culture needed for AI to learn and improve.

Then, consider Amazon. Their success with AI is, in my view, deeply intertwined with their cultural fabric. AI isn't treated as a separate entity; it's woven into their daily operations and decision-making. They've built a culture where employees are encouraged to experiment, learn from failures, and continuously refine AI applications. This cultural embrace fuels their innovation and, ultimately, their competitive edge. Their leaders understand that AI integration requires board-level cultural attention, modeling AI-centric behavior and reinforcing AI's role as a co-pilot.

In this chapter, I explore this critical link between culture and AI success. I dig into why building a culture where AI can thrive is paramount, the common pitfalls I've observed when culture is neglected, and the actionable strategies I've developed to help you create an AI-ready organization.

Definition and Relevance: Why AI Adoption Requires a Thriving Culture

For me, a thriving AI culture goes beyond simply training employees on new software. It requires actively cultivating an evolving organizational DNA – a mindset where AI maturity requires a learning culture, teams are empowered to experiment, and curiosity and humility are culture catalysts.

I believe this is essential for three core reasons:

- **Building Trust:** Trust is the foundation of all meaningful AI integration. When we help employees understand how AI works, what its limitations are, and how it supports, not replaces, their decision-making, trust follows. But this happens only through transparency and inclusion. I teach leaders to bring employees into the AI process early:

  o Involve them in testing.

  o Ask for their feedback.

  o Show how decisions are made.

  This type of transparency signals respect, and trust is built on respect.

- **Driving Adoption:** Adoption doesn't happen because you mandated a new tool. It happens when teams feel safe to explore and energized to innovate. This is why building a culture of innovation is so critical to success with AI. I challenge leaders to create research & development (R&D) space - time, budget, and psychological safety - for employees to tinker, test, and iterate.

o When people know they won't be penalized for trying something new (or for surfacing a problem), they'll bring their best ideas forward. That's where AI gets sticky.

This isn't innovation for innovation's sake. Adoption grows when employees believe the AI actually helps them win, whether that's saving time, serving customers, or solving meaningful problems.

- **Fostering Innovation Through Iterative Learning:** This is where I push leaders to rethink their definition of ROI:
  o "Do you only count ROI when something works perfectly, or are you capturing the value of what you've learned when it doesn't?"
  o In organizations with thriving AI cultures, learning is capitalized. A failed AI pilot isn't a waste. If it generates insight, it becomes part of your next success. That's why I emphasize failure-absorbent cultures: ones where people aren't punished for taking intelligent risks, and where lessons are celebrated as part of the journey, not seen as setbacks.

AI success isn't linear; it's iterative and layered. And the most innovative teams track their learning as carefully as they track their metrics.

Common Pitfalls: What Goes Wrong and Warning Signs

I've seen so many promising AI initiatives never get off the ground (or quietly unravel) not because the technology failed but because the culture wasn't ready to support it. When employees don't trust the system, when leaders fail to invest in learning, or when teams are afraid to experiment, even the best AI tools go unused or misapplied.

The result? A growing gap between what's *possible* with AI and what actually delivers value. These aren't isolated incidents; they're cultural patterns I've seen over and over again. The following are the five most common pitfalls I watch for, and the warning signs leaders should never ignore.

Pitfall #1: Fear of Failure Stifles Experimentation

- **Mistake:** The organization punishes failure or avoids taking risks, preventing teams from testing, learning, or iterating with AI.
- **Example:** A global insurance company launched a small AI initiative to streamline claims processing. Early tests showed promise, but there were gaps - glitches in data mapping, a few misrouted claims, and some

confusion around how to override AI decisions. Instead of treating this as part of the learning curve, leadership hit the brakes. They paused the pilot, assigned blame, and demanded that the next version be "fully accurate before we try again." The result? Months of paralysis. Innovation teams became gun-shy, employees avoided proposing new ideas, and AI adoption flatlined. What could have been a valuable iterative process - refining the model, improving workflows, and learning from frontline feedback - was shut down in favor of perfection.

- **Warning Sign:** No AI pilot projects, limited iteration, and a culture of perfectionism over learning.
- **Leadership Check:** Are your teams allowed to test, fail, and learn, or are they waiting for permission to get it "right" before they even start?

Pitfall #2: Employees Resist AI Due to Lack of Trust

- **Mistake:** AI is rolled out without involving employees in its design, testing, or purpose, creating fear, confusion, and skepticism.
- **Example:** A Fortune 500 retailer deployed an AI forecasting system, but store managers ignored it, relying on gut instinct instead. They didn't trust the AI, because they hadn't been included in the process and didn't understand what factors were behind the recommendations. With their jobs on the line if they performed badly, they were more comfortable relying on their own historic knowledge and approach than on an unknown system.
- **Warning Sign:** Low adoption rates, vocal resistance, and employees using workarounds to bypass AI recommendations.
- **Leadership Check:** Are you asking people to trust a system they've never seen, shaped, or understood?

Pitfall #3: AI Initiatives Clash with Organizational Norms

- **Mistake:** AI is introduced without aligning with the company's values, workflows, or ways of thinking, creating cultural friction.
- **Example:** A retail chain introduced an AI-driven scheduling tool to optimize labor costs, but it ignored employee preferences and local manager autonomy. The system clashed with long-held values around flexibility and employee empowerment, so store managers began manually overriding it.
- **Warning Sign:** Teams perceive AI as disruptive or top-down; collaboration between AI and business units is minimal or strained.
- **Leadership Check:** Does your AI initiative fit how your people actually work, or does it fight against your culture?

Pitfall #4: No Investment in AI Literacy

- **Mistake:** Organizations fail to educate and prepare employees to work alongside AI, leaving them unsure how to engage or what to expect.

- **Example**: A national logistics company rolled out an AI-powered routing platform to optimize delivery schedules and reduce fuel costs. The tech worked beautifully on paper. But drivers and dispatchers weren't trained on how to interpret the AI's suggestions or understand its logic. They didn't know when to trust it or when to override it, and they weren't given a voice in shaping the rollout. As a result, teams quietly reverted to old workflows. One regional supervisor described it bluntly: "I'm not going to follow a robot if I don't understand what it's doing."
- **Warning Sign**: Employees struggle to explain what the AI does, rely on outdated practices, or show low confidence in AI outputs.
- **Leadership Check**: Have you equipped your workforce to engage with AI, or are you expecting them to trust something they can't explain?

Pitfall #5: Governance Becomes a Substitute for Action

- **Mistake:** Leadership overemphasizes AI policy, compliance, and risk frameworks without actually building anything. It becomes a stalling tactic rooted in fear, not strategy.
- **Example:** A global enterprise spent 18 months developing AI governance frameworks. They held committee meetings, published internal white papers, debated risk thresholds, and even mailed out crystal trophies to recognize the AI Governance Council's contributions. But despite all the activity, not a single AI pilot had been tested or deployed. Innovation teams were stuck in neutral, waiting for approvals, guidelines, or clarity that never quite arrived. Eventually, employees began to joke that "AI" stood for *"Always Inactive."* Behind the scenes, frustration mounted. Product teams lost confidence and stopped working on AI-related ideas. Leaders who had once championed AI quietly distanced themselves or left the company. And when budget season came around, AI funding was cut, not because the tech lacked promise, but because no one had seen results.
- **Warning Sign:** Endless planning and meetings with no progress, over-reliance on documentation, and a reluctance to launch anything not fully "perfected."
- **Leadership Check:** Are you spending more time talking about AI than building it?

Leadership Case Studies: How Executives Drive AI Culture

The organizations who reap the most business benefit from AI are led by leaders who prioritize building a culture where AI can thrive. They understand that fostering a growth mindset, promoting collaboration, and building trust are essential for unlocking AI's transformative potential.

Microsoft - Satya Nadella

Satya Nadella exemplifies this approach through his emphasis on creating psychological safety and continuous learning. His "learn-it-all" rather than "know-it-all" philosophy transformed Microsoft's culture from one of competition to collaboration. By encouraging employees to embrace curiosity and view challenges as opportunities for growth, Nadella created an environment where AI innovation flourishes. His leadership style emphasizes that mistakes are learning opportunities, leading to breakthrough developments in Microsoft's AI capabilities.

DBS Bank - Piyush Gupta

Piyush Gupta demonstrates how leaders can systematically build an AI-ready culture. Under his guidance, DBS launched comprehensive AI literacy programs and created innovation spaces where employees could experiment with AI solutions. By establishing hackathons and dedicated innovation labs, Gupta fostered a culture where employees at all levels feel empowered to contribute to AI initiatives. His approach proved that cultural transformation doesn't just come down to top-down directives; it necessitates creating opportunities for hands-on engagement with AI.

Walmart - Doug McMillon

Doug McMillon shows how board-level commitment to AI culture drives enterprise-wide transformation. By consistently communicating AI's strategic importance and backing these messages with substantial resource allocation, McMillon demonstrated that cultural change requires visible leadership support. He ensured that AI initiatives received not just financial backing but also the organizational attention needed for success. His approach included regular updates to the board on AI progress and establishing clear metrics for measuring cultural transformation in AI adoption.

These leaders all demonstrate a key truth I teach often: AI culture is built, not declared. And while their organizations are large and well-resourced, the principles they follow - trust, clarity, continuous learning - apply just as powerfully to early-stage startups. I've had the opportunity to put these beliefs into practice from day one as the CEO of my own AI company,

Neuro Collective Exchange (NCX). What follows is a firsthand look at how we built cultural foundations with the same level of discipline we apply to our AI strategy.

NCX - Dr. Lisa Palmer

At NCX, we recognized early that integrating AI into organizations isn't just a technical challenge; it's a cultural one. If we wanted to build an AI-native company that actually delivers impact, we couldn't treat culture as an afterthought. We had to design it with the same rigor we apply to products, systems, and strategy.

Our cultural design process started with purpose. Our founding team aligned around a shared mission: empowering forward-thinking humans, fueled by technology, to create thriving, healthy organizations. But for us, that wasn't just a mission statement; it became our operational north star. Every decision, from partnerships to product direction, had to serve that outcome.

From there, we defined three core cultural beliefs that would shape our approach:

- **Together We Innovate** (Humans + Machines)
- **Access Unlocks Potential**
- **Balanced Boldness**

What makes our approach different is that we didn't stop at language. We turned our beliefs into decision infrastructure.

We built a **Decision Evaluation Framework:** a practical tool that forces cultural clarity at every key inflection point. It's a spreadsheet, yes. But it's also a discipline. Before we greenlight any new initiative, we use the framework to assess alignment with our principles.

- **Under Together We Innovate, we ask:** Are we bringing in diverse perspectives - human and machine? Is there mutual trust? Shared understanding?
- **Under Access Unlocks Potential, we evaluate:** Will this decision democratize access to insight or tools? Will it make modern technologies more usable?
- **Under Balanced Boldness, we challenge ourselves:** Is this move ambitious *and* structured? Are we chasing signal or just noise?

These aren't theoretical questions. They shape who we work with, how we prioritize roadmap features, how we evaluate investors, and how we lead ourselves. When we talk about *applying culture*, this is what we mean: real-time accountability through shared decision filters.

We saw the value of this system early on, especially when evaluating our first major funding opportunity. The framework pushed us beyond checking boxes on a term sheet, forcing us to ask harder, more strategic questions: Does this investor align with our belief in democratizing access to intelligence? Will they embrace our commitment to human + AI collaboration, not just tolerate it? Will they support our balance of bold vision and disciplined execution?

We walked away from offers that looked attractive on paper but failed to meet our cultural criteria. Drawing on both my professional experience and doctoral research - research that clearly links culture to AI business success - we knew these weren't philosophical decisions. They were strategic filters designed to protect our trajectory and maximize long-term enterprise value. The future valuation of our company will reflect the cultural discipline we've applied from the start.

This process has proven especially valuable in complex AI decisions. It prevents us from defaulting to short-term wins or performative governance. It keeps us aligned with our core belief that humans, not technology, must remain at the center of business efforts to create the best outcomes.

Our experience reinforces what I teach: a strong AI culture isn't something you talk about; it's something you build. And you build it by translating beliefs into systems that shape real decisions. That's how you create a culture where AI can thrive and where the people behind it can lead with clarity, courage, and purpose.

Why Leadership Is the Key to Building a Culture Where AI Thrives

These case studies reveal a crucial truth: business success with AI is fundamentally impacted by the environment leaders cultivate. The most successful AI initiatives don't happen by chance; they flourish because leaders proactively create the conditions where AI can thrive.

Their approach consistently includes these key elements:

- **Championing AI Literacy:** Leaders go beyond providing basic training; they foster a deep understanding of AI's capabilities and limitations across all levels of the organization. They ensure everyone, from the C-suite to the frontline, can engage confidently with AI.

- **Modeling a Growth Mindset:** They actively promote experimentation, viewing failures as learning opportunities and rewarding calculated risk-taking. They emphasize that continuous learning and adaptation are essential for AI's evolution.

- **Embedding AI Ethos:** AI isn't treated as a separate initiative; it's integrated into the organization's core values, decision-making processes, and long-term vision. Leaders ensure AI principles become part of the organizational DNA.

- **Empowering Collaboration:** They break down silos, fostering cross-functional teams where diverse perspectives shape AI development and deployment. They create an environment where collaboration is the norm, not the exception.
- **Communicating with Transparency:** Leaders prioritize open and honest communication about AI's purpose, benefits, and limitations. They build trust by ensuring stakeholders understand AI's decision-making processes and its impact.

In essence, these leaders recognize their role as architects of an AI-ready environment. Their actions, communication, and priorities determine whether AI becomes a genuine catalyst for growth or remains just another underutilized tool. By building cultures where AI is not merely accepted but actively championed, they create environments where technology and teams can reach their full potential. The data is clear: organizations that prioritize AI culture at the leadership level consistently achieve faster adoption, higher ROI, and sustainable competitive advantages.

Actionable Framework: How to Build an AI-Ready Culture

In my work, I've found that creating and sustaining a thriving AI culture requires a multifaceted approach, and I've developed a framework based on these steps:

1. **Champion AI as an Enabler:** I advise organizations to avoid presenting AI as a job replacement tool. Instead, I emphasize its potential to augment human capabilities, automate mundane tasks, and free employees to focus on more strategic and creative work. I encourage sharing success stories and examples of how AI has enhanced employee roles in other organizations.

2. **Invest in AI Literacy:** I strongly recommend providing comprehensive training and education programs that cater to different levels of technical expertise. I stress the importance of focusing on practical applications and real-world use cases, demystifying AI and making it accessible to everyone. This is crucial for trust-building (e.g., offer workshops that explain AI concepts in plain language and provide opportunities for hands-on interaction with AI tools).

3. **Foster a Culture of Experimentation:** I urge leaders to create an environment where employees feel safe to explore AI's potential, test new

ideas, and learn from both successes and failures. I advocate for creating safe spaces for experimentation and celebrating learning as a valuable outcome. This reflects the principle that AI maturity requires a learning culture (e.g., establish dedicated "AI labs" or innovation sprints where teams can experiment with AI without fear of negative consequences).

4. **Promote Collaboration:** I emphasize the need to break down silos between technical teams and business units, fostering cross-functional collaboration and knowledge sharing. I encourage creating opportunities for employees from different backgrounds to work together on AI projects, leveraging their diverse perspectives and expertise. This is essential for an innovation culture (e.g., form AI project teams that include members from different departments, with diverse skill sets, and varied backgrounds).

5. **Lead by Example:** I believe leaders must champion AI adoption by modeling the mindset they want the organization to embrace. That means showing a personal willingness to learn, experiment, and adapt alongside their teams. When senior leaders visibly engage in AI conversations, not just delegate them, they send a clear message: *this matters.*

This is more than theory. I've had a dozen CEOs ask me to host a private cohort on generative AI so that they could build their own fluency and lead from the front. These were not tech executives; they were business leaders who understood that credibility in AI leadership requires more than sound bites. It requires active participation.

I emphasize that leaders must back their words with action. Leadership shapes culture. If AI is just something "the tech team handles," adoption stalls, or never starts. But when AI shows up in board-level conversations, executive workflows, and strategic priorities, it becomes part of how the organization thinks.

AI culture requires purposeful design, active engagement, and daily commitment. The most successful organizations *intentionally* cultivate the conditions in which AI can thrive. That means investing in literacy, encouraging experimentation, leading from the front, and embedding collaboration into every layer of the enterprise. Bold AI Leaders have the courage to lead with clarity, humility, and curiosity. When you build a culture where people feel trusted, included, and empowered to learn, AI doesn't just work better; it delivers *real*, lasting business value.

The Culture Playbook for AI-Ready Organizations

Dr. Lisa Palmer, Founder of NCX and Fortune 500 AI Advisor
Culture doesn't "happen." It's built one decision at a time. It's shaped, tested, and reinforced daily. This is the leadership playbook I use to help organizations design cultures where AI thrives.

1. **Champion AI as an Enabler**
   - Reframe AI as a partner, not a replacement.
   - Share stories that highlight how AI augments human talent.
2. **Invest in AI Literacy**
   - Make AI understandable and usable for *everyone*.
   - Provide practical training grounded in real business use cases.
3. **Foster a Culture of Experimentation**
   - Encourage iteration and reward learning, not just outcomes.
   - Build failure-absorbent systems that treat mistakes as fuel for growth.
4. **Promote Collaboration**
   - Break down silos. Build cross-functional teams.
   - Invite diverse voices to shape and scale your AI initiatives.
5. **Lead by Example**
   - Learn out loud. Engage personally in AI discussions.
   - Show (don't just tell) that AI is a strategic priority.

AI culture requires purposeful design, active engagement, and daily commitment. Bold leaders don't just talk about AI. They live it.

Case Study and Lessons Learned: Real-World Applications

To illustrate the importance of building a culture where AI can thrive, consider these real-world examples:

Success Story: Amazon - AI Adoption as a Cultural Advantage

- **Challenge:** Scaling AI across diverse operations, including logistics, retail, and cloud computing.
- **Solution:** Amazon cultivated a culture of AI experimentation and continuous learning, embedding AI into decision-making at all levels and empowering employees to innovate.
- **Results:** AI became a core driver of efficiency and customer loyalty, powering everything from product recommendations to warehouse automation, demonstrating that a thriving AI culture fuels business success.

Lesson Learned: The Hospital That Ignored AI Culture

- **Challenge:** Implementing a comprehensive clinical AI system across five hospitals, designed to predict patient deterioration, optimize surgical scheduling, recommend care pathways, and assist with radiology triage.

- **Mistake:** The organization treated it as a pure technology deployment, failing to involve clinicians in development, provide context for AI decisions, or create feedback channels. Training focused on mechanics rather than meaningful integration into clinical workflows, while success metrics emphasized adoption over outcomes.

- **Outcome:** The $15M system was largely ignored or actively worked around by clinical teams who maintained parallel processes they trusted more. Emergency physicians experienced alert fatigue, surgeons kept separate scheduling systems, and radiologists bypassed the triage tools. The project defaulted to basic administrative functions, missing the opportunity for true care transformation and highlighting how cultural readiness determines AI's clinical impact.

Key Takeaway: AI is only as good as the people who trust and use it. Building a culture where AI can thrive is a foundational requirement for realizing AI's transformative potential.

Chapter Checklist and Next Steps

Before moving on, ensure you've addressed these key considerations for building a culture where AI can thrive:

- ☐ **AI as an Enabler:** Have we clearly communicated AI's role as a tool to augment human capabilities, not replace them?

- ☐ **AI Literacy:** Are we investing in comprehensive AI training and education for all stakeholders, fostering understanding and trust?

- ☐ **Culture of Experimentation:** Are we creating a safe space for experimentation, where learning from failures is valued and encouraged?

- ☐ **Collaboration and Inclusion:** Are we fostering cross-functional collaboration and ensuring diverse perspectives are included in AI initiatives?

- ☐ **Leadership Commitment:** Are leaders actively using AI, championing AI adoption, and modeling the desired AI-ready mindset?

- ☐ **Balance of Governance and Action:** Are we pairing responsible oversight with real progress - actually building, testing, and learning from AI?

Next Chapter Preview: Data as a Strategic Asset

AI's potential is powered by people. When you build a culture that encourages learning, trust, and experimentation, you create the conditions for AI to thrive. But culture alone isn't enough. **AI also needs fuel, and that fuel is data.**

In the next chapter, we'll explore how to treat data as a strategic asset: high-quality, accessible, and ethically managed. Because without the right data, even the most collaborative AI culture can't deliver on its promise.

Final Thoughts

Building a culture where AI can thrive isn't a one-time project; it's an ongoing commitment. By prioritizing trust, learning, collaboration, and ethical considerations, organizations can unlock AI's transformative power and create a future where humans and AI work in true partnership.

CHAPTER 10

Data as a Strategic Asset

High-Quality Fuel for AI

While helping organizations to adopt AI, I emphasize this simple truth: AI is only as effective as the data it's built on. You can't separate the performance of your AI solutions from the quality of your data. That's why treating data as a strategic asset is both a technical best practice and a business imperative.

In this chapter, I show how organizations move beyond passive data collection toward purposeful data stewardship. We'll examine why AI-ready data must be complete, accessible, and trustworthy, and how modern approaches like synthetic data, AI-powered governance, and automated bias detection are reshaping the way smart companies handle their data. If culture sets the tone for AI, data sets the pace. This chapter gives you the tools to accelerate with confidence.

Building on the strategic priorities introduced in earlier chapters, this one sets the stage for scalable, trustworthy AI by setting a solid foundation.

The Hidden Cost of Bad Data

AI's potential is immense, but its performance is only as strong as the data used to create it. When models are trained on inaccurate, incomplete, or inconsistent data, the consequences ripple across the business (see Figure 10.1):

- AI outputs become unreliable, reducing confidence in results.
- Stakeholder trust erodes as skepticism about AI decisions grows.
- Opportunities for insight and automation are missed or misdirected.
- Business strategies falter, guided by flawed or misleading information.

**The Hidden Cost
of Bad Data**

- **Inaccurate Results**
- **Loss of Trust**
- **Wasted Insights**
- **Misguided Decisions**

FIGURE 10.1 Inaccurate or incomplete data undermines AI performance at every level, leading to faulty insights, stakeholder skepticism, and failed strategic outcomes.

Consider This Real-World Example: In 2021, a major financial institution launched an AI-powered credit risk model to streamline loan approvals. The promise? Fewer defaults and greater financial inclusion. The reality? Complaints poured in. Qualified borrowers were rejected, while risky applicants got the green light. The cause? Incomplete, biased, and outdated training data that compromised the model's effectiveness from the start.

Now compare that with Tesla, which has mastered the use of synthetic data to train its self-driving AI. By generating realistic, high-quality data that mimics rare or risky road scenarios, Tesla avoids the limitations of real-world data, speeds up model development, and improves safety without compromising privacy or performance.

The Takeaway: AI is only as good as the underpinning data. Organizations that treat data as a strategic asset and actively invest in synthetic and structured data are positioned to win. Those that ignore data quality will pay for it in poor performance, missed insights, and lost trust.

Definition and Relevance: Why Data Quality and Synthetic Data Matter

Data quality encompasses the accuracy, completeness, consistency, timeliness, and validity of data. For AI initiatives, high-quality data is non-negotiable; it's the foundation upon which reliable models and trustworthy insights are built. Furthermore, I see quickly growing importance of synthetic data - artificially generated data that mirrors real-world data's statistical properties - as a powerful tool to augment or even replace real data, particularly when addressing privacy and bias concerns.

These concepts are strategically relevant because:

- **Reliable AI:** High-quality data is essential for building AI models that are reliable, accurate, and trustworthy.
- **Bias Mitigation:** Effective data management, including the use of synthetic data, plays a crucial role in mitigating bias and ensuring the ethical use of AI.
- **Efficient AI Development:** A robust data foundation is critical for enabling the efficient development and seamless scaling of AI initiatives across the enterprise.
- **Data Privacy:** Synthetic data provides a means to unlock AI innovation while addressing growing concerns around data privacy and regulatory compliance.

Data isn't just fuel for AI; it's the foundation. When organizations treat data as an afterthought, AI is unstable and unscalable. But when they treat data as capital, AI becomes a strategic advantage. Because in every case, AI performance flows directly from data quality.

Common Pitfalls: What Goes Wrong and Warning Signs

Organizations often stumble by failing to recognize data's strategic importance. Here are common pitfalls and the warning signs that indicate potential problems:

Pitfall #1: Treating Data as a Byproduct, Not an Asset

- **Mistake:** Failing to recognize data's strategic value, leading to unstructured and underutilized data. Failing to recognize data's strategic value, leading to unstructured and underutilized data.
- **Example:** A global retailer accumulates petabytes of customer data across systems, but with no unified infrastructure or ownership, the data becomes more noise than fuel. Personalization suffers, and the AI recommendations feel generic rather than tailored.
- **Warning Sign:** AI outputs are inconsistent or irrelevant because data is poorly labeled, fragmented, or inaccessible across teams.

Pitfall #2: Failing to Address Bias in AI Training Data

- **Mistake:** Using historical data without scrutiny, perpetuating existing biases in AI systems.

- **Example:** A hiring platform trained on legacy data favored resumes from candidates with Ivy League backgrounds, marginalizing highly qualified talent from nontraditional paths.
- **Warning Sign:** AI outcomes consistently favor one group over another, triggering ethical and legal concerns, internal pushback from employees, and eroding stakeholder trust.

Pitfall #3: Over-Reliance on Real-World Data

- **Mistake:** Neglecting synthetic data, hindering AI development due to data scarcity or privacy concerns.
- **Example:** A healthcare AI project stalled due to the unavailability of diverse patient data. By not exploring synthetic data, they lost months of potential progress and innovation.
- **Warning Sign:** AI projects stall due to data access issues or limited data diversity.

Pitfall #4: Boiling the Ocean Instead of Prioritizing Precision

- **Mistake:** Attempting to overhaul many systems at once, delaying AI implementation and diluting focus.
- **Example:** An enterprise team tried to launch a "360-degree customer view" across all products, regions, and channels before deploying even a single personalization use case. After a year of investment, no live AI product had launched.
- **Warning Sign:** Teams are stuck in data wrangling mode indefinitely, AI initiatives fail to launch, and business value remains unrealized.

Why Smart Data Strategy Is the Future of Scalable AI

Companies that succeed with AI don't treat data quality and governance as back-office tasks; they treat them as core enablers of AI performance, trust, and longevity.

- AI models perform better, faster, and with fewer errors when trained on structured, clean, well-managed data.
- Built-in data governance ensures compliance isn't bolted on later but embedded from the start.
- Bias detection becomes proactive, not reactive, reducing ethical risk and protecting customer trust.

The organizations I work with that scale AI most successfully share a key insight:

AI doesn't just need good data. AI should help create good data.

By positioning AI as both a user *and* a steward of enterprise data, these companies build AI systems that are more resilient, more compliant, and more aligned with long-term strategy. This approach builds the foundation that AI can stand on for years to come.

Actionable Framework: How to Treat Data as a Strategic Asset

To unlock the full potential of data for AI, organizations need a proactive and strategic approach. Here's a framework to guide you:

1. **Shift from Data Hoarding to AI-Optimized Data:**
    - **Why?** I advise organizations to move beyond simply storing large volumes of raw data and instead focus on curating and structuring data specifically for AI applications.
    - **Example:** A manufacturing company implements a data catalog to organize and standardize sensor data from its equipment, making it readily available for AI-powered predictive maintenance.
    - **Quick Win:** Map your organization's key data sources and assess their "AI-readiness" in terms of quality, structure, and accessibility.
2. **Use Synthetic Data to Overcome Challenges:**
    - **Why?** I recommend exploring the use of synthetic data to augment real-world data, address privacy concerns, and mitigate bias in AI training.
    - **Example:** A financial institution generates synthetic transaction data to train a fraud detection AI, without exposing sensitive customer information.
    - **Quick Win:** Identify a specific AI use case where synthetic data can be applied to improve data availability or address privacy limitations.

Foundational Enabler: Use AI to Manage the Data That Fuels AI

Before diving into step 3, it's worth highlighting a key insight I emphasize in my work: AI should not only depend on high-quality data; it should help create it. The most advanced organizations use AI to actively manage, clean, and protect the very data their models rely on. This isn't just a technology upgrade; it's a smart shift in how we build trustworthy, scalable systems.

Here are a few ways I see organizations doing this well:

- **Automating Data Governance:**

  AI tools now help track how data is used, flag risky activity, and ensure compliance with laws like GDPR or HIPAA *automatically*.

  - **Example:** A global payments company uses AI to monitor its financial data in real time, making sure nothing violates privacy rules or creates risk.

- **Cleaning Up Data Before It Causes Problems:**

  AI can detect and fix issues in data like missing fields, duplicate entries, or inconsistent labels *before* those issues affect business outcomes.

  - **Example:** A large bank uses AI to check loan records for errors. What used to take weeks of manual work now happens in hours, and the results feed directly into more accurate risk models.

- **Spotting Bias Before It Gets Baked In:**

  Before data ever reaches an AI model, fairness tools can identify if certain groups are underrepresented or treated unfairly so teams can fix it early.

  - **Example:** A recruiting platform ran a fairness audit on its historical hiring data and discovered the system was unintentionally favoring male applicants. They used AI tools to rebalance the data before retraining their model.

The takeaway? **Let AI help prepare the data AI needs.** These tools are like digital quality-control teams - scanning, flagging, and fixing problems faster and more reliably than people ever could. They free up your teams to focus on the work that matters, while building trust in the AI systems your business will rely on.

3. **Improve Data Quality with AI-Driven Techniques:**
   - **Why?** I emphasize the importance of employing AI to automate data cleaning, validation, and enrichment, ensuring data accuracy and consistency.
   - **Example:** An e-commerce company uses AI-driven data validation to clean product descriptions, improving the accuracy of its recommendation engine.
   - **Quick Win:** Pilot an AI-driven data quality tool on a small dataset to evaluate its effectiveness in improving data accuracy and completeness.
4. **Integrate Data Governance and Compliance:**
   - **Why?** I stress the need to establish robust data governance policies and practices to manage data security, privacy, and ethical use in AI applications.

- **Example:** A technology company implements an AI-powered data governance platform to track data lineage and ensure compliance with data privacy regulations in its customer service AI.
- **Quick Win:** Conduct a data governance audit to identify potential risks and areas for improvement in data handling practices.

5. **Continuously Monitor and Evolve:**
   - **Why?** I advocate for regularly reviewing and updating your data strategy to adapt to evolving AI technologies, business needs, and regulatory requirements.
   - **Example:** A media company establishes a recurring review process to assess the performance of its AI-driven content recommendation system and identify opportunities to incorporate new data sources and improve accuracy.
   - **Quick Win:** Schedule a recurring meeting to discuss data strategy and identify emerging trends and best practices.

Case Study and Lessons Learned: Real-World Applications

The principles in this chapter come to life when you see how organizations navigate real data challenges. Whether accelerating AI learning with synthetic data or confronting the consequences of historical bias, these examples show that data strategy isn't merely theoretical - this business approach has real-world consequences. The following stories highlight both what's possible and what to avoid when treating data as a strategic asset.

Success Story: Tesla - Scaling AI with Synthetic Data to Accelerate Edge Learning

- **Challenge:** Training autonomous driving systems requires exposure to millions of rare and dangerous edge-case scenarios - situations like sudden pedestrian crossings at night, multi-vehicle accidents in fog, or unpredictable driver behavior. Collecting enough of these events from real-world driving is not only time-consuming; it's risky and ethically complex.
- **Solution:** Tesla turned to high-fidelity synthetic data generation, creating virtual driving scenarios that mirror real-world complexity without endangering lives or breaching privacy. These simulations allowed the AI to "experience" a wide range of edge cases at scale.

- **Results:** Tesla's self-driving AI improved its learning curve dramatically, accelerating model maturity while maintaining safety standards. Synthetic data also helped Tesla navigate regulatory scrutiny by reducing reliance on sensitive real-world footage.

Insight: Synthetic data isn't just a workaround; it's a strategic accelerator for companies working in data-constrained or high-risk domains.

Lesson Learned: The Financial AI Model That Reinforced Historical Bias

- **Challenge:** A large financial institution deployed an AI system to streamline loan approvals. Over time, leaders noticed a troubling trend: the AI disproportionately denied applications from minority borrowers, even when applicants had comparable creditworthiness.
- **Mistake:** The model was trained exclusively on historical loan approval data that reflected decades of systemic bias. Because no corrections or compensations were introduced during training, the AI didn't just replicate the bias; it amplified it at scale.
- **Outcome:** The model was pulled from production, and the organization had to retrain it using a more representative dataset, including synthetic data intentionally designed to balance demographic variables and mitigate embedded bias.

Insight: If your training data reflects historical inequity, your AI will replicate it both faster and at greater scale. Fairness must be designed into the dataset, not assumed from its availability.

Key Takeaway: AI models are only as fair, effective, and scalable as the data they're trained on. Real-world data may be rich, but it's rarely neutral. Leaders must treat data quality, representation, and augmentation (like synthetic data) as strategic imperatives. It's not enough to ask "Do we have data?" You have to ask "Do we have the right data to power the future we want to build?"

Chapter Checklist and Next Steps

In this chapter, we've explored a fundamental truth: AI's potential is unleashed when organizations recognize and treat data as a strategic asset. By focusing on data quality, implementing robust governance, and strategically employing techniques like synthetic data, businesses can create the bedrock upon which AI thrives. The challenge now shifts to demonstrating the power of this data-driven AI. We must *show* the world how this carefully constructed foundation translates into real-world business impact.

Before moving on, ensure you've addressed these essential elements of a modern, AI-ready data strategy:

- ☐ **Data as a Strategic Asset:** Are we treating data as capital, not just a byproduct, and are we actively curating it to support business outcomes and AI goals?
- ☐ **AI-Ready Data Quality:** Have we assessed whether our data is accurate, complete, consistent, timely, and structured for AI consumption?
- ☐ **Use of Synthetic Data:** Are we using synthetic data strategically to overcome privacy, scarcity, or representational challenges in our datasets?
- ☐ **Bias & Fairness Mitigation:** Do we have practices in place to detect and reduce bias in training data before it impacts real-world AI outcomes?
- ☐ **AI-Powered Data Management:** Are we using AI itself to automate data cleaning, governance, and compliance, turning quality into a scalable advantage?
- ☐ **Focused Data Prioritization:** Are we resisting the urge to "boil the ocean" and instead focusing on the specific, high-value data needed to power targeted AI efforts?
- ☐ **Alignment with Business Strategy:** Is our data infrastructure designed to fuel our most important business initiatives, not just collect more data for data's sake?

Final Thoughts

AI isn't just powered by data; it's defined by it. If your data is biased, fragmented, or unclear, your AI will be too. That's why treating data as a strategic asset is foundational. It means curating what matters, cleaning with intent, protecting with precision, and designing with purpose. And in an era where velocity often trumps strategy, smart organizations slow down just enough to get their data right, this is the essence of applying "speed with rigor" as we discussed in Chapter 2.

The most effective AI leaders don't chase quantity; they prioritize quality. They don't hoard data; they activate it. And they don't wait until things go wrong to fix their data; they invest early to scale wisely.

Because when you treat data not as exhaust, but as enterprise capital, you give AI something solid to stand on. And that's how you unlock real value, not just from your models but from your business.

Looking Ahead to Part 3: Bringing It All Together, From AI Strategy to Scalable Execution

In Parts 1 and 2, we laid the essential groundwork for achieving business success with AI. Part 1 explored how to cultivate the **Bold AI Leadership** mindset, grounded in four core principles: Business Value, Speed with Rigor, Simplicity, and Human-Centricity. Part 2 then introduced my five research-backed strategic **AI Success Pillars**, equipping you with a structured approach to align AI efforts with enterprise priorities:

1. **Business Value:** Ensures AI initiatives address real business problems and drive measurable impact
2. **Customer-Centricity:** Keeps AI grounded in delivering exceptional experiences and loyalty
3. **Collaborative Teams:** Unites business and technical leaders around a shared vision
4. **Cultural Shifts:** Builds organizational readiness through trust, training, and transparency
5. **Data as a Strategic Asset:** Powers AI with high-quality, ethical, and relevant information

Together, these pillars help organizations avoid the common pitfalls that cause AI efforts to stall, misalign, or fizzle out.

In Chapter 5, we met Sarah, a senior executive leading a high-potential AI initiative that had all the right ingredients - strong talent, solid infrastructure, and quality data. But despite this, her project stalled. Even with the right strategies in place, true transformation demands more than frameworks; it requires action.

Sarah's stalled initiative didn't fail because of a lack of technology, talent, or data. It faltered because her team lacked three vital enablers:

- **Enterprise-wide buy-in**
- **Disciplined, momentum-driven execution**
- **Clear alignment between AI initiatives and business goals**

Sarah's challenge wasn't technical; it was strategic. Her story reveals a common reality: AI success depends not just on vision or tools, but on your ability to lead across functions, earn trust, and execute with focus.

This realization leads us to Part 3, where we shift from designing strategy to delivering results. The central question now becomes:

How do organizations operationalize AI at scale to achieve sustainable business impact?

Bold AI Leadership requires vision, intent, and thoughtful execution. In Part 3, we'll unpack how leaders overcome the critical execution gap by addressing three core challenges:

1. **Gaining Stakeholder Buy-In:** Turning AI from an abstract idea into a shared, tangible opportunity for teams, leaders, and customers

2. **Overcoming Execution Barriers:** Navigating resistance and embedding AI into real-world workflows

3. **Scaling for Long-Term Success:** Designing AI systems that evolve, integrate, and deliver sustained value across the enterprise

To tackle these challenges, Sarah turned to one of the most underleveraged tools in the AI leadership playbook: visualization.

The Power of Visualization in AI Execution

As introduced through Sarah's journey and formalized in the **AI Performance Flywheel**, visualization plays a pivotal role in each phase of AI maturity, from Foundation to Execution, Scale, and Innovation Momentum.

In Part 3, we'll explore how visual tools help leaders:

- **Accelerate alignment and buy-in** by making the business impact of AI tangible and shareable

- **Drive disciplined execution** by aligning cross-functional teams around clearly communicated priorities

- **Enable scaling** by distilling complexity into accessible insights for decision-makers at every level

You'll learn how to apply these tools in the chapters ahead:

- **Chapter 11**: Gain stakeholder buy-in through persuasive, business-oriented visualization

- **Chapter 12**: Break through resistance with visualization that translates vision into action

- **Chapter 13**: Orchestrate AI success across functions with scalable, system-level visual frameworks

Sarah turned a stalled initiative into an enterprise success story by making AI's value visible and actionable. Now it's your turn. Part 3 shows you exactly how.

Key Takeaways from Part 2: How the Five AI Success Pillars Fuel AI Execution

In Part 2, we explored the five strategic AI success pillars that create the conditions for successful, scalable AI. These aren't abstract ideas; they're the guardrails that keep AI efforts focused, aligned, and value-driven. From defining real business outcomes to building collaborative teams and preparing high-quality data, these pillars are the engine behind sustained AI momentum. Together, they give leaders a practical playbook to navigate complexity and accelerate results. And when applied collectively, they bring the AI Performance Flywheel to life, transforming strategic priorities into measurable business outcomes.

The Five AI Success Pillars provide the foundation for sustained AI success. Each one addresses a common reason AI initiatives stall, ensuring that your efforts remain aligned, purposeful, and scalable:

- **Business Value focuses the work:** It ensures every AI initiative drives meaningful outcomes, tying technology investment directly to performance.
- **Customer-Centricity keeps AI grounded:** It aligns solutions with real-world needs and expectations, increasing adoption and long-term loyalty.
- **Collaborative Teams break down barriers:** Cross-functional alignment ensures technical and business leaders build together, not in silos.
- **Cultural Shifts create space to learn:** AI thrives in organizations that value curiosity, embrace iteration, and lead with clarity and trust.
- **Data as a Strategic Asset powers the system:** High-quality, curated, and well-governed data fuels reliable, ethical, and scalable AI outcomes.

Together, these pillars activate the Flywheel. They bring structure to each phase - Foundation, Execution, Scale, and Innovation Momentum - ensuring progress never stalls and value compounds over time.

Now, it's time to shift from strategy to execution. Part 3 shows how Bold AI Leaders turn vision into reality through alignment, discipline, and the power of visual storytelling.

PART 3

Bringing AI to Life (Visualization as a Catalyst for Change)

Welcome to the practical heart of our journey! This is where AI potential becomes measurable business impact, where bold ideas transform into tangible results.

Throughout this book, I've introduced my **Bold AI Leadership Model**, a pragmatic framework for AI success, built on three essential layers:

- **Mindset:** The guiding principles for confident AI decisions
- **Strategy:** The five success pillars that focus AI efforts
- **Action:** Visualization tools and frameworks to execute AI strategy

This final part of the book focuses on action. Here, I show you how to activate the **AI Performance Flywheel**, a structured approach to building and sustaining AI momentum through four key phases:

- **Foundation Momentum:** Converting skepticism into trust with clear results
- **Execution Momentum:** Moving AI from pilot to operational success
- **Scale Momentum:** Expanding AI for enterprise-wide impact
- **Innovation Momentum:** Embedding AI for continuous improvement

To secure buy-in, demonstrate value, and scale AI successfully, leaders must do more than tell people about AI's potential; they must show its value. That's why visualization tools are so powerful!

How Visualization Drives AI Impact

Visual Dartboarding is a technique I developed to accelerate decision-making and stakeholder alignment. Instead of starting from a blank page, I create a visual draft of a plan, model, or concept, giving stakeholders something to react to and transforming abstract discussions into productive collaboration. This shift shortens solutioning, encourages collaboration, and turns skeptics into co-creators - a critical factor in AI adoption.

I've seen too many forward-thinking leaders struggle with AI adoption, not for lack of ideas, but because the impact wasn't clear. That pattern inspired me to write this book, drawing from my repeated success using visual storytelling to turn stalled technology initiatives into scaling successes. When an abstract AI concept becomes a clear, visual story, resistance fades and buy-in accelerates. A complex machine learning model becomes a clear ROI dashboard. A neural network's decision-making process transforms into an intuitive workflow diagram. Suddenly, leaders aren't just approving AI investments; they're asking how to scale them faster.

To successfully scale AI, leaders must think like architects, building momentum, trust, and alignment block by block. That's why I developed the Visualization Tool Decision Framework, a systematic approach to selecting and applying the right visualization tools to tackle specific challenges, data complexities, and organizational goals. These tools don't just explain AI; they ensure every stakeholder has the right blueprint to contribute, making AI adoption a structured, iterative process.

Each visualization is a building block, carefully chosen to meet the needs of different stakeholders and stacked together to create business results (see Figure P3.1):

- **Executive Leaders (Vision & Alignment):** Strategy visualization dashboards, business value roadmaps, and AI opportunity portfolios act as the master blueprint and owner's vision, defining what success looks like and how to get there. These visual tools help executives align teams, prioritize investments, and communicate bold direction across the organization.

- **Board Members (Strategy & Governance):** Governance risk heatmaps and competitive capability radar charts serve as structural blueprints and foundation plans, ensuring AI initiatives are compliant, well-governed, and aligned with business strategy, just as a building needs solid architectural plans and proper permits before construction begins.

- **IT Teams (Infrastructure & Integration):** System architecture flowcharts and API performance dashboards form the critical infrastructure, like the plumbing, electrical, and HVAC systems that keep a building functioning. These technical visualizations ensure AI systems are well-integrated, performant, and maintainable.

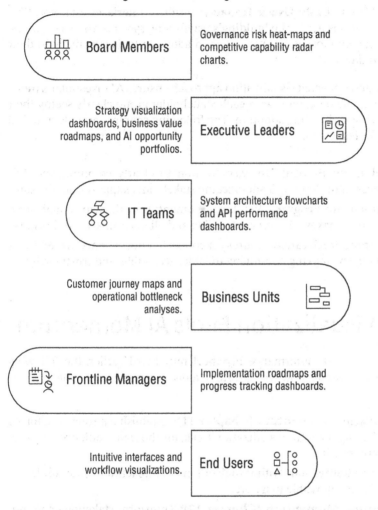

VISUAL COMMUNICATION
The Right Tools for the Right Audience

Board Members — Governance risk heat-maps and competitive capability radar charts.

Strategy visualization dashboards, business value roadmaps, and AI opportunity portfolios. — Executive Leaders

IT Teams — System architecture flowcharts and API performance dashboards.

Customer journey maps and operational bottleneck analyses. — Business Units

Frontline Managers — Implementation roadmaps and progress tracking dashboards.

Intuitive interfaces and workflow visualizations. — End Users

FIGURE P3.1   From Vision to Buy-In: Clear, targeted visuals drive action. Use the right tools for the right audience to drive action.

- **Business Units (Execution & Operation):** Customer journey maps and operational bottleneck analyses shape the engaging spaces where value happens, like the lobbies, offices, and meeting rooms where daily business occurs. These visualizations reveal how AI enhances business processes and drives efficiency.

- **Frontline Managers (Adoption & Implementation):** Implementation roadmaps and progress tracking dashboards serve as construction schedules and project milestones, keeping teams aligned and progress visible, just as construction managers rely on clear timelines and checkpoints.

- **End Users (Daily Use & Impact):** Intuitive interfaces and workflow visualizations act as the building's wayfinding systems and user guides, ensuring employees can navigate and adopt AI tools effectively in their day-to-day work.

This interconnected visualization approach ensures AI investments translate into tangible outcomes, with each stakeholder group clearly seeing their role in driving and scaling adoption. The following chapters provide practical guidance for leaders to:

- **Build Early Buy-In:** Use visualization to clearly communicate AI's business value, helping leaders secure stakeholder support from the start.
- **Demonstrate Progress:** Reinforce momentum with clear, visual storytelling that makes AI's impact tangible and aligns teams around results.
- **Overcome Resistance:** Address skepticism, ethical concerns, and fear of change by making AI understandable, accessible, and trustworthy.

How Visualization Fuels AI Momentum

Building on the AI Performance Flywheel introduced earlier, the following chapters demonstrate how visualization tools accelerate each phase of AI adoption:

- **Foundation Momentum (Chapter 11):** Establish a strong case for AI by selecting the right visualization tools, for the right audience, and create early buy-in.
  - ○ **Key Theme:** Start with visualizations so impactful to your audience, they're impossible to ignore.
- **Execution Momentum (Chapter 12):** Transform stakeholder skepticism into support through pain point-specific visualization.
  - ○ **Key Theme:** Match each visualization to stakeholder pain points.
- **Scale & Innovation Momentum (Chapter 13):** Scale proven AI solutions across business units and functions.
  - ○ **Key Theme:** Connect successful implementations to multiply business impact.

By the end of this part of the book, you'll have the practical knowledge to fully execute my Bold AI Leadership Model, turning AI potential into sustained organizational impact. Let's dive in!

CHAPTER 11

From Strategy to Buy-In

Creating Foundation Momentum

"**S**how me."

These two words changed everything for Sarah Chen.

After weeks of presenting slide decks and forecasts about AI-powered claims processing, she had covered every angle: stats, models, projections. Yet the board remained skeptical. Then the CFO leaned forward and said those two words.

That's when Sarah realized her mistake. She had been telling when she needed to be showing.

Every AI-powered transformation reaches a moment like this - the tipping point between strategy and belief. It's not enough to have a compelling roadmap; adoption depends on whether stakeholders can see the impact.

Welcome to the **Foundation Momentum** phase.

The Buy-In Barrier

For many leaders, the first major roadblock isn't the AI itself; it's convincing others to believe in its value. This is what Sarah encountered in her meeting with the board. Like many leaders launching AI initiatives, she had fallen into the trap of explaining AI's potential instead of demonstrating its impact.

It reminded her of the Southwest Airlines story, how a billion-dollar idea was born from a triangle sketched on a bar napkin. Maybe her claims transformation plan needed less polish. . .and more marker (see Figure 11.1).

FIGURE 11.1 **SWA Visual Dartboard:** In 1971, Southwest Airlines' founders Rollin King and Herb Kelleher sketched a simple triangle on a napkin in a San Antonio bar, connecting Dallas, Houston, and San Antonio. That napkin captured their entire business model: fast, frequent flights between three major Texas cities. Though the story has been embellished over time, it endures as a powerful symbol of how clarity and simplicity can launch billion-dollar ideas. It's the ultimate Show Not Tell moment - a quick visual collaboratively created turning into a legendary business blueprint.

Source: © 2021 Southwest Airlines Co.

Sarah's challenge reflects a critical moment in every AI journey - the need to transform abstract potential into visible impact. This is where the Foundation Momentum phase begins and where many promising AI initiatives stall. Leaders have the vision, and often piles of detailed numbers and ineffective charts, but struggle to translate them into compelling visual storytelling tools that drive buy-in and build unstoppable momentum.

To overcome this challenge, leaders must address two critical dimensions: demonstrating the benefits of action and highlighting the risks of inaction. My **Visualization Tool Decision Framework** provides a systematic approach to selecting and applying visualization tools that accomplish both goals.

Sarah sat at her desk, scrolling through a sea of visualization tools, each promising to simplify complex ideas. She was finally aware that visualization of business impacts was the key to getting the approval that she needed, but which one would actually convince the board? She had spent weeks preparing technical diagrams, predictive analytics models, and efficiency charts, yet none had resonated. She needed a different approach.

Visual Dartboarding: Accelerating Buy-In Through Co-Creation

A beloved teacher, Carolyn Catlin, who changed the course of my life by introducing me to an entirely new world through literature and writing, once told me, "there is no desire greater than to alter someone else's draft." This insight has proven invaluable throughout my career, especially in complex AI initiatives. People naturally engage more deeply when they can react to something concrete rather than starting from scratch.

Visual Dartboarding emerged from years of complex enterprise selling, where I discovered that success depends not just on what you present, but how you engage stakeholders in shaping the solution. In AI adoption, this principle becomes even more critical—instead of pushing for immediate buy-in on a polished proposal, we create visual drafts that stakeholders can react to, refine, and ultimately co-own.

Start with Outcomes

Before creating any visual draft, establish your "backstop" - the specific business outcome that defines success. This ensures every visualization connects directly to measurable value. Also, identifying any specific desired measurable outcomes or timelines will ensure that you understand what will motivate stakeholders to action.

The Five Steps of Visual Dartboarding

Visual Dartboarding follows a five-step process, captured in Figure 11.2. Each stage builds alignment by making ideas visible, collaborative, and actionable. In AI and transformation work, the way you present ideas often matters just as much as the ideas themselves. Too often, leaders default to "polish and pitch," but that approach invites evaluation, not collaboration. Visual Dartboarding flips that script.

It's a method I use with executive teams to turn early ideas into shared solutions, quickly, visibly, and with far more buy-in. The goal isn't perfection; it's momentum. You'll start rough, invite edits, and turn static proposals into interactive tools for alignment. Each step is designed to shift the dynamic from "selling your idea" to "building it together."

Visual Dartboarding Process

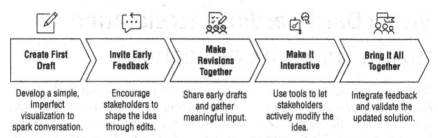

Create First Draft	Invite Early Feedback	Make Revisions Together	Make It Interactive	Bring It All Together
Develop a simple, imperfect visualization to spark conversation.	Encourage stakeholders to shape the idea through edits.	Share early drafts and gather meaningful input.	Use tools to let stakeholders actively modify the idea.	Integrate feedback and validate the updated solution.

FIGURE 11.2 **Visual Dartboarding:** From rough draft to real alignment. This step-by-step process transforms early-stage ideas into shared ownership through simple, iterative, collaborative visualization. Each phase builds clarity, engagement, and momentum, because when people can see it, they can understand it, and they can support it.

My Visual Dartboarding process includes five essential steps, each designed to accelerate collaboration, build lasting alignment, and create shared mental ownership. Here's how to do it.

Step 1: Create Your First Draft (Start Rough)

Too many teams inadvertently kill progress by spending weeks refining presentations, aiming for perfection before sharing anything. This is exactly the WRONG thing to do! Instead, focus on creating what I call a **minimum viable visualization**, just enough structure to make an idea visible and give stakeholders something concrete to react to. This shifts the dynamic from "present and defend" to "explore and enhance," inviting input and strengthening alignment from the start.

To begin, ask yourself, "What's the simplest way to make this idea visible?"

- If you're improving customer service, sketch a rough flowchart of the support process.
- If you're optimizing revenue, draft a quick diagram highlighting areas where profits leak.
- If you're introducing AI, create a vendor capability map to show where external AI solutions integrate with your existing systems.

The format doesn't matter. It simply needs to clarify the business challenge you're addressing. The sooner you make the idea real, the sooner your stakeholders can engage, refine, and take ownership, accelerating progress toward a solution that works for everyone

Why Rough Works Better   The power of imperfection in business planning might seem counterintuitive, but it's backed by experience. When you present a polished, perfect-looking proposal, you inadvertently create barriers to collaboration. Stakeholders often hesitate to "mess up" something that looks finished, even if you encourage feedback. In contrast, rough drafts send a clear message: "This is a starting point, and we need your expertise to make it better."

There's power in imperfection. A rough sketch sends the message: "This is a starting point, not a finished product." That signal invites edits, ideas, and shared ownership, exactly what builds momentum.

Making Your First Draft Work   Start with the basics - simple shapes, arrows, and clear labels that anyone can understand and modify. Include real numbers from your current business state, but present them in a way that makes them obviously adjustable. A key success factor is leaving strategic white space around your core ideas; these blank areas serve as implicit invitations for additions and improvements.

Keep your tools simple and accessible. Erasable markers and removable sticky notes aren't just convenient; they're psychological signals that everything is up for discussion. Create obvious places for improvement suggestions by marking areas with questions or deliberately incomplete sections. Think of your draft as a conversation starter rather than a finished product.

Step 2: Invite Early Feedback (Check Your Ego at the Door)   Your first draft isn't meant to be perfect; it's meant to start the conversation. Yet, many leaders struggle with detaching from their initial ideas. The moment you present something, it's tempting to defend it. But true momentum happens when you shift from "my idea" to "our solution."

How to Mentally Prepare for Feedback:

- **Adopt a Facilitator Mindset:** You're guiding a discussion, not pitching a finished idea.
- **Expect and Welcome Changes:** The best stakeholder response is "What if we changed this?"
- **Celebrate Edits as Engagement:** Every revision means your audience is invested.
- **Practice Your Response:** Instead of defending, say:
  - "That's a great angle I hadn't considered!"
  - "I love that tweak. Let's explore it further."
  - "This is exactly why I brought this draft. Let's build on it."

Why This Works When stakeholders shape the solution, they stop judging and start driving. A board member adjusting your investment model or a claims manager refining the workflow, they aren't just giving feedback; they're taking ownership. That's when momentum kicks in.

Step 3: Make Revisions Together (Share Early, Share Rough)

Many leaders make the mistake of holding onto an idea too long, refining and perfecting it before revealing it to stakeholders. But the later you introduce a concept, the harder it is to get meaningful input, because by that point, people see their role as evaluators, not contributors.

Instead, use early sharing as a momentum accelerator. Get a rough draft in front of stakeholders as soon as possible, not for approval, but to spark discussion.

How to Share for Maximum Engagement:

- **Send Materials 48 Hours Before Meetings:** This gives people time to think without feeling pressured.
- **Set the Expectation for Feedback:** Frame it as:
  - "This is an early draft. Let's refine it together."
  - "This is just a starting point. Your insights will help shape the final approach."
  - **Ask a Specific Question:** Instead of "Thoughts?," guide their thinking:
  - "Which of these assumptions feels off?"
  - "What's missing that would make this stronger?"
  - "How would you explain this to someone in your role?"

Why This Works Early input turns critics into co-creators. You're no longer defending a pitch; you're leading a conversation where everyone feels invested.

Step 4: Make It Interactive (This Is Where the Magic Happens)

Nothing accelerates buy-in faster than getting stakeholders physically involved in shaping the solution. Whether on a whiteboard, sticky notes, or digital collaboration tools, turning a presentation into a working session changes passive observers into active contributors.

How to Spark Engagement in a Working Session:

- **Start with "How Can We Make This Better?" and Not "Do You Like This?":** Avoid any questions that can be answered with a simple yes or no.
- **Hand Stakeholders the Marker:** Encourage them to draw, move elements around, or annotate.

- **Use Color Coding:** Different colors for risks, priorities, or unknowns spark engagement.
- **Document Changes in Real Time:** Watching their input take shape reinforces ownership.

Energy Boosters for High-Impact Sessions:

- **Stand Up and Move Around:** Physical movement keeps people engaged.
- **Take Photos of Each Iteration:** Capture the evolution of ideas.
- **Celebrate Breakthrough Moments by Calling Out Shifts in Thinking:**
  - "That's a game-changer. Let's build on that!"
  - "We just solved a major roadblock!"
  - "This is exactly the kind of collaboration AI success requires."

Step 5: Bring It All Together (Build Shared Ownership)

Now comes the most critical phase: showing stakeholders how their input has shaped the solution. This reinforces shared ownership and ensures momentum for implementation.

When stakeholders see their feedback reflected in the next version, their mindset shifts from "your idea" to "our solution." That sense of co-creation is what turns passive observers into active champions.

The Refinement Process: How to Integrate and Validate Feedback

- **Compile All Feedback:** Review discussion notes, workshop photos, and written input. Identify recurring themes and the most impactful suggestions.
- **Create Version 2.0:** Incorporate key changes, ensuring the solution remains aligned with business objectives and stakeholder priorities.
- **Reconvene the Group:** Bring stakeholders back together. You may need multiple rounds of discussions before you reach final refinements and sign-off.
- **Showcase the Evolution:** Present the updated visualization side-by-side with the original. Use phrases like:
  - "Here's how your input strengthened the concept. . ."
  - "This change came directly from our last discussion. . ."
  - "We refined this based on your feedback about X. . ."
- **Embrace Additional "Tweaks":** Small refinements signal engagement. If stakeholders still have suggestions, it means they're invested!

Success Signals: How You Know It's Working

- **Stakeholders start calling it "our solution"** instead of "your proposal."
- **Spontaneous refinement suggestions emerge,** showing ongoing engagement.

- **The conversation shifts to implementation** like "How do we roll this out?"
- **Energy in the room increases**, with excitement replacing skepticism.
- **New possibilities emerge** as people see how the framework can be extended.

At this stage, resistance has transformed into momentum. Instead of selling an idea, you've co-created a solution, one that stakeholders are eager to bring to life!

Putting It to Work

Visual Dartboarding shines can be a powerful early step when tackling complex AI-powered business transformations. By giving stakeholders something to see, touch, and modify, leaders can shift AI discussions from theoretical to actionable. The following visualization approaches consistently drive engagement, accelerate buy-in, and uncover insights that traditional presentations miss.

Process Transformation Maps: Showing the Journey   Think of these as your "before and after" stories, but with a crucial twist: they're designed to be modified. Start by mapping your current workflow, then overlay potential AI enhancement points. The magic happens when stakeholders can physically move these AI touchpoints around, debating where automation will have the most impact. One client used erasable markers to draw their existing claims process, then used different colors to show where AI could reduce processing time. This simple visualization sparked a two-hour discussion that would have been impossible with static slides. The reason? Seeing workflows visually allowed the team to spot bottlenecks and dependencies that weren't obvious before.

Prioritization Matrices: Making Tough Choices Visual   When faced with multiple AI opportunities, a well-designed prioritization matrix brings clarity and alignment to decision-making. The most effective approach? Make it interactive.

Create a simple four-quadrant grid showing impact vs. effort (see Figure 11.3), but instead of presenting a fixed analysis, use movable sticky notes (or virtual equivalents) to let stakeholders debate, adjust, and shift priorities in real time. This small change transforms the matrix from a passive report into an active decision-making tool. Technical teams and business leaders naturally negotiate trade-offs as they move initiatives across quadrants, creating a shared sense of ownership rather than a top-down directive.

Impact/Effort Matrix

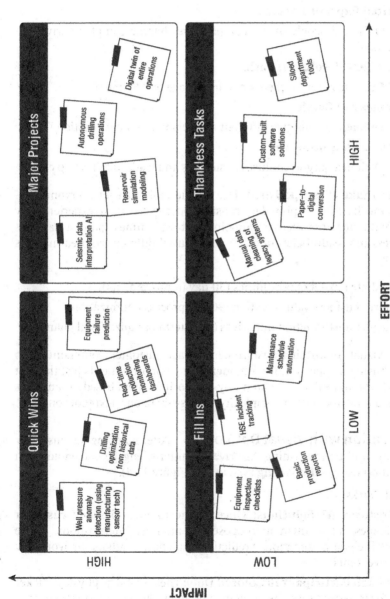

FIGURE 11.3 Impact/Effort Matrix for AI Initiatives in Upstream Energy: This sample matrix demonstrates how brainstormed AI initiatives can be quickly captured by a team working together, in person or virtually, allowing stakeholders to co-prioritize in real time. From quick wins to major projects, this tool sparks debate and fosters alignment. By turning prioritization into an interactive experience, leaders and technical teams create shared accountability and clarity around where to focus first.

Customer Experience Maps: Finding Pain Points

Start with a rough sketch of your customer's journey, highlighting the five most common frustrations:

- **Delayed Responses**

  "Our average response time is 72 hours when customers expect 24."
- **Limited Expertise Access**

  "Only two people in the company can handle complex derivatives questions."
- **Inefficient Resolution Paths**

  "Customers repeat their story an average of 3.5 times."
- **Inconsistent Service**

  "Different agents give different answers to the same question."
- **Unclear Communication**

  "Technical jargon confuses customers and leads to follow-up calls."

Don't make it too polished. Use simple tools that let everyone contribute. One healthcare provider transformed their patient experience by starting with business metrics: appointment wait times, patient satisfaction scores, and readmission rates. The team used different colored markers to indicate:

- Immediate impact opportunities (30-day improvements)
- Midterm business value creation (90-day process optimization)
- Strategic transformation initiatives (long-term organizational change)

This visual approach transformed abstract customer complaints into concrete business opportunities. But identifying opportunities is just the first step. Next, you'll need a systematic way to prioritize them based on business impact and implementation complexity. That's where our next tool comes in.

Prioritization with Visual Dot Voting

After mapping out customer pain points and brainstorming AI-driven solutions, engage stakeholders in prioritization using a **dot voting** system (see Figure 11.4).

How It Works:

Brainstorm AI Solutions: Once the team identifies key customer challenges, allow them to propose potential AI interventions. These might include automation, predictive analytics, chatbots, or workflow improvements.

Give Each Participant 10 Colored Dots: These could be physical sticker dots for in-person sessions or digital voting markers in a virtual setting.

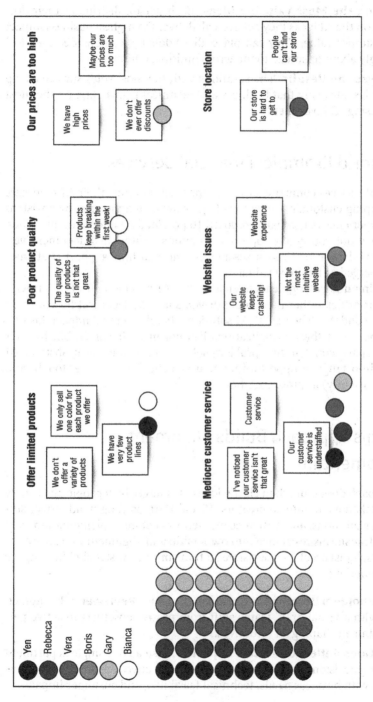

FIGURE 11.4 Visual Dot Voting: Turning Ideas into AI Action: After mapping pain points and brainstorming AI solutions, teams use dot voting to prioritize what matters most. Each stakeholder gets 10 colored dots to vote on the ideas with the highest potential impact. The visual clustering of dots quickly reveals consensus, aligning business and technical teams around the most valuable AI opportunities.

Vote on the Most Valuable Ideas: Each person distributes their dots based on the AI ideas they believe will deliver the highest business impact or customer value. They can place all 10 dots on a single idea they feel strongly about or spread them across multiple options.

Analyze the Results: The solutions with the most votes surface as top priorities, ensuring that business and technical teams align on the most promising AI investments.

Real-World Example: Financial Services

A financial services company used this approach to refine their AI roadmap. After mapping customer frustrations (e.g., slow loan approvals, inconsistent chatbot experiences), the team proposed 10 potential AI interventions. When they applied dot voting, the top three solutions - automated document verification, AI-driven loan risk assessments, and real-time support chatbots - clearly emerged as the most valuable.

By using **dot voting**, leaders ensure that AI adoption efforts align with business priorities rather than being driven solely by technical feasibility or executive mandates. The result? AI solutions that deliver real impact, faster.

The power of these visualizations lies not in their polish, but in their ability to spark collaborative problem-solving. They transform abstract AI concepts into tangible opportunities that stakeholders can see, touch, and (most importantly) improve together.

Why This Approach Builds Alignment and Momentum

This approach does more than clarify ideas; it changes how people engage. By turning stakeholders into co-creators, Visual Dartboarding builds trust, surfaces better solutions, and generates momentum before implementation even begins. It transforms resistance into ownership and alignment into action.

It doesn't just accelerate decisions; it transforms how stakeholders engage with AI adoption:

- **Stakeholders Become Co-Creators, Not Just Reviewers:** By interacting with a visual draft, teams shift from passive observers to active participants in shaping AI initiatives.
- **Solutions Reflect Collective Expertise:** Instead of a single department driving decisions, input from multiple perspectives ensures AI solutions align with business needs, technical feasibility, and customer impact.

- **Ownership Develops Before Implementation:** When stakeholders see their ideas reflected in the solution, they're more likely to champion AI adoption rather than resist it.

- **Resistance Transforms into Engagement:** Addressing concerns early and collaboratively reduces skepticism, making AI feel like a shared opportunity rather than a top-down mandate.

By fostering collaboration from the start, this approach ensures that AI adoption isn't just approved; it's embraced.

How to Know It's Working

The true impact of Visual Dartboarding isn't just in faster decisions; it's in the lasting alignment and engagement it creates. Here's how to gauge its effectiveness:

- **Faster Stakeholder Alignment:** Are decisions being made more quickly with less debate?

- **Higher Engagement in Planning Sessions:** Are more people contributing ideas and refining concepts?

- **Fewer Revision Cycles:** Are initial drafts leading to final decisions with minimal rework?

- **Stronger Implementation Success:** Are AI initiatives moving from approval to execution smoothly?

- **Greater Cross-Functional Collaboration:** Are technical, business, and executive teams working together more effectively?

Key Takeaways for Leaders

Visual Dartboarding is more than a planning method; it's a leadership power move. These takeaways show how bold leaders use it to align teams faster, spark co-creation, and turn AI strategy into outcomes that actually stick:

1. **Never Start from Scratch:** A rough visual is always better than a blank page.

2. **Expect and Welcome Feedback:** Every edit is a sign of engagement, deepening buy-in, and momentum.

3. **Keep the Focus on Business Outcomes:** Tie visuals to desired business results, not just ideas. AI adoption isn't about the technology; it's about the value it creates.

4. **Involve the Right People Early:** The best solutions come from diverse perspectives.

5. **Iterate Visually and Rapidly:** The faster you refine, the sooner you build momentum.

Visual Dartboarding turns abstract AI ideas into visible, collaborative plans from day one. It shifts the dynamic from "I approve your idea" to "this is our shared idea," building true co-ownership, deeper alignment, and enduring commitment from kickoff to execution.

The Visualization Tool Decision Framework

Sarah's challenge isn't unique. Many leaders recognize that visualization is essential but struggle with knowing which tool, for which audience, at which moment. That's why I developed the **Visualization Tool Decision Framework**, a structured approach to making those decisions. This framework helps leaders answer three fundamental questions:

"What am I trying to achieve?" (Goals – Needed Business Outcome)
- Is the primary goal to show ROI, identify risks, convey urgency, build trust, foster collaboration, simplify complex concepts, optimize customer experience, or drive cultural change?
- Each goal requires specific visualization tools matched to the desired outcome.

"What can we realistically implement?" (Resources and Data)
- Does your organization have simple or complex data?
- What level of budget and expertise can you access?
- The key is choosing tools that match your current capabilities.

"Who needs to understand this and what's stopping them?" (Resistance)
- What roles and perspectives are you addressing?
  - Strategic (executives, board members)
  - Operational (department heads, managers)
  - Technical (IT teams, developers)
  - Front-line (end users, operators)
- What's their current relationship with technology?
  - Technical literacy level
  - AI familiarity and comfort
  - Industry-specific mental models

- What specific concerns or resistance points do they have?
  - Fear of the unknown
  - Skepticism about ROI
  - Regulatory and ethical concerns

The Framework in Action

Sarah learned the hard way that having a systematic approach would be crucial to her success. Her first attempt used a complex 3D data landscape that impressed her technical team but left board members confused and defensive. She hadn't considered that her audience (seasoned insurance executives) thought in terms of risk portfolios and actuarial tables, not neural networks and machine learning models.

To overcome this challenge, my framework provides a three-step process to answer these questions systematically (see Figure 11.5).

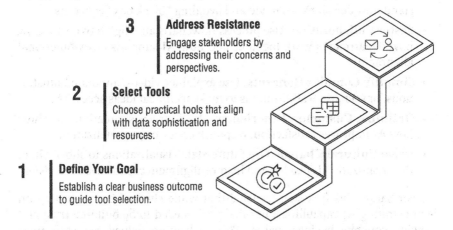

Visualization Tool Decision Framework

3 Address Resistance
Engage stakeholders by addressing their concerns and perspectives.

2 Select Tools
Choose practical tools that align with data sophistication and resources.

1 Define Your Goal
Establish a clear business outcome to guide tool selection.

FIGURE 11.5 Steps to Implement the Visualization Tool Decision Framework: This figure illustrates the three-step process leaders can follow to select and apply visualization tools effectively: Defining AI adoption goals (Step 1), matching tools to data and resource complexity (Step 2), and addressing resistance to AI adoption through targeted visualizations (Step 3).

Step 1: Define Your Goal - What Business Outcome Do We Need to Achieve?

Before selecting any visualization tool, leaders must first clarify why they're communicating in the first place. What specific business outcome are you hoping to drive with this AI initiative?

This step helps you move beyond showcasing technical features and toward delivering a message that resonates with the audience's needs, fears, and expectations. Instead of starting with "What can the technology do?" begin by asking "What exactly are we trying to achieve?"

Each goal requires a different visualization strategy. Here are common business goals and the visualization types that support them (see Figure 11.6):

- **Show ROI:** Use interactive heatmaps and side-by-side comparisons to demonstrate financial ROI.
- **Identify Risks:** Use regulatory maps, simulations, and what-if scenarios to surface potential vulnerabilities or compliance issues.
- **Convey Urgency:** Visualize the cost of inaction. Show projected revenue loss, market erosion, or rising costs if nothing changes.
- **Build Trust:** Use governance flowcharts, audit trails, and decision logic diagrams to create clarity and confidence, helping stakeholders understand how decisions are made and avoiding "black box" concerns.
- **Foster Collaboration:** Use process flowcharts and digital twins to show how departments work together and how AI supports cross-functional alignment.
- **Simplify Complex Concepts:** Use explainer videos, annotated illustrations, or scenario walkthroughs to make technical ideas accessible.
- **Optimize Customer Experience**: Use journey simulations to show how AI improves satisfaction, responsiveness, or personalization.
- **Drive Cultural Change:** Use future-state visualizations to show where the organization is headed and inspire alignment around a shared vision.

For Sarah, this first step revealed that while she had been focusing on demonstrating AI capabilities, her real goal needed to be building trust and showing concrete business value. This realization helped her shift from technical demonstrations to business impact visualizations.

STEP 1: DEFINE YOUR GOAL
Each Goal Requires Its Own Visualization Strategy

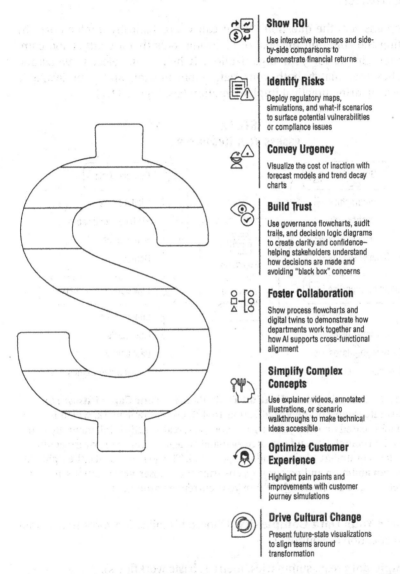

Show ROI

Use interactive heatmaps and side-by-side comparisons to demonstrate financial returns

Identify Risks

Deploy regulatory maps, simulations, and what-if scenarios to surface potential vulnerabilities or compliance issues

Convey Urgency

Visualize the cost of inaction with forecast models and trend decay charts

Build Trust

Use governance flowcharts, audit trails, and decision logic diagrams to create clarity and confidence—helping stakeholders understand how decisions are made and avoiding "black box" concerns

Foster Collaboration

Show process flowcharts and digital twins to demonstrate how departments work together and how AI supports cross-functional alignment

Simplify Complex Concepts

Use explainer videos, annotated illustrations, or scenario walkthroughs to make technical ideas accessible

Optimize Customer Experience

Highlight pain paints and improvements with customer journey simulations

Drive Cultural Change

Present future-state visualizations to align teams around transformation

FIGURE 11.6   Matching Visualization Strategies to Business Goals: This figure illustrates Step 1 of the Visualization Tool Decision Framework, which is defining the business outcome you're trying to achieve. Each goal requires a distinct visualization approach tailored to decision-makers' needs. By aligning your tools to your intended impact, you shift from showcasing technology to influencing business outcomes with clarity and purpose.

Step 2: Select Tools - What Can We Realistically Implement?

This step answers the question "What can we realistically implement?" by preventing the common mistake of choosing tools that are either too complex or too simple for your organization. It helps you select visualization approaches that match both your data sophistication and your available resources, ensuring practical implementation (see Figure 11.7).

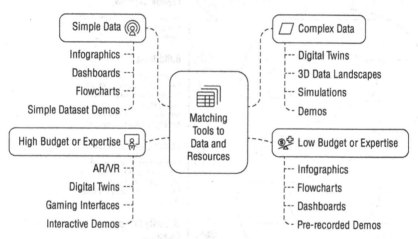

STEP 2
Assess Your Resources

FIGURE 11.7 **Selecting Visualization Tools That Fit Your Capabilities:** This figure illustrates Step 2 of the Visualization Tool Decision Framework, which is selecting tools based on what your organization can realistically implement. By mapping both data complexity and resource availability, leaders can avoid overreaching on flashy tools or underutilizing available potential. The goal is to strike the right balance between ambition and practicality, ensuring that chosen visualizations are not only effective but also executable within your current environment.

Assess Your Data Complexity: Choose visualization tools that match the sophistication of your data.

- **Simple data** (e.g., summaries, metrics, basic workflows):
    Use infographics, dashboards, and flowcharts.
- **Complex data** (e.g., dynamic, multidimensional, or predictive):
    Use simulations, digital twins, or immersive 3D data landscapes.

Evaluate Your Resources: Select tools based on your team's time, budget, and skill level.

- **Limited budget or expertise:**

    Stick to lightweight tools - infographics, simplified flowcharts, or pre-recorded demos.

- **Robust budget and technical capacity:**

    Leverage more advanced platforms - interactive demos, AR/VR, or gaming-style environments.

    Match Tools to Organizational Maturity: Choose tools that are sustainable, not just impressive.

- Even the most powerful tool is ineffective if no one knows how to use it or maintain it. Pick visualization approaches that align with your organization's current stage, tech infrastructure, and internal skillsets.

    Sarah's rational assessment of "What can we realistically implement?" led to a two-tiered visualization approach based on available data:

- For **basic claims data:** Interactive dashboards showing processing times and error rates, plus process flowcharts comparing current vs. AI-enhanced workflows.

- For **deeper analysis:** Journey simulations visualizing end-to-end processing improvements and risk reduction.

- To stay within **budget and comfort zone:** She used pre-recorded demos and simplified visuals in familiar insurance terminology to maximize clarity and buy-in.

Step 3: Address Resistance - Who Needs to Be Convinced, and What's Holding Them Back?

This step answers the critical question, "Who needs to understand this and what's getting in their way?" By identifying each stakeholder group's unique concerns and perspectives, you can select visualization tools that transform resistance into engagement. Instead of using a one-size-fits-all approach, it ensures each audience sees the impact of AI in terms that resonate with their priorities and concerns (Figure 11.8).

Use this step to identify:

- **Which groups need to be persuaded?**
- **What's causing their hesitation?**
- **Which visuals will resonate most?**

The framework provides guidance for common scenarios:

Stakeholder Profile	Resistance Scenario	Visualization Strategies	Key Messaging
Executive	ROI Skepticism	Interactive ROI Dashboard, Comparative Analysis Charts, Predictive Analytics Simulations	"This dashboard allows you to stress-test our assumptions and see the potential financial upside."
Employee	Job Displacement	Workflow Transformation Maps, AI Collaboration Storyboards, Skill Augmentation Visuals	"AI will handle the routine tasks, freeing you up for more complex and rewarding work."
IT	Integration Complexity	System Architecture Diagrams, Data Flow Visualizations, API Performance Dashboards	"We've designed a phased integration plan that minimizes disruption to your existing systems."
Middle Manager	Loss of Control	Process Monitoring Dashboards, Exception Handling Flowcharts, Decision Support Maps	"AI provides data-driven insights to support your decisions, not replace your judgment."
Customer Service Agent	Impersonal Interactions	Customer Journey Maps with AI Touchpoints, Sentiment Analysis Displays, Personalized Communication Mockups	"AI will help us respond faster and provide more personalized service, leading to happier customers."
Legal/Compliance	Regulatory Risks	AI Governance Frameworks, Audit Trail Visualizations, Bias Detection Reports	"These tools ensure transparency and compliance, mitigating potential legal and regulatory issues."
Marketing Team	Creative Constraints	AI-Powered Content Generation Demos, A/B Testing Visualizations, Performance Prediction Charts	"AI can help us personalize campaigns and predict performance, allowing for more effective creative strategies."
Sales Team	Lead Quality Concerns	Lead Scoring Accuracy Charts, Opportunity Conversion Forecasts, Customer Segmentation Maps	"AI will provide you with higher-quality leads and insights to close deals faster."
Operations Manager	Operational Disruption	Predictive Maintenance Dashboards, Supply Chain Optimization Maps, Resource Allocation Simulations	"AI will optimize our operations, reduce downtime, and improve resource allocation."

FIGURE 11.8 Tailoring Visualizations and Messaging to Stakeholder Resistance: This figure illustrates Step 3 of the Visualization Tool Decision Framework. By aligning stakeholder concerns with tailored visualization strategies and targeted messaging, leaders can move beyond resistance and build alignment. These pairings help each group understand how AI supports their goals, positioning it as a tool for empowerment, not disruption.

Counter Common Objections with the Right Tools: *Use visualization strategies to move people from resistance to curiosity and ultimately to action.*

- **Fear of the unknown**

    Use demos, infographics, and explainer videos to make AI approachable.
- **Skepticism about ROI**

    Use interactive comparisons and ROI heatmaps to make financial benefits tangible.
- **Regulatory or legal concerns**

    Show governance flows, audit trails, and bias detection visuals to demonstrate oversight.

Tailor to Stakeholder Roles and Mindsets: *Each audience processes information differently. Match your message to how they think and what they need.*

- **Strategic stakeholders** (e.g., board members, executives):

    Focus on ROI, risk mitigation, and business alignment visuals.
- **Operational leaders** (e.g., department heads):

    Emphasize workflow improvements, resource impacts, and simulations.
- **Technical teams** (e.g., IT, data science):

    Provide architecture diagrams, system integration maps, and tooling overviews.
- **Front-line staff** (e.g., claims processors, customer support):

    Use before-and-after visuals to show how AI makes their jobs easier, not obsolete.

Sarah applied these principles when mapping her key audiences, identifying distinct resistance patterns and needs. Board members expressed skepticism about ROI and governance, while department heads feared operational disruption. Claims processors worried about job security, and the IT team raised questions about technical integration.

Understanding these different perspectives helped Sarah develop a targeted visualization strategy. When she analyzed her organization, she found clear patterns of resistance:

- **Board members** were skeptical of ROI and governance.

    She used **interactive heatmaps** and **flowcharts** showing oversight.
- **Department heads** worried about operational disruption.

    She showed **journey simulations** highlighting process improvements.

- **Claims processors** feared job loss.

   She created **before-and-after visuals** to show how AI supported (not replaced) their work.

- **The IT team** was concerned about integration complexity.

   She provided **technical diagrams** that clearly mapped AI components into the current stack.

The key to her success was recognizing that each group processed information differently based on their technical literacy, primary concerns, and decision-making criteria. By tailoring visualizations to each group's lens, Sarah didn't just explain AI; she made it *relevant* to everyone.

What Changed: The Momentum Shift   With a new visual approach, Sarah didn't just explain AI; she changed how people responded to it. Board members who previously crossed their arms now leaned forward, engaging with visualizations that spoke their language. Department heads who feared disruption could now see clear process improvements. Claims processors who worried about job security understood how AI would enhance their capabilities rather than replace them.

The power of this systematic approach lies in its interconnected nature. Each step builds upon the others, creating a visualization strategy that drives understanding and builds unstoppable momentum. More than just presenting data, this framework helps leaders tell compelling stories that resonate with each audience's unique needs and concerns, laying the foundation for successful AI adoption.

Breakthrough Insight: Hidden Patterns in Plain Sight (Sumo Match Fixing)

In 2000, two economists uncovered something unexpected in sumo wrestling. They weren't searching for fraud. They were simply analyzing match outcomes. But when they visualized the data, a pattern jumped off the page.

Wrestlers who needed one more win to reach a crucial milestone were winning at statistically suspicious rates, especially when their opponents had nothing to lose. The match results had always been public. But it took a simple visual - plotting wins against tournament standings - to expose a years-long match-fixing scandal.

The Power of Visual Pattern Recognition   That sumo story shows what happens when you stop scanning rows of data and start seeing relationships.

The same shift is transforming businesses.

At Central States Insurance, AI-powered visualization helped uncover bias in how claims adjusters handled similar cases. Once they made decision flows visible, they cut inconsistencies by 18%. The numbers had always been there, but the truth only emerged when people could see it.

What Might Be Hiding in Your Data?   AI visual tools reveal invisible dynamics all across your business. Here's where to look:

Human Behavior and Decision Bias

- Unconscious bias in hiring, promotions, and reviews
- Time-of-day effects on judgment and performance
- Groupthink patterns in meeting decisions
- Experience-based blind spots in leadership calls

Workflow Bottlenecks and System Gaps

- Legacy habits masking inefficient steps
- Bottlenecks caused by unclear handoffs or role confusion
- "Shadow processes" operating outside formal systems
- Lags and loops hidden in cross-functional flows

Revenue Leaks and Missed Opportunities

- Missed pricing optimization or bundling chances
- Customer behaviors signaling unmet needs
- Cross-sell moments buried in frontline workflows
- High-value micro-interactions going unnoticed

Compliance, Risk, and Governance

- Early signs of regulatory exposure or audit risk
- Gaps in oversight during key process stages
- Anomalies that flag potential fraud or error
- Risk stacking across departments or systems

Customer Experience Blind Spots

- Repetition loops frustrating customers
- Drop-off points in self-service tools
- Cross-channel friction that erodes loyalty
- Pain points masked by average satisfaction scores

From Numbers to Narrative   Think of your business like a table covered in puzzle pieces. The data is there. But until you connect the pieces visually, the picture stays blurry.

The sumo scandal wasn't exposed by more data. It was exposed by a better way of seeing what was already there.

Your data holds the same potential. The breakthrough won't come from collecting more. You'll find it when you ask: *What patterns are we missing because we haven't visualized them yet?*

Key Takeaway: The data was always there. Visualization made it impossible to ignore.

Chapter Reflection: Visuals That Win Support and Build Momentum

As we've explored in this chapter, the journey from AI potential to business impact begins with making the invisible visible. Leaders like Sarah Chen don't fail because they lack data, but because they lack the right way to communicate it. **Visual Dartboarding** and the **Visualization Tool Decision Framework** provide the means for building **Foundation Momentum** - transforming abstract AI initiatives into compelling, high-impact stories that secure buy-in and drive execution.

But tools alone aren't enough. Success depends on thoughtful application, stakeholder engagement, and continuous iteration.

Key Chapter Insights

- **Visualization as Collaboration:** Visualization isn't merely presenting data; it's creating a shared language for change. When stakeholders can see and interact with AI's potential impact, abstract discussions become concrete solutions.

- **Stakeholder-Specific Clarity:** Just as every stakeholder brings unique concerns, they require different visual approaches to build trust. A CFO might need financial impact visualizations, while operations leaders require process flow insights. Success lies in matching the visualization to the viewer.

- **Start Rough, Build Better:** The "minimum viable visualization" concept teaches us that perfection is the enemy of progress. Those early, imperfect drafts often spark the most valuable discussions and insights. By giving stakeholders something to react to, we transform critics into collaborators.

- **Co-Creation Drives Adoption:** When stakeholders help shape visualizations, they develop solution ownership. This shift - from defending AI initiatives to co-creating them - transforms resistance into advocacy. The visualization becomes not just yours, but theirs.

- **Revealing Hidden Patterns:** Like the sumo wrestling analysis showed, critical insights often hide in plain sight. The right visualization doesn't just present data; it reveals patterns that change how we understand our business. Sometimes, we don't need more data; we simply need a new way to see it.

Your Turn: Build Momentum Through Shared Vision

AI buy-in doesn't happen because of another polished slide deck. It happens when people *see* what's possible and feel like they're part of the process.

Now it's your turn.

You've seen how rough visuals spark real conversations and how co-creating the solution turns skeptics into supporters. It's time to turn theory into traction.

The tools are here. The mindset shift is yours to make.

Use the prompts below to map your buy-in barriers, sketch your first draft, and get the right people in the room. Whether you're launching your first AI pitch or trying to turn "not yet" into "let's go," this is how momentum starts.

Building Foundation Momentum

- What's one AI visualization you could implement today that would be impossible to ignore in your organization?
- Which stakeholder group would benefit most from a **Visual Dartboarding** session?
- How could you use visualization to overcome your organization's biggest AI adoption barriers?

Applying the Framework

- Which of the three Visual Tool Decision Framework steps presents your biggest challenge, and why?
- What resources do you need to start implementing these visualization approaches?
- How will you measure the impact of improved visualization on AI adoption?

Your Organization's Story

- What's your equivalent of Sarah's claims-processing visualization?
- Where do you suspect the hidden patterns in your organization are waiting to be revealed?
- How could better visualization transform your current AI initiatives?

Your Action Plan

Quick Wins (Next 30 Days)

- Identify your highest-impact visualization opportunity.
- Schedule your first **Visual Dartboarding** session.
- Map your key stakeholders' visualization needs.

Building Momentum (60–90 Days)
- Implement your first visualization framework.
- Collect and measure early success stories.
- Expand visualization tools across teams.

Scaling Success (90+ Days)
- Create visualization standards and best practices.
- Build visualization capabilities across the organization.
- Integrate visualization into AI governance and strategy.

Next Chapter Preview: Execution Momentum

As we move into Chapter 12, we'll build on this foundation to explore how visualization drives **Execution Momentum** - transforming stakeholder skepticism into active support through pain point-specific visualization. Then, in Chapter 13, we'll examine how visualization enables **Scale and Innovation Momentum**, helping organizations multiply business impact across functions and units.

Final Thoughts

I created Visual Dartboarding years ago because I needed to help people collaborate and co-own solutions, moving quickly from ideation to business impact. As I watched leaders struggle to drive value with AI, it was clear that one-time buy-in wasn't enough; success required a repeatable approach. That's why I developed the Visualization Tool Decision Framework. Together, leaders can use these tools to turn skeptics into champions. When stakeholders can see the impact, resistance fades, and momentum builds.

Now that we've established Foundation Momentum, let's focus on turning resistance into support.

CHAPTER 12

From Resistance to Results

Driving Execution Momentum

Every AI initiative must evolve from strategy to successful execution. Winning approval for AI is one thing. Successfully integrating change into daily operations, workflows, and decision-making is another entire level of challenge.

Too often, AI projects stall after a successful pilot. Leaders secure buy-in, launch an initiative, and expect momentum to carry it forward only to run into unexpected resistance. Teams push back on new workflows. IT raises integration concerns. Employees question AI's reliability. Executives worry about how to measure success.

This isn't a technology problem. It's an **execution problem**.

Sarah Chen had built a strong business case for AI-powered claims processing. She'd convinced her board, aligned her leadership team, and proven AI's value in a controlled environment. But now, as AI moved from proof-of-concept to day-to-day operations, she encountered a new set of barriers, ones that wouldn't be solved by another strategy meeting.

AI adoption doesn't fail because of a lack of potential. It fails when organizations don't account for the human, operational, and strategic barriers that surface during execution.

In this chapter, we'll explore:

- **Why AI initiatives often stall after a promising start**
- **The seven major barriers to AI execution and how to overcome them**
- **How visualization can break resistance and accelerate implementation**
- **The role of stakeholder-specific visual strategies in building Execution Momentum**

Sarah knew that pushing AI forward required more than just logic or persuasion; it required helping people see AI's impact in a way that resonated with them. The right visualization tools wouldn't just explain AI's role; they would make it impossible to ignore.

The Execution Gap: Why AI Fails to Deliver Business Value

Sarah Chen had secured buy-in for her AI-powered claims processing initiative, but she quickly realized that buy-in doesn't equal execution.

With board approval in hand, she expected enthusiasm to spread through the organization. Instead, she faced a new wall of resistance. IT worried about system compatibility. Claims managers feared disruption to their workflows. Executives asked, "How will we know it's working?"

Sarah had tackled the strategy-to-buy-in gap, but now she had to bridge the buy-in-to-execution gap.

She wasn't alone in this struggle. Across industries, leaders championing AI often find their projects stuck at this stage. The reasons? **Execution resistance**.

The AI Execution Problem: More than 80% of AI initiatives fail to deliver business value, not because the technology is flawed, but because the wrong projects are chosen or they never make it past internal barriers.

Why does this happen? Too often, organizations approach AI like this:

"We have AI, now where can we use it?"

Instead of: *"Here's our business problem. What's the best way to solve it?"*

This lack of business focus has created an AI reputation problem. Executive teams have heard horror stories of wasted money, poor ROI, and unpredictable AI behaviors. Regulatory concerns add another layer of uncertainty. Many leaders don't fully grasp the difference between traditional, rules-based systems and AI models that learn, adapt, and evolve.

Sarah realized that to succeed, she had to systematically dismantle execution barriers, not through more reports, but through visualization.

The Seven Barriers to AI Execution: How Sarah Broke Through AI Resistance

Sarah Chen stood in her office, staring at the stakeholder map on her whiteboard. Seven different groups, seven different forms of resistance. The board members questioned whether AI aligned with the company's long-term strategy. The CFO doubted the financial return. The risk and compliance teams worried about regulatory exposure. IT leaders saw an integration nightmare. Business unit managers feared AI-driven decisions would erode trust, while frontline employees worried it would replace them entirely. And claims processing teams, the people who would use the AI daily, felt AI was disrupting a system that already worked just fine.

Each group had valid concerns, shaped by their unique responsibilities and perspectives. But Sarah also knew that these concerns, if left unaddressed, would become roadblocks. The success of her AI rollout depended not just on the technology itself, but on how well she could communicate its value in a way that each stakeholder could see, understand, and trust.

A one-size-fits-all approach wouldn't work. She couldn't just explain AI; she had to show them what it meant for their world. Each group needed a tailored visualization to help them move from skepticism to support.

Taking a deep breath, Sarah picked up a marker. It was time to break the resistance, one visualization at a time.

Over the next several days, Sarah worked through each group, adapting her message, refining her visuals, and addressing the concerns that mattered most. What follows is a play-by-play of how she tackled the seven most common execution barriers with role-specific visualization strategies.

The AI Adoption Toolkit: Visual Solutions for Real-World Challenges

Overcoming resistance to AI is dramatically simplified with the right visualization tools used with strategic intent. Here are three powerful categories:

- **For Building Trust:** Use Explainability Dashboards and Impact Simulations to help stakeholders understand how AI works and, crucially, what value it brings.
- **For Workflow Alignment:** Use Process Maps and Integration Flowcharts to illustrate how AI fits into current operations while minimizing disruption.
- **For Strategic Vision:** Use Capability Radar Charts and ROI Dashboards to directly connect AI initiatives to key business goals and performance metrics.

These categories align directly with the core challenges leaders face during AI execution, which we explore in Sarah's journey through seven common resistance scenarios.

The Front Lines: "This Isn't How We Work"

It started with the claims processing teams. Sarah watched as veteran claims processor Jim Martinez crossed his arms during her presentation. "We've been doing this job for 20 years," he said. "AI is just going to mess up a system that works."

Sarah recognized the fear behind his words. These weren't just processes she was changing; they were people's livelihoods. Her response? She pulled up a split-screen visualization showing a typical claims journey.

"Look at this," she said, pointing to the left side. "Right now, our customer satisfaction scores show 40% of complaints come from slow claims processing, because you're forced to spend 60% of your time on basic data entry instead of helping customers. On the right, that's your day with AI. By automating routine tasks, you can focus on complex cases where your expertise directly improves customer outcomes. Our pilot showed this approach reduced complaint rates by 35% and increased customer satisfaction scores by 25%."

The room shifted. Jim uncrossed his arms. "So we'd be doing less paperwork and more actual problem-solving?"

Middle Management's Trust Gap

But winning over the front lines was just the beginning. Business unit leaders like Maria Rodriguez had different concerns. "If AI makes a wrong decision," Maria challenged, "it's my team that faces the consequences."

Maria managed a team handling $50 million in annual claims, and she'd seen before the high costs of bad decisions. "A single mishandled claim costs us an average of $15,000 in rework. And, it damaged customer relationships that we've spent years building," she explained. "How can I trust AI with those stakes?"

Sarah's solution? She unveiled an explainability dashboard that tracked every AI decision in real time. "Watch this," she demonstrated, clicking through a recent claims decision. The system displayed each factor considered, confidence levels, and exactly where human oversight kicked in.

"And here's the best part," Sarah added, pulling up another screen. "You can see every decision pattern, track accuracy rates, and adjust oversight levels whenever needed."

Maria leaned forward. "So we're not just turning everything over to a black box?"

Executive Alignment and Strategic Fit

In the boardroom, the questions changed again. CEO David Chen cut straight to the point: "How does this fit our five-year strategy?"

Sarah was ready. Her competitive capability radar chart filled the screen, showing their position against key competitors, revealing stark business impacts. "These red zones represent $2.3 million in lost revenue last quarter," she explained. "Our major competitor, RapidClaims, has been processing similar claims 40% faster with 50% fewer errors, translating to 15% lower operating costs and 12% higher customer retention rates. Their market share grew 4% last quarter, mostly from our customer base. Our pilot results show we can close this gap significantly. We're already achieving 30% faster processing with 40% fewer errors. With full implementation, we'll match or exceed their performance levels within six months."

The board sat up straighter. Now she had their attention.

Risk and Compliance: Reducing Exposure

Legal counsel Jennifer Wu's concerns were different entirely. "Regulatory compliance isn't optional," she reminded everyone. "One AI mistake could cost us millions."

Sarah's governance risk heatmap made the risks clear. "Actually, Jennifer, our manual processes pose the bigger threat," she said, pointing to the red zones across their existing workflow: human error in data handling, inconsistent General Data Protection Regulation (GDPR) compliance, and gaps in decision documentation.

She quantified the stakes: "Last year, our manual approach exposed us to $5.2 million in regulatory penalties. Data handling errors led to three reportable GDPR incidents, each carrying potential fines of up to 4% of global revenue. The AI solution automates compliance checks, which would have prevented all three incidents. Plus, it creates complete audit trails, reducing our liability exposure by an estimated 60%."

Then she switched views. "Here's the same map with AI governance in place. Complete audit trails. Automated compliance checks. Real-time risk monitoring."

Jennifer actually smiled. "Now that's interesting."

IT: Integration Without Disruption

The IT team had their own doubts. "Our systems weren't built for this," warned CTO Mike Chang. Sarah's response? A detailed system architecture flowchart showing how AI would integrate with their existing infrastructure.

"We're not replacing systems," Sarah clarified. "We're enhancing them." Then, she pulled up real-time API performance data from their pilot program. The numbers spoke for themselves.

Her system architecture flowchart made the business impact clear. "By integrating AI with our existing systems rather than replacing them, we'll save $1.4 million in implementation costs," she explained. "Pilot data shows a 30% reduction in processing time while maintaining 99.99% system uptime. That means we can handle 600 more claims per day, a 60% increase in volume capacity, without adding infrastructure costs."

CFO Demands: Proving ROI

CFO Robert Torres remained skeptical until Sarah showed him the AI performance scorecards. "These aren't projections," she emphasized. "This is actual data from our pilot."

Sarah showed the CFO hard numbers from the pilot: "During the pilot, we've seen:

- $750,000 reduction in operating costs
- 30% faster processing, allowing us to handle 600 more claims per day
- 40% fewer errors, eliminating an estimated $300,000 in rework costs
- Customer retention improved 8% for accounts processed through the AI system
- Employee satisfaction scores are up 15% due to reduced manual workload
- An ROI over 127% in the first year"

The numbers told a story even a skeptical CFO couldn't ignore.

Turning Resistance into Momentum

By addressing each group's concerns with targeted visuals, Sarah turned resistance into momentum. She didn't just roll out AI; she built support by showing each audience how it served their goals.

"The key," she later explained, "wasn't convincing everyone to see AI the same way. It was helping each group see how AI solved their specific challenges. Different visualizations, same story: AI driving real business value."

Sarah knew that overcoming these barriers required more than arguments or documentation. She needed to show, not just tell.

Tailoring Your Visual Strategy

"I don't see how AI will improve our customer experience," the Board Chair said, frowning at yet another dense PowerPoint presentation. "And what about the risks?"

Sarah, the Chief Digital Officer, had anticipated this reaction. Three months earlier, she'd watched another AI initiative die in a boardroom, buried under technical jargon and vague promises.

But this time was different.

She'd experienced an *aha* moment since that last project pitch. She now realized that each stakeholder group wasn't just looking for different information; they needed different ways of *seeing* that information. "I was speaking AI," she'd reflected, "when I should have been speaking risk management to the board, system architecture to IT, and customer experience to our service teams."

Ready with her new approach, she pulled up a governance risk heatmap that immediately caught the Board's attention. Red zones highlighted their current high-risk areas: manual handling of customer financial data, inconsistent GDPR compliance in customer communications, and lack of systematic oversight on service decisions. The visualization then showed how AI automation would transform these red zones to green through standardized data protocols, automated compliance screening, and complete audit trails of every customer interaction.

Next, she revealed a competitive capability radar chart. The visualization told a compelling story: their competitors were rapidly advancing in AI-enabled customer service, shown by larger footprints across key metrics like response time and resolution rates. Their company's smaller footprint made the gap (and opportunity) immediately clear.

"Now I see what we're up against," the Chair nodded. "What's next?"

With board approval secured, Sarah faced her next challenge: the IT team's concerns about system integration. Rather than overwhelming them with requirements, she shared a clear system architecture flowchart showing how the AI would complement their existing platforms. The team leaned in, especially when she pulled up real-time API performance dashboards from a pilot program.

"This we can work with," the Chief Technology Officer said, already sketching ideas on his tablet.

But the business units proved to be her toughest audience. Customer service managers worried about losing the human touch. That is, until Sarah showed them customer journey maps highlighting how AI would eliminate frustrating hold times and repetitive queries, freeing their teams to handle complex cases requiring emotional intelligence.

The operational bottleneck analysis sealed the deal: clear visualizations showed how AI would reduce ticket backlogs by 60% and cut average resolution time in half.

Same AI Project, Different Story for Each Group

Sarah later explained: "Each group needed something different, but the outcome was the same: a clear, shared understanding of AI's value."

With alignment across all key execution stakeholders, Sarah had transformed AI from a top-down directive into a collaborative effort.

Momentum had shifted. AI execution was no longer a push; it had become a pull.

Key Takeaways: Driving AI Execution with Visualization

- **Execution Resistance Is Predictable, But Solvable.**

  Every AI leader faces skepticism, but knowing where resistance will come from allows for a proactive strategy.

- **Different Stakeholders Need Different Visuals.**

  A single AI presentation won't work. Tailor visualization to each group's concerns.

- **Make the Invisible Visible.**

  Seeing how AI fits, enhances and delivers results, removes barriers, and builds momentum.

Next Up: Scaling AI Beyond the Pilot Stage

Sarah had moved AI from approval to execution, but her next challenge was even bigger:

→ **How do you scale AI across the enterprise?**

→ **How do you maintain alignment and avoid fragmentation?**

In Chapter 13, we'll explore how visualization fuels **Scale and Innovation Momentum** - turning successful pilots into enterprise-wide transformation.

Breakthrough Insight: The Hidden Costs of Performance Blind Spots

In 1999, researchers studying emergency room efficiency made a surprising discovery. Conventional wisdom suggested that the biggest cause of patient delays was a shortage of doctors. Hospitals responded by hiring more physicians, yet wait times remained stubbornly high.

It wasn't until researchers mapped out patient flow visually that they saw the real issue: the bottleneck wasn't the doctors; it was the intake process. Nurses were spending too much time on paperwork before patients were even seen, causing a backlog that no amount of additional staffing could solve.

By making a simple change - shifting some administrative tasks away from intake nurses - hospitals reduced wait times by over 30% without hiring a single additional doctor. The problem had never been a lack of medical expertise; it was a process inefficiency hiding in plain sight.

Sarah Chen had her own version of this ER dilemma.

On paper, her AI-driven claims process looked like a success. Automation was reducing manual data entry, processing speeds were improving, and approval rates were stable. But complaints from both employees and customers told a different story: delays, inconsistencies, and cases inexplicably getting stuck.

Much like the hospital administrators who assumed the problem was a lack of doctors, Sarah's team initially believed the issue was that AI recommendations weren't accurate enough. But when she visualized the end-to-end claims process, the truth became clear: the slowest point wasn't AI decision-making; it was human hesitation.

- **Less Experienced Adjusters Were Flagging Too Many Claims for Manual Review:** Worried about making mistakes, they defaulted to requiring supervisor approvals, even when AI had correctly identified low-risk cases.
- **Inconsistent Decision-Making Created Hidden Rework:** Two adjusters handling identical claims sometimes reached completely different conclusions, forcing time-consuming overrides.
- **Claims Weren't Being Routed Efficiently:** The AI was trained on historical patterns, but it wasn't accounting for real-time workload imbalances, leading to lopsided workloads.

Just like in the ER, the problem wasn't a lack of AI sophistication; it was a workflow inefficiency that had never been fully visible before.

AI Doesn't Just Automate. It Exposes Weaknesses.

This is one of the paradoxes of AI adoption: Instead of simply optimizing existing processes, AI often reveals flaws that were previously invisible. If those flaws aren't addressed, AI won't solve the problem; it will amplify inefficiencies at scale.

Sarah's solution wasn't to tweak the AI model itself. Instead, she focused on changing how decisions were made:

- **Heatmaps of decision bottlenecks** revealed where claims were getting stuck.
- **Side-by-side AI vs. human comparisons** helped adjusters build trust in AI's recommendations.
- **Confidence score dashboards** showed adjusters exactly when and why they could trust AI insights.

These small but crucial interventions didn't just improve AI adoption; they fundamentally transformed how claims were processed, reducing decision time by 40% and increasing accuracy across teams.

Key Takeaways

The lesson from both hospital ERs and AI adoption is the same: What you think is broken might not be the real problem. If you don't look at the full picture, you'll waste resources fixing the wrong things.

AI's greatest value isn't just automation; it's illumination. It helps leaders see the real story hidden inside their business before they scale what's broken.

Chapter Reflection: From Resistance to Results

Business success with AI doesn't happen simply by building great technology. It demands that leaders create an approach that works, repeatedly, in the real world. As Sarah Chen discovered, buy-in is just the beginning. The real challenge starts when AI meets execution, and resistance begins to surface.

This chapter explored how **Execution Momentum** is often blocked by hidden barriers - from trust issues and workflow disruption to misaligned business strategies and unclear ROI. But as Sarah's experience showed, these barriers aren't roadblocks; they're invitations to rethink how AI is introduced, integrated, and communicated.

Key Chapter Insights

- **Execution Resistance Is Predictable and Solvable**

  AI adoption follows a pattern: initial excitement, followed by skepticism when implementation gets real. Knowing where resistance will come from lets you prepare for it.

- **Different Stakeholders Need Different Visuals**

  A single AI presentation won't work. Board members care about governance and ROI, IT needs system integration details, and frontline employees want to see how AI makes their work easier. Matching the visualization to the audience transforms opposition into engagement.

- **AI Doesn't Just Automate. It Exposes Performance Blind Spots.**

  AI has a way of surfacing inefficiencies that were previously invisible. Leaders who embrace this reality can fix systemic issues rather than just automating broken processes.

- **Visualization Moves AI from "Their Project" to "Our Solution"**

  When stakeholders see their fingerprints on an AI initiative, they shift from resisting change to driving its success. The right visualization tools accelerate this shift.

Your Turn: Break Through AI Resistance Visibly

Let's be real: AI resistance isn't surprising. This isn't just another tech rollout. AI changes how people work, shifts power dynamics, and challenges what's familiar. Of course it sparks pushback.

But here's the good news: resistance is predictable, and it's absolutely solvable.

You don't need more data. You need better ways to show what AI actually *means* for your people, your workflows, and your bottom line.

This toolkit gives you the questions that matter. Start by pinpointing where things are stuck, then use targeted visual strategies to break through confusion, build trust, and get everyone moving in the same direction.

Whether you're facing skeptical executives, hesitant teams, or clunky processes, this is how you move from vision to visible value.

Step 1: Assess Execution Momentum

Identify where your rollout is stalling and why.

- What's your biggest AI execution challenge right now?
- Which stakeholder group is showing the most resistance, and what's driving it?
- Where are the hidden bottlenecks slowing down adoption in your workflows?

Step 2: Apply Visualization to Break Resistance

Choose the right visual tools to shift mindset and behavior.

- Which execution-stage visualization (e.g., process maps, trust dashboards, role-based playbooks) would have the biggest impact in your organization?
- How can you tailor communication for each stakeholder group to build buy-in?
- What small but visible AI success story can you highlight right now?

Step 3: Scale What Works

Turn successful adoption moments into enterprise momentum.

- How will you track execution success (e.g., speed, accuracy, adoption rates)?
- What's your next step to make AI part of daily operations, not a special project?
- How can you build a culture where AI is seen as an asset, not a threat?

Pro Tip

Each visualization is a trust-building tool. The more your stakeholders can *see* how AI works for them, the faster you turn resistance into results.

Next Chapter Preview: Scale and Innovation Momentum

With **Execution Momentum** driving progress, the next challenge is ensuring AI doesn't stall in isolated projects or single departments. When AI is scaled effectively, it fuels continuous innovation, turning early wins into a self-sustaining cycle of business impact.

In the next chapter, we'll explore **Scale and Innovation Momentum**, two critical phases of the **AI Performance Flywheel**. We'll look at how visualization fuels enterprise-wide AI adoption, orchestration keeps initiatives aligned, and scale unlocks new opportunities, ensuring AI doesn't just expand, but becomes a lasting driver of business growth and competitive advantage.

Final Thoughts

Every leader advocating for AI encounters resistance, not because people reject innovation, but because they struggle to see how it fits into their world. After all, it's human nature to be cautious about what we don't understand. That's why I created a repeatable process to make AI's value crystal clear, transforming abstract potential into visible, practical impact. When people can see AI's value, they stop questioning it and start driving it.

Now that we've tackled Execution Momentum, let's shift our focus to scaling AI across the enterprise.

CHAPTER 13

Scale and Innovation Momentum

Turning Wins into a Wave

Securing buy-in is a milestone. Executing successfully is a break-through. But true transformation? That comes in the next two phases of the AI Performance Flywheel: **Scale and Innovation Momentum** (Figure 13.1).

This is where scattered wins become a wave, where AI shifts from isolated projects to enterprise force. But scale alone isn't enough. Without orchestration, alignment, and visibility, you don't get transformation. You get chaos.

This chapter explores how organizations activate these next phases by focusing on:

Real-world examples like:

- Sarah's company scaling AI from claims to customer service
- Malik's factory electrification moment that revealed the *real* scaling barrier
- Maria's leadership breakthrough as innovation shifted from R&D to frontlines

Practical frameworks including:

- The AI Performance Flywheel in action
- Visual Dartboarding for innovation orchestration
- Innovation Networks and Scale Visualization Tools

The business unlocks of true scale:

- Moving from automation to opportunity discovery
- Creating compound effects across siloed initiatives
- Orchestrating AI across maturity levels and use case types

Scaling and Innovation Momentum Cycle

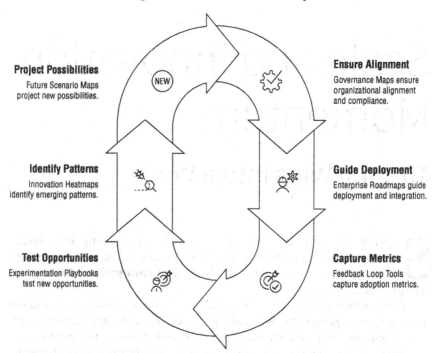

Project Possibilities

Future Scenario Maps
project new possibilities.

Ensure Alignment

Governance Maps ensure
organizational alignment
and compliance.

Identify Patterns

Innovation Heatmaps
identify emerging patterns.

Guide Deployment

Enterprise Roadmaps guide
deployment and integration.

Test Opportunities

Experimentation Playbooks
test new opportunities.

Capture Metrics

Feedback Loop Tools
capture adoption metrics.

FIGURE 13.1 Scaling and Innovation Momentum Cycle: Successful AI adoption doesn't stop at deployment; it thrives on continuous alignment and discovery. This cycle illustrates how scaling AI (right side) ensures structured deployment and governance, while innovation tools (left side) unlock new business opportunities. By integrating feedback loops, organizations transform AI from a static solution into a self-sustaining engine for growth, adaptability, and long-term competitive advantage.

The shift from early wins to sustainable innovation isn't automatic. But when leaders scale with visibility, alignment, and intention, AI stops being a tool and becomes a force multiplier.

Scaling AI for Enterprise-Wide Impact (Section 1)

As AI moves from early wins to company-wide impact, organizations reach a turning point. Sarah's claims processing success created excitement, but scaling brings new hurdles: coordinating teams, managing data across systems, establishing guardrails, and keeping initiatives connected to business goals. This section explores how leaders can expand AI without losing focus or creating disconnected projects. We follow Sarah's practical approach to turning isolated success into a foundation for broader transformation that strengthens the entire organization.

Scaling Without Losing Focus

Sarah stood back from her latest visualization: a large sheet of paper covered with a "success map" of their claims processing AI implementation. Green sticky notes showed efficiency gains. Yellow notes captured lessons learned. Red flags marked potential scaling challenges. String connected related elements, creating a physical depth that flat diagrams couldn't match.

"This worked in claims processing," the CEO said, studying the map. "Now, we need AI in customer service, risk assessment, and pricing analytics. How soon can we scale this across the enterprise?"

Sarah picked up a marker and moved to the whiteboard. She drew a simple circle labeled "Claims AI Success." Around it, she sketched rough arrows pointing outward in all directions, each marked with "Scale here?" The CEO's request to expand AI across the enterprise suddenly looked a lot messier on paper.

The Scaling Illusion: Why Expansion Isn't Enough

"Before we discuss timeline," Sarah replied, "let's visualize what scaling really means." She knew the real question wasn't how soon but instead how to scale AI without losing focus, creating silos, or overwhelming the organization. She had seen other companies rush AI expansion, only to end up with a disconnected mess of tools, inconsistent governance, and teams working at odds.

Rethinking AI's Value

Before continuing with Sarah's scaling journey, take a moment to explore this section. See how organizations are moving beyond basic automation to discover entirely new markets, products, and business models. These insights will be essential as you scale your own AI initiatives.

1. **Expanding into New Products and Services**
   - **Spotify's AI-Generated Playlists:** Spotify uses AI to analyze listening habits and generate personalized playlists like "Discover Weekly." This AI-powered service keeps users engaged and creates new revenue streams through premium subscriptions.

- **AI-Powered Virtual Try-Ons (L'Oréal, Sephora):** Beauty brands use AI to let customers virtually try on makeup via augmented reality. This service enhances online shopping and increases product sales without physical sampling.

2. **Creating Innovative Business Models**
   - **Tesla's Autonomous Ride-Sharing Network:** Tesla plans to use self-driving AI to enable a fleet of robotaxis, shifting its business from selling cars to providing transportation as a service (TaaS).
   - **AI-Driven Financial Services (Ant Group, PayPal):** AI-driven credit scoring enables fintech companies to offer microloans without traditional credit history checks, opening new financial service models for underbanked populations.

3. **Reshaping Competitive Landscapes**
   - **Netflix's AI Content Recommendations:** By leveraging AI to predict viewer preferences, Netflix creates competitive differentiation and influences content production decisions, making data-driven original series like Stranger Things a global success.
   - **AI-Optimized Drug Discovery (DeepMind, Moderna):** AI accelerates pharmaceutical R&D by predicting how molecules will interact, reducing drug development time from years to months and disrupting traditional healthcare innovation.

Each of these examples goes beyond efficiency gains, showing how AI creates entirely new opportunities that redefine industries and competitive strategies.

The Scale-Up Challenge: Making Complexity Visible

Using her signature Visual Dartboarding approach, Sarah started with three rough circles on a fresh whiteboard: "Claims (Working!)," "Customer Service (??)," and "Risk Assessment (???)." The arrows connecting them were intentionally dotted and messy. "This is what scaling really looks like," she explained, adding question marks where processes weren't clear.

Next to this first sketch, she began a "Risk Map," a visualization technique she'd learned from systems thinking. Three overlapping zones emerged, covered next.

Fragmentation Zone

She drew islands, actual tiny islands, representing each department's AI plans. Marketing's island had a "Customer Prediction" flag. Sales' island flew a "Lead Scoring" banner. Operations' island displayed "Process Automation" in bold. Between the islands, she drew rough waves with labels like "Data doesn't flow" and "Communication gap?"

"See these islands?" she asked, adding dotted lines between them. "Right now, every department is planning their own AI voyage. In isolation, each makes sense. But together…" She drew squiggly lines between the islands, representing failed connections.

Misalignment Territory

For this, Sarah pulled out her impact-effort matrix cards, a physical tool she used for strategic planning. On the whiteboard, she quickly sketched a 2x2 grid:

- **X-axis:** "Business Value" (with "?" to "!!!")
- **Y-axis:** "AI Complexity" (with "Simple" to "Help!")

As team members called out proposed AI projects, she placed cards in different quadrants. Most landed in "High Complexity, Value???," a visual wake-up call about their current trajectory.

Governance Gaps

For this challenge, Sarah drew a simple hub-and-spoke diagram on the whiteboard, a visualization technique she often used to map dependencies. "Governance" sat in the center, with spokes radiating out to key elements: "Compliance," "Bias Testing," "Security," "Ethics."

As she drew dotted lines between these elements, gaps became obvious. "Each new AI project impacts every part of this wheel," she explained, drawing a quick journey line that zigzagged through multiple spokes. "But look what happens when we add a second project." She drew another line in a different color, then a third, until the simple diagram revealed a complex web of intersections and potential failure points.

"And this is just tracking the basics," she added, putting down her marker. "We haven't even mapped data privacy requirements or model drift monitoring."

"Foundation First," she wrote in bold letters at the top, circling it twice.

Standing back, Sarah let the visuals sink in. The messy reality of their scaling challenge was now impossible to ignore. But more importantly, it was now something they could discuss, debate, and improve together.

The Data Reality: Mapping the Messier Truth

Sarah's next Visual Dartboard was brutally simple: a rough Venn diagram where Marketing's circle barely overlapped with Sales' and Finance's data lived in its own isolated bubble. "This is our data reality," she said, shading the tiny overlap area with red marker. "AI needs to live in these gaps."

"Think of AI like a high-performance engine," she explained, quickly sketching a car on the whiteboard. Under it, she drew two fuel tanks: one labeled "Clean Data" (tiny) and another labeled "What We Actually Have" (much larger, filled with question marks).

Using her whiteboard toolkit, just markers and sticky notes, she mapped out three critical patterns:

The Complexity Trap

Sarah drew a simple flowchart of their current data movement. Each department got its own box, with arrows showing data flow. As she added more arrows, team members called out additional connections. Soon, the clean flowchart became a tangle of intersecting lines.

"Hold on," said the Marketing VP, standing up. "That arrow is wrong. We send data to Sales weekly, not daily." He grabbed a marker and updated the diagram.

"Actually," the Sales Director chimed in, "we're not receiving that data at all." She added a big X over the arrow.

Within minutes, the team had transformed Sarah's basic flowchart into a more accurate (if messier) representation of their data reality.

The Scale-Up Challenge

Next to the tangled flowchart, Sarah drew two columns (see Table 13.1).

TABLE 13.1	Mapping Today's Claims AI Complexity Against the Scale-Up Challenges of Enterprise AI	
Claims AI (Now)	**Enterprise AI (Future?)**
One data source	Dozens (or hundreds) of data sources
Standard format	Multiple, often conflicting formats
Single department	Cross-department, cross-functional AI
Clear ownership	Unclear or fragmented ownership
Well-defined governance	Diverse compliance & security requirements
AI trained on curated data	AI operating on live, evolving data
Limited risk exposure	Expanded risk across interconnected AI systems

The Quality Cascade

For this, Sarah used a technique she called the "Quality Cascade" to explain how small data issues can snowball into large-scale AI problems. She began with a simple question - "Where do quality problems begin?" - and mapped how minor data issues compound over time. At the narrow end of the funnel, small problems seem isolated. But as they cascade forward, they branch into other systems, causing ripple effects that escalate into system-wide disruptions and ultimately major AI failures (see Figure 13.2).

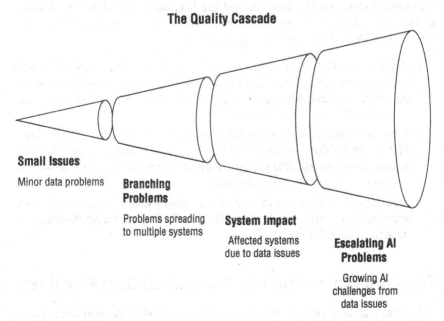

The Quality Cascade

Small Issues
Minor data problems

Branching Problems
Problems spreading to multiple systems

System Impact
Affected systems due to data issues

Escalating AI Problems
Growing AI challenges from data issues

FIGURE 13.2 Sarah's **Quality Cascade** illustrates how small data issues expand into cross-system problems and ultimately grow into major AI challenges.

"Every part of this funnel affects multiple systems," she explained. "Fix it early, or watch the problems grow."

The room fell quiet as everyone studied the visualizations. What had seemed like abstract data challenges were now concrete problems they could see (and solve) together.

Building the Foundation for Scale: Making the Invisible Visible

Sarah recognized that successful enterprise AI management extended beyond infrastructure development. It required making complex systems visible and understandable to everyone involved. Leveraging her Visual Dartboarding approach, she mapped out three Fundamental Elements essential to supporting AI at scale, covered next.

Fundamental Element 1: Centralized Data Architecture

Centralized Data Architecture formed the backbone of scalable AI. Sarah's preliminary assessment revealed significant gaps in understanding how information flowed through the organization.

- Hand-drawn flowchart of key departments (Sales, Marketing, Finance) with very rough arrows showing where data should flow. Arrows are dotted lines to indicate uncertainty. Question marks next to each arrow: "Does this flow actually happen?"

- A simple table (drawn on a whiteboard) with three columns: "Data Field," "Definition (Maybe)," "Who Owns It?" Many cells are blank or have question marks. She snapped a photo to ensure she could email it to everyone before they met to discuss it.

- A tangled web of boxes and lines (intentionally messy) representing data sources. Some lines are broken. The label "Hidden Dependencies?" is written in large letters.

Fundamental Element 2: Automated Data Pipelines

Automated Data Pipelines would determine whether AI solutions could operate reliably at scale. Sarah's visual assessment highlighted several critical issues standing in the way:

- A very basic bar graph (drawn quickly) showing "Data Quality Score" for different data sources. The scores are estimates, and some bars are missing entirely.
- A drawing of a pipeline with a large clog in the middle. The word "Bottleneck?" is written next to it.
- A series of boxes representing data transformation steps, connected by arrows. Some boxes have question marks: "What happens here?" There are sticky notes attached with suggestions for improvement.

Fundamental Element 3: Scalable Governance

Scalable Governance provided the guardrails for responsible AI expansion. Sarah's documentation revealed blind spots in how the organization monitored and managed its data and models:

- A simple table showing "Data Source," "Last Updated," "Who Approved It?" Many cells are blank or have "Unknown" written in them.
- A rough chart showing "Bias Score" for different AI models. The scores are estimates, and there's a large question mark: "Is this accurate?"
- A map of the organization with different areas shaded to represent data sensitivity. The shading is uneven and imprecise. The label "Privacy Concerns?" is written in large letters.

"We can't manage what we can't see," Sarah explained, spreading her collection of rough sketches across the conference table. "These aren't pretty, but they're getting people talking about the right problems."

The visual approach sparked real conversations:

- Business leaders stopped nodding politely and began drawing additions: "Actually, this process is broken here," and "You forgot this connection."
- IT brought their own markers to meetings, eagerly updating the data pipeline sketches with newly discovered bottlenecks.
- Compliance teams flagged risks using the privacy maps, circling hotspots and adding "YIKES!" annotations where data handling required immediate attention.

"Perfect diagrams make people think everything's under control," Sarah noted, pointing to a particularly messy flowchart covered in question marks and sticky notes. "But these rough sketches? They give people permission to admit what they don't know, and that's where real progress starts."

This section is already strong. It captures the messy reality of AI scaling and the importance of tackling foundational issues before expanding. The following is a refined version that maintains the practical, visual approach while sharpening the language for clarity and impact.

From Insight to Action: When the Whiteboard Meets Reality

Sarah knew the hardest part wouldn't be identifying the problems; it would be turning insights into action. She opened a fresh whiteboard and started sketching what she called a **Reality Check Map** to separate assumptions from facts.

TABLE 13.2	The Reality Check Map forced the team to confront hidden breakdowns and knowledge gaps, before scaling made them worse.	
WORKING	**BROKEN**	**UNKNOWN**
✓ Claims Data	✗ Sales/Mktg Data	? HR Data Quality
✓ Basic AI Models	✗ Data Flow Gaps	? Model Drift
✓ Small Team	✗ Governance Issues	? True Costs

At the top, she wrote three columns (see Table 13.2).

Then, she started mapping dependencies with simple arrows. Within minutes, the board became a tangle of connections, some solid, some dashed, representing assumptions.

The CTO pointed at one. "That's not right. Customer data flows through three different systems before AI even touches it." He grabbed a marker and added the missing steps, revealing an even messier picture.

"Perfect," Sarah said. "The mess is what we need to see."

By the end of the hour, the whiteboard told an uncomfortably honest story:

- **Dotted lines** showed assumed data flows that nobody could verify.
- **Red X's** marked known failures.
- **Yellow sticky notes** highlighted compliance risks.
- **Question marks** clustered around critical systems that nobody fully understood.

Sarah took a photo. "It's ugly, but it's true. And truth is what we need right now."

She turned to another whiteboard and drew a simple timeline (see Figure 13.3).

```
| NOW  →    Quick Wins  →  90 Days  →  6 Months → 1 Year  |
| ------------ | ------------- | ------------- | ------------- | ------------- |
| [Fix What's Broken] | [Connect Systems] | [Scale Up] | [Optimize] |
```

FIGURE 13.3 Sarah's Phased Roadmap made transformation feel doable by stacking early wins into sustainable progress.

Under "Quick Wins," she listed immediate actions:

- **Map actual data flows** (not what we assume)
- **Fix broken connections** in Sales/Marketing
- **Document "mystery processes"** (all those "???" marks)
- **Start weekly data quality checks**

She paused. "Notice what's not on this list?"
Silence.
"No new AI projects," she said. "We fix the foundation first."
The CEO, watching quietly, finally spoke. "Show me where it hurts most."
Sarah circled the densest tangle of arrows and question marks. "Right here. Customer data should flow between systems, but it doesn't. Fix this, and we unlock everything else."
She added one final note at the bottom of the board:

- **Start with what's broken**
- **Fix what we can see**
- **Document what we don't know**
- **Then (and only then) scale**

"This," she said, tapping the board, "is our real digital transformation. Not the one in PowerPoint decks, the one that starts by admitting what's actually broken."

The Synthetic Data Revolution: Scaling AI Without Scaling Risk

To scale effectively, Sarah knew she needed to address two fundamental challenges: data and talent. She started with the data challenge. For years, companies have treated data as an asset to be hoarded, believing that the more they stored, the greater their competitive edge. But Sarah's team had hit a harsh reality: 93–97% of corporate data wasn't AI-ready. Worse, maintaining massive data stores wasn't just inefficient; it was a legal and operational liability.

"We're not just storing data; we're storing risk," Sarah pointed out in a leadership meeting. She referenced recent shareholder lawsuits under Delaware's 2023 fiduciary duty ruling, where companies were being held accountable for unstructured, non-compliant data. She drew a quick visual to punctuate her point about risk (see Figure 13.4).

```
RISK LEVEL:
[Low]--- | ---[Med]--- | ---[HIGH!]
        ↑
     Previous
                      ↑
                     Now
```

FIGURE 13.4 The team's mindset shifted when Sarah **showed that storing more data meant inheriting more risk.**

The solution? High-fidelity synthetic data.

Sarah knew synthetic data wasn't just a research tool anymore. It had evolved into a strategic asset, one that could accelerate AI development while sidestepping privacy concerns, compliance risks, and the inherent biases of real-world datasets.

The Shift: From Hoarding Data to Generating Intelligence

To help her team visualize the shift, Sarah sketched a simple comparison on the whiteboard (see Table 13.3).

TABLE 13.3	To break old habits, Sarah contrasted Legacy Data Beliefs with Modern AI Thinking, focused on AI readiness, not data volume.	
Old Thinking	**New Thinking**	
Raw Data = Value	AI-Ready Data = Value	
Quantity Wins	Quality Wins	
Store Everything	Generate as Needed	

Next, she mapped out how synthetic data fundamentally changed their approach (see Table 13.4).

The Shift from Traditional to AI-Optimized Data Workflows

Sarah knew she needed to make the impact concrete. On the whiteboard, she created a stark comparison that silenced the room (see Table 13.4).

TABLE 13.4	**Traditional vs. Synthetic Workflows:** Showing That Traditional Workflows Come with Delay and Risk; Synthetic Workflows Come with Speed and Control			
Stage	**Traditional Workflow**	**Time to Execution**	**Synthetic Data Workflow**	**Time to Execution**
Data Preparation	Collect real-world data → Clean → Store	Weeks–Months	Generate high-fidelity synthetic data	Hours–Days
Compliance & Privacy	Wait for approvals → Address privacy risks	Months	No privacy risk → Immediate usability	Instant
AI Training	Train AI models on historical data	Weeks	Train AI on structured, bias-controlled data	Days
Testing & Refinement	Identify biases/errors → Retrain models	Weeks–Months	Test & refine AI with synthetic edge cases	Hours–Days
Deployment	Deploy AI with limited validation	High Risk	Deploy AI with validated real-world adjustments	Lower Risk

Key Takeaway: Synthetic data compresses AI development cycles from months to days, eliminates compliance roadblocks, and enables faster, bias-controlled iteration. The companies that win in AI won't be the ones hoarding data; they'll be the ones generating and refining AI-ready data at scale.

"Look at the speed difference," she said, circling the workflows. "With synthetic data, we can start testing tomorrow."

She added one final note at the bottom:

- **Traditional:** Six to eight months to deployment
- **Synthetic:** Two to three weeks to deployment

"The question isn't whether to use synthetic data," she concluded. "It's why we waited so long to start."

The CEO checked his watch. "How soon can we implement this in customer service?"

Sarah smiled. "We already started generating the data this morning."

The Hidden Cost of Data: Visualizing the True Picture

Sarah knew budget discussions needed clear visuals. She divided the whiteboard into two sections and started mapping out costs (see Table 13.5). Although a close look at the comparison she shared was incredibly compelling, it took mental effort to discern. This was intended to help leadership see it not just as a technical shift, but as a strategic financial decision

TABLE 13.5	Showing How Synthetic Data Slashes Expenses Across Storage, Compliance, and Operations	
Aspect	**Current Approach**	**Synthetic Approach**
Storage Costs	Growing 40%/year	Dropping 25%/year
	New compliance requirements	Pay-as-you-go
	Backup requirements	No storage needed
Compliance Overhead	$2M/year reviews	$500K/year
	$1M/year audits	No privacy reviews
	$800K legal	No PII concerns
Time Costs	Data cleaning: three to four months	Ready in days
	Privacy reviews: 2+ months	Instant start
	Validation: six to eight weeks	Quick iteration
Process Costs	High due to privacy reviews and compliance	Lower due to fewer privacy reviews and less overhead

She added a quick table comparison between traditional costs and synthetic costs (see Table 13.6). Again, great information, but the furrowed brow of the CFO as he absorbed the information made it clear to Sarah that a graphic would be more effective.

TABLE 13.6	Illustrating How Traditional Data Costs Escalate Over Time, While Synthetic Data Offers Compounding Savings and Reduced Operational Burden	
Year	**Traditional Data Costs**	**Synthetic Data Costs**
2023	High costs across storage, compliance, and processes	Lower generation costs, no storage needs, minimal compliance
2024	Costs continue to rise (40% in storage)	Generation costs drop (25% per year)
2025	Increased backup and audit costs	Pay-as-you-go, reduced process costs

She then drew a simple cost trajectory (see **Figure 13.5**).

FIGURE 13.5   Sarah's **cost trajectory sketch** made the choice unmistakable: while traditional data costs compound year after year, synthetic costs decline predictably over time.

Below this, she sketched three circles representing data value (see Figure 13.6).

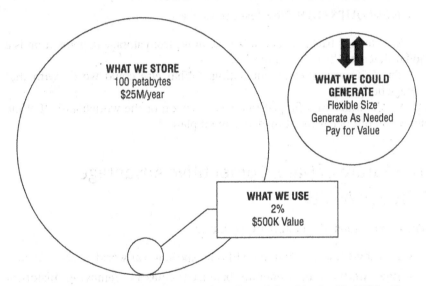

FIGURE 13.6   Sarah's **data storage visual** challenged the old-school belief that "more is better" when it comes to data stored. Sarah exposed the hidden cost of hoarding (most data sits unused), while synthetic data offered a flexible, value-driven alternative.

The CFO leaned forward. Sarah's shift from sharing tables to simple graphics had fully captured his attention. "Show me the Claims project numbers." He was ready to see a simple data view now.

Sarah quickly added a case study box (see Table 13.7). The synthetic approach cut time and spend by two-thirds while more than doubling results.

TABLE 13.7 **Exposing the Inefficiency of the Traditional Model**: Longer Timelines, Higher Costs, and Lower Success		
Metric	**Traditional Data Approach**	**Synthetic Data Approach**
Development Time	8 months	3 months
Total Spend	$2.4M	$800K
Success Rate	40%	85%

Finally, she wrote her key question in large letters:

- **OLD QUESTION:** How much data can we store?
- **NEW QUESTION:** How fast can we learn?

She stepped back. "Every dollar we move from storage to generation is a dollar that actually drives value."

The CFO was already calculating. "What else could we do with that storage budget?"

Sarah smiled and flipped to a clean section of the whiteboard. "Let me show you our department-by-department plan..."

The Future of Data: Competitive Advantage Through Agility

The implications of this shift are profound:

- **Privacy-First AI:** Train AI without exposing real-world sensitive data
- **Bias Reduction:** Generate balanced datasets, removing historical discrimination
- **Regulatory Compliance:** Sidestep GDPR, HIPAA, and other data constraints
- **Speed to Market:** Deploy AI faster by eliminating data acquisition delays

Sarah realized that data was no longer just an asset; it was an enabler. The companies that won in AI wouldn't be those hoarding petabytes of raw data. They'd be the ones with the agility to synthesize, structure, and deploy AI-ready data faster than their competitors.

Moving Forward: Scaling AI with Smarter Data

As Sarah and her team expanded AI across departments, they no longer viewed scaling AI as a problem of "Do we have enough data?" Instead, they asked: "How quickly can we create the right data?"

This wasn't just an operational shift; it was a strategic one. AI scaling meant no longer just storing data. It meant learning faster, and with synthetic data, that future was within reach.

AI Talent and Upskilling – Scaling AI Literacy Across the Workforce

With a clear data strategy in place, Sarah turned to an equally crucial challenge: preparing her people for AI at scale. The talent challenge was as fundamental as the data challenge. Sarah's pilot had succeeded because of seamless collaboration between AI specialists and claims processors who deeply understood their business. But as she contemplated scaling across the organization, she saw a widening gap between technical expertise and business knowledge.

"We can't hire an AI team for every department," she realized. "And even if we could, that's not the right approach." The pilot's success hadn't come from technical expertise alone; it came from claims processors being active participants in solution development, not passive users. How could they recreate that level of engagement across the entire organization?

Sarah recognized that scaling AI meant more than deploying technology; it meant empowering people to use it effectively. Her upskilling strategy focused on three key areas: educating leadership about AI's strategic role, training cross-functional teams to leverage AI insights in their daily workflows, and redefining roles to embrace an AI-augmented approach where technology enhanced rather than replaced human capabilities.

Initially, Sarah faced resistance from employees who feared automation would replace their expertise. But as she introduced AI literacy programs, something unexpected happened. Teams began moving from resistance to innovation, proactively identifying new use cases in their workflows. AI transformed from a top-down initiative into a collaborative tool driving meaningful business impact.

"AI isn't just for data scientists," Sarah explained to her leadership team. "It requires collaboration across all functions to deliver value. Without broad AI literacy, even sophisticated models fail to gain traction."

The best AI organizations, Sarah had learned, don't just scale models; they scale their people's capacity to create value. That's why she made infrastructure and talent development the backbone of her AI scaling strategy.

Orchestrating the AI Symphony: Managing Multiple Initiatives

Having both data and talent wasn't enough. Sarah needed a way to coordinate multiple AI initiatives across the organization. Standing before her office window late one evening, Sarah studied the whiteboard behind her, covered with sticky notes representing AI initiatives sparked by their claims processing success. Unlike her focused pilot, she now faced a complex web of possibilities, each needing to progress through its own Foundation → Execution → Scale → Innovation cycle.

"It's like conducting an orchestra," she murmured, seeing how each initiative played its own part in a larger symphony. Claims Processing AI was already in its Innovation phase, predicting claim complexity and detecting fraud patterns. The Customer Service Chatbot was scaling across digital channels, while Risk Assessment AI was just beginning its execution phase. Meanwhile, new use cases in pricing analytics were still laying their foundation.

Sarah's key insight was powerful: scaling AI wouldn't happen as a linear expansion. It demanded careful orchestration of multiple initiatives at different stages of maturity. She developed four key principles to manage this complexity:

1. **Visual Orchestration Tools**
   - AI workflow sketches for team alignment
   - Side-by-side comparisons to build trust
   - Feedback loop visualizations to track progress
2. **Resource Orchestration**
   - Balancing talent and computing power across initiatives
   - Transferring knowledge from mature systems to new deployments
   - Managing shared infrastructure and data pipelines
3. **Risk and Governance Orchestration**
   - AI Explainability Dashboards for transparency
   - Bias Detection Heatmaps across systems
   - Compliance tracking at scale

4. Performance Orchestration
- Cross-system impact measurements
- Adoption heatmaps across departments
- Efficiency and growth metrics

"Each AI initiative is like an instrument," Sarah explained to her team. "Individually, they create value. But orchestrated together, they create something much more powerful." She knew success required more than just scaling; it required sustainable orchestration that kept every initiative aligned, integrated, and governed.

This meant ensuring every AI deployment was:

- Connected to clear business outcomes
- Designed to work across departments
- Protected by robust governance
- Supported by skilled teams
- Built on quality data foundations

The real challenge wasn't just scaling AI; it was conducting this complex symphony of initiatives to create lasting business value.

For a detailed breakdown of orchestration principles and tools, see Appendix I: Orchestrating Principles for Scaling AI available among the resources at the book's companion website, **DrLisa.ai/snt-book-resources**.

Scaling AI with Visualization: Tools to Maintain Alignment

Sarah developed a set of visualization tools to keep AI expansion on track. Using them ensured that AI remained ethical, aligned, driving business value, and continuously improving as it scaled across the organization.

One of her key tools was **AI Governance Maps**, which helped ensure AI stayed compliant, ethical, and aligned with corporate objectives. By visually mapping governance frameworks, Sarah made it easier for teams to understand regulatory requirements, bias mitigation strategies, and accountability measures, ensuring AI was used responsibly.

She also leveraged **Enterprise AI Roadmaps**, which provided a long-term view of AI's integration and strategic alignment. These roadmaps helped leadership teams see where AI initiatives were heading, how they connected to business goals, and what adjustments were needed to maintain momentum.

AI Feedback Loops were also key tools. They allowed teams to track how AI was performing in production, spot emerging risks, and adjust models dynamically to keep AI solutions relevant and effective.

These tools were never allowed to become static reports. They were living, evolving tools that adapted as AI scaled, helping leaders stay aligned and make better decisions in real time.

Breakthrough Insight: Scaling Doesn't Mean Success Unless You Rethink the System

In the 1920s, factory owners replaced steam engines with electric motors, yet productivity barely budged. Why? They plugged new tech into old layouts. The real breakthrough came when they redesigned workflows around electricity itself.

Today's AI leaders face the same trap. Scaling AI into existing systems doesn't deliver transformational value; it just automates the old way of working.

Malik James, CDO of a global auto manufacturer, lived this firsthand. His $50M investment in AI-powered forecasting hit diminishing returns, until he mapped the real issues:

- Distribution centers were "safety padding" AI forecasts, holding 15–20% more inventory than recommended
- Regional managers were overriding AI suggestions during peak seasons, creating excess stock
- Some centers were sharing corrected forecasts with suppliers without flagging the manual adjustments

The takeaway? You don't just scale AI, you redesign the business around what AI makes possible. You don't get exponential results with linear thinking.

The AI Feedback Loop – How Scaling Becomes Launchpad for Innovation

As Sarah watched the AI initiatives scale across their company's operations, she noticed something unexpected. Instead of simply driving more volume as she expected from the core premise of "scaling," scaling was revealing entirely new possibilities. The AI systems, now processing thousands of claims daily, were surfacing patterns that would have been impossible to spot with human analysis alone.

For instance, the AI began detecting subtle correlations between certain types of home insurance claims and future fraud attempts, patterns that only became visible at scale. It identified clusters of approval steps that created consistent bottlenecks in the workflow. Perhaps most valuable were the early warning signals of customer dissatisfaction, patterns of interaction that predicted potential policy cancellations months before they occurred.

Sarah realized they were witnessing what she called the "Scaling Feedback Loop." As AI processed more claims, it generated insights that revealed new business opportunities. Data about AI adoption across departments highlighted workflow inefficiencies that could be addressed. Performance feedback from multiple AI systems drove continuous refinements and sparked ideas for new innovations.

The challenge was no longer just implementing AI; it was having the right visualization strategy to make these emerging opportunities visible to decision-makers. "We need to be able to see the forest and the trees," Sarah explained to her team. "Each individual AI solution is valuable, but the real breakthroughs come from understanding the patterns that emerge when they work together at scale.

This realization would become crucial as they moved from scaling AI to leveraging it for innovation, a journey that would require new ways of thinking about how technology and human insight combine to create value.

Turning Scale into Innovation (Section 2)

Once AI moves beyond pilots and becomes embedded across the enterprise, a new challenge emerges: how to capture the unexpected value AI generates at scale. This section explores how leaders like Sarah use visualization not only to execute with clarity, but to uncover, connect, and accelerate innovation across systems.

The Innovation Challenge: AI's True Value Emerges at Scale

Most organizations approach AI deployment with a clear end state in mind: automate this process, optimize that workflow, reduce these costs. But Sarah was discovering a counter-intuitive truth: AI's most significant value often emerges after deployment, in ways no one initially predicted.

At CSIG, this pattern kept repeating. Their claims' processing AI was doing its intended job: accelerating approvals and reducing errors. But it was also identifying fraud patterns they hadn't known existed. Their customer service AI was successfully reducing wait times, but more importantly, it was revealing service gaps in their product offerings that no one had previously identified.

"We're seeing compound effects," Sarah explained to her leadership team. "When multiple AI solutions operate at scale, they create value in unexpected ways. The challenge isn't just implementing AI; it's systematically capturing and amplifying these emerging innovations."

Creating Compound Effects: How Scaling AI Unlocks Innovation

Sarah's team began documenting these "AI network effects" - cases where scaling AI in one area created value elsewhere. The pattern was clear: AI solutions, once embedded deeply enough in business processes, started reshaping decisions far beyond their original scope.

For example:

- Their claims approval AI wasn't just processing claims faster; it was identifying patterns that led to the creation of entirely new fraud prevention protocols.
- Their customer service AI wasn't just reducing wait times; it was surfacing insights that drove the development of new insurance products.
- Their cost optimization AI wasn't just reducing expenses; it was revealing opportunities for dynamic pricing models they hadn't considered possible.

Visualization Tools for Amplifying AI-Driven Innovation

To help stakeholders see and act on AI's expanding impact, Sarah's team developed three key visualization approaches:

- **Innovation Pattern Maps**

  Simple, compelling visualizations showing how AI solutions interact and create unexpected value. For example:
  - Heatmaps showing where multiple AI systems were creating compound effects
  - Flow diagrams revealing how insights from one AI system sparked improvements in others
  - Impact trees showing how single AI implementations branched into multiple value streams

- **Cross-System Value Trackers**

     Visual dashboards that captured and displayed connections between different AI implementations:

  - Before/after comparisons showing combined impact
  - Connection diagrams highlighting synergies between AI systems
  - Visual ROI tracking across interconnected AI initiatives

- **Opportunity Spotlights**

     Dynamic visualizations that helped teams identify and communicate new AI opportunities:

  - Visual highlights of emerging patterns
  - Simple graphics showing potential expansion areas
  - Clear visual stories of how one AI success could lead to another

Chapter Reflection: Flywheel Momentum in Action

AI doesn't create momentum. Leaders do.

Driving business impact with AI demands more than technology. It requires leaders to turn complexity into clarity, clarity into action, and action into momentum. This chapter explored how leaders activate the AI Performance Flywheel, using visualization, orchestration, and scale to unlock AI's full potential.

- **Visualization Creates Clarity and Fuels Action**

     Visualization breaks down complexity, making AI's impact visible and actionable. It turns technical insights into business speak, helping teams see how AI connects to real-world decisions. When leaders use visualization to highlight opportunities and risks, alignment happens faster, skepticism turns into engagement, and AI gains momentum across the organization.

- **Orchestration Keeps AI Efforts Aligned and Moving Forward**

     AI efforts don't succeed in isolation. Without coordination, initiatives compete for resources, create silos, and slow progress. Orchestration ensures AI efforts work together, aligning priorities, governance, and execution. Instead of disconnected projects, AI becomes a cohesive strategic enabler that builds momentum with each success.

- **Scale Transforms AI into an Engine for Discovery and Innovation**

     At scale, AI shifts from optimizing workflows to uncovering new opportunities. As more systems connect, unexpected patterns emerge, revealing insights that aren't visible in isolated deployments. Efficiency gains turn into strategic advantages, and AI moves beyond automation into a continuous driver of business growth and innovation.

Connecting the Dots: The AI Performance Flywheel in Action

Scaling AI happens when organizations activate the AI Performance Flywheel. With a strong Foundation in place and Execution momentum propelling progress, the Scale and Innovation Momentum phases accelerate AI's impact. By leveraging visualization tools, multi-effort orchestration practices, and the insights uncovered through scaled AI efforts, organizations create a self-sustaining cycle of increasing returns.

It starts with clear visualization, making complex AI relationships understandable and turning technical details into actionable business insights. When leaders can see AI's impact holistically, they make better decisions, secure stakeholder buy-in, and turn skepticism into engagement.

With this clarity, strong orchestration becomes possible. AI initiatives across different departments and maturity levels are no longer siloed but aligned into a coordinated strategy. Governance improves, resources are optimized, and AI projects feed into each other, rather than competing for attention.

As AI reaches scale, its full innovation potential emerges. What started as isolated efficiency gains evolves into strategic advantages, unlocking patterns and insights that were previously invisible. AI doesn't just optimize existing processes; it creates new opportunities that compound over time, accelerating growth and competitive differentiation.

This flywheel effect ensures that AI isn't just another tool; it becomes an engine for continuous business reinvention, where each phase amplifies the next. Organizations that master this shift don't just scale AI; they turn AI at scale into a force for sustained innovation, new business value creation, and long-term competitive advantage.

Key Questions for Leaders

To drive business impact with AI, leaders need to balance tactical execution with strategic vision. These questions help assess both immediate scaling challenges and emerging opportunities for innovation:

Scaling Challenges
- What barriers prevent AI from expanding beyond successful pilots?

- Where do misalignments exist between AI capabilities and business processes?
- How can visualization tools reveal hidden obstacles to scale?

Innovation Opportunities

- How can AI move beyond efficiency to enable new products, or even new business models?
- What unexpected patterns and insights have your AI solutions revealed?
- Are you capturing and acting on these emerging opportunities?

The Big Idea

AI success isn't measured by how much you implement; it's measured by how well AI is connected, scaled, and turned into a continuous source of business value.

Instead of asking "How do we scale AI?," leaders should ask, "What new possibilities does AI reveal?"

Companies that master this evolution don't just scale AI; they turn AI at scale into lasting competitive advantage.

Final Field Test: Sarah's AI Flywheel Comes Full Circle

Sarah grabbed her markers and started fresh on the whiteboard. No PowerPoint today. No polished presentations. Just her, three colors of markers, and a room full of executives ready to tackle their next big AI challenge.

They had seen this before. Over the past few months, Sarah's sketches, data maps, AI maturity grids, feedback loops, and dozens of other visual tools had helped them cut through complexity, align priorities, and turn scattered AI projects into real business impact. Whether diagnosing roadblocks, orchestrating scale, or uncovering new opportunities, visualization had become their most powerful tool for making AI work.

Today, they would use it again, not just to reflect on where they had been, but to map out where they needed to go next.

"Before we talk about what's next," Sarah said, drawing three rough circles, "let's map out what we've actually built." Inside each, she scrawled:

- "Claims AI: Working!"
- "Customer Service AI: Getting There"
- "Risk AI: Just Started"

The CFO shifted in his seat. He still wasn't comfortable with Sarah's rough visualization style. But he had stopped asking for "cleaner" slides months ago, especially after her messy data reality maps had exposed critical process gaps that had been costing them millions.

Sarah drew dotted lines between the circles. "Here's where it gets interesting." She started filling in the spaces where the circles overlapped.

"Claims is catching fraud patterns – great. But look what happened when we connected it to Risk." She scribbled "!!!" in the overlap and then added: "Found 3 new risk signals?"

The CTO leaned forward. "Hold on. Are those from last week's anomaly report?"

"Exactly." Sarah handed him a marker. "Help me show them what else we found."

The CTO circled the overlap and added: "Predicting fraud BEFORE claims are filed?"

The Risk Manager stood up. "Wait. If Claims is catching early fraud patterns and Risk is adjusting models faster. . .does that mean we're pricing policies wrong?"

Sarah tapped the center of the diagram. "Not just pricing them wrong. We've been underpricing low-risk customers *and* losing high-value customers we should have saved."

The CFO sat up straight. "Are you saying AI is identifying revenue leakage?"

Sarah nodded. "We didn't build AI to fix pricing. But AI at scale doesn't just optimize processes; it uncovers patterns we didn't know to look for."

A pause. Then the Customer Service VP pointed at the board.

"Hold on. Are those retention signals the same ones that flagged VIP customers for special handling?"

Sarah underlined the connection. "They are. And," she added an arrow, "customers in that segment renewed at double the normal rate."

The CFO exhaled sharply. "Show me the numbers."

Scaling Creates Opportunity. . .and Risk

Sarah grabbed a fresh section of whiteboard and sketched a before-and-after timeline:

Before:

- Three separate AI projects = Three separate results
- Fraud detection stayed in Claims
- Risk modeling adjusted too late
- Customer Service flagged issues reactively

Now:

- Claims catches fraud → Risk adjusts models in real-time
- Risk spots pricing gaps → Customer Service retains high-value customers
- Customer Service feedback → Claims gets smarter, detecting trends earlier

She circled everything. "We're not just connecting systems. We're creating business impact."

The CFO, still processing, leaned back. "This is powerful. But if we scale this further - more systems, more connections - it could get. . . chaotic."

Sarah pulled out a red marker. "Exactly. That's what we need to map next. Where does scale create risk?"

She drew a cloud labeled "Scaling Risks?"

The CTO grabbed the marker first. "Data bottlenecks." He drew thick red knots between AI systems. "More connections mean more data flow. We're already hitting limits."

The Risk Manager added a red outline around the diagram. "Governance gaps." He underlined the problem. "Every new AI connection needs oversight. Who's making sure this doesn't spiral?"

The Customer Service VP sketched wavy red lines. "Timing. If AI expands too fast in one area but lags in another, it creates friction instead of efficiency."

Sarah let the concerns fill the board. This was the power of visualization: it made risks visible without making them overwhelming.

"Okay," she said, pulling out a green marker, "now let's map solutions. Where do we already have answers?"

The CTO drew a bold green line through his data bottleneck. "We're already building better data pipelines between Claims and Risk. We can reuse that framework to connect other systems."

The Risk Manager marked green checkmarks next to governance risks. "We built an oversight model for Claims AI. It actually scales well; we just need to expand it."

The Customer Service VP added green steps. "What if we match rollout speed to where AI creates the fastest returns?"

Sarah watched as the green solutions started balancing the red risks. The messy diagram was telling a new story, not just about problems, but about how to solve them together.

Scaling AI Is About Discovery, Not Just Expansion

The CFO tapped the overlapping circles again. "Hold on. You marked some of these connections with stars earlier. What do those mean?"

Sarah smiled. "Those are the discoveries we never planned for."

She underlined them:

- New fraud detection patterns
- Unexpected retention insights
- Hidden pricing signals

"Every time we connect AI systems, new patterns emerge. But don't take my word for it. Let's trace one. See these fraud detection patterns?" She taps a starred connection on the board. "We only found them after linking Claims AI and Risk AI. And over here," she points to Customer Service, "this retention spike? AI flagged it before we even knew it mattered. The more we connect, the more AI reveals."

The CFO's face changed. "So when we scale. . ."

". . .We're not just scaling what we know. We're scaling our ability to discover what we don't know yet."

Sarah finished his thought, circling the entire whiteboard.

From Theory to Action in Two Weeks The CFO exhaled. "This is the clearest view of our AI future I've seen yet." He turned to Sarah. "What happens next?"

Sarah grabbed a fresh marker. "We strengthen these AI connections we mapped today. Then," she added dotted lines, "we leave space for what we'll discover next."

The room felt different now. The skepticism had turned into focused energy.

The CFO smirked. "Send me a photo of this before you erase it."

Sarah smiled. Same time next week? She was already reaching for a fresh marker.

Lessons from Sarah: Turning AI Complexity into Momentum

Sarah never positions herself as an AI expert with all the answers, because AI isn't about having the right answers; it's about asking the right questions. She believes wholeheartedly in "Show AI—Don't Tell It." She doesn't just explain AI's potential; she demonstrates it.

Whether through interactive dashboards, real-time insights, or hands-on decision-making tools, she puts AI where it creates business impact: in the hands of the people who drive the business. She understands that AI works best when humans lead the way, shaping its design, validating its decisions, and uncovering new opportunities together.

Her leadership doesn't aim to force AI adoption; it's aims to reveal AI's impact. Her ability to turn fragmented AI projects into enterprise-wide momentum comes down to five key leadership moves.

Move #1: She Puts AI in the Hands of Decision-Makers   AI can't create impact from the sidelines. Sarah ensures that leaders don't just read about AI insights; they interact with them. Whether through data visualizations, live dashboards, or scenario simulations, she turns AI outputs into decision-making tools that enhance, rather than replace, human judgment.

By designing AI for collaborative intelligence, she makes complex patterns intuitive, helping decision-makers not just understand AI, but trust and act on it. She ensures AI projects are aligned with measurable business goals such as cost savings, revenue growth, or competitive advantage to demonstrate tangible business value.

Move #2: She Connects AI Systems to Unlock Compounding Value
AI works best when it's connected, and so do people. Sarah doesn't allow AI initiatives to remain siloed. Instead, she reveals hidden links between systems, ensuring that:

- Data flows seamlessly across departments
- Insights get shared, not trapped in single-use models
- AI-driven discoveries build on each other, compounding their impact

By doing this, she turns AI from a collection of disconnected projects into a force multiplier for business growth. She also works with AI governance teams to ensure that AI systems are being used responsibly, reducing risks related to bias, compliance, and security.

Move #3: She Orchestrates AI Like a Conductor, Not a Controller   AI success is about orchestration, not rigid, top-down control. Sarah sees AI as a symphony, where teams, processes, and technology must work in harmony.
Instead of forcing AI adoption through mandates, she:

- Aligns teams around shared business goals
- Builds adaptability into AI strategies
- Fosters iterative learning, where AI adapts to business needs, not the other way around.

She scales not just automation, but Human + AI interactions, ensuring that people and AI evolve together, rather than AI dictating the pace. By embedding AI governance practices, she ensures these initiatives remain transparent, fair, and accountable.

Move #4: She Designs for Discovery, Not Just Efficiency   Most organizations use AI to optimize what they already do. Sarah goes further. She designs AI as a discovery engine.

She helps teams shift from "How can AI automate this?" to "What new opportunities can AI uncover?" This mindset opens doors to emerging trends that no one is watching, hidden market gaps, and AI-driven business models.

By embracing AI as a tool for exploration, Sarah ensures that AI doesn't just make the business more efficient; it makes it more innovative.

Move #5: She Turns AI into a Continuous Learning Loop AI isn't a project; it's a living system that must evolve. Sarah makes sure AI doesn't just generate insights, but learns from real-world feedback. Then, she partners with fellow leaders to ensure that AI innovation aligns with long-term enterprise strategy rather than short-term experimentation.

She builds feedback loops where:

- AI refines itself based on new data
- Teams challenge and validate AI's outputs
- AI-driven decisions improve over time

Most importantly, she empowers people to shape AI's evolution by integrating strong governance frameworks that oversee AI learning, mitigate risks, and drive continuous innovation. This structured approach ensures that humans and AI collaborate, adapt, and improve together, compounding business value with every iteration. Sarah's leadership style isn't "I'm the expert. Do what I say." She's a visionary, a facilitator, and a change agent who guides others in seeing AI's impact firsthand. AI doesn't drive momentum; leaders do. Whether through visualization, orchestration, or scaling AI into innovation, she puts the AI Performance Flywheel into motion, ensuring AI isn't just implemented, but continuously refined for compounding business impact.

How will you activate AI momentum in your organization?

Your Turn: Turn Scale into a Discovery Engine

Successfully scaling AI across an enterprise is like conducting an orchestra. Every section must play in harmony. A few isolated AI projects might show promise, but true impact comes when those scattered wins evolve into a coordinated, enterprise-wide force.

The good news? Visualization is the conductor's baton. It turns fragmented efforts into visible momentum, helping teams connect initiatives, spotlight compound effects, and surface untapped opportunities.

Use these questions to diagnose your scale friction and build a visualization strategy that drives unified, enterprise-wide momentum. Whether you're hitting walls with coordination, missing innovation signals, or struggling to sustain progress, these prompts will help you shift from scattered experiments to compounding impact.

Find Your Scale Friction:
- Where are AI projects getting stuck or scaling unevenly?
- Which teams are working in silos instead of in sync?
- What valuable insights might be hiding between disconnected systems?

Use Visualization to Connect the Dots:
- Which visual tools would reveal cross-functional impact (e.g., compound effect maps, orchestration dashboards)?
- How can you show leadership the risks of fragmented scale and the rewards of alignment?
- What's one quick win that could demonstrate the value of scaling with visibility?

Shift from Expansion to Innovation:
- What new insights has AI surfaced that weren't part of the original plan?
- How can you turn those insights into new offerings, services, or business models?
- Where can you embed AI feedback loops to spot the next big opportunity before anyone else?

Call to Action: Your Scale Starts Here

You've now seen how visualization fuels momentum across execution, scale, and innovation. Let's turn that insight into action:

1. Complete the **AI Performance Flywheel Momentum Checklist** (see Appendix E).
2. Choose your first visualization challenge to tackle.
3. Map your next 90 days of scale progress.
4. Start your flywheel, and build toward exponential impact.

   "Your visualization journey starts with one insight that changes how people see the system. What will yours be?"

Pro Tip

You don't scale AI for efficiency. You scale it for discovery.

Final Thoughts: Making AI Momentum Self-Sustaining

Every organization scaling AI hits the same challenge: fragmentation. Not because teams resist collaboration, but because they can't always see beyond their immediate objectives. That's why I built visualization strategies into the AI Performance Flywheel. When teams can *see* how their work connects, silos dissolve, alignment builds, and momentum compounds.

The companies I see thriving with AI don't treat it as a one-time implementation; they treat it as a living system. Scaling AI expands value. Innovating with AI multiplies it. And visualization is the connective tissue - the tool that reveals patterns, unlocks alignment, and keeps progress moving.

The most powerful visualizations don't just inform. They accelerate. They transform abstract concepts into shared conviction, and that's what turns momentum into sustained business impact.

Conclusion: Lead Boldly. Show What's Possible

As you reach the end of this book, I hope you're not just thinking differently about AI. I hope that you're ready to lead it differently.

I wrote this for bold, forward-thinking leaders who don't want more theory. You want traction. You want transformation. You want real business impact.

Throughout this book, I've shared the **Bold AI Leadership Model** that I've developed and tested through years of research and hundreds of real-world AI implementations. I've shown you how to think, plan, and act with clarity, even when the path feels complex. You've learned how to:

- Anchor AI in business value, not technical novelty
- Build cultures where curiosity, experimentation, and trust drive momentum
- Treat data as strategic capital, not digital clutter
- Communicate visually to gain buy-in and accelerate execution
- Scale AI into a system that doesn't just automate but continuously uncovers, learns, and unlocks new innovations

And most importantly, I've shown you how to **stop talking about AI, and start showing it**.

In my experience, that's what changes everything. When you visualize the opportunity, when you reveal the connections, when you help others see the impact, people engage. They align. They take action. That's how AI creates real business value.

You don't need to have every answer. But you do need a system. You need the mindset, the strategy, and the tools to lead with confidence, particularly in the face of uncertainty.

That's why I created the **AI Performance Flywheel**: to give you a repeatable way to build momentum, align your organization, and transform curiosity into outcomes.

So here's my challenge to you:

- Start small, but make it visible.
- Don't wait for the perfect moment. Create a momentum moment.

- Use the frameworks in this book to design your next bold move.
- Lead in a way that shows others what's possible.

Your team is waiting.
Your stakeholders are watching.
And your future with AI is unwritten.
Don't just talk about AI.
Show it. Lead it. Build it.
Let the results you *show* speak for themselves.
I'll be right here, cheering you on.

—Dr. Lisa

PART 4

Appendices

APPENDIX A:
Visualization Tool Example for Business Value

How to Use This Appendix

This appendix introduces the **Customer Experience Pulse**: a dynamic visualization tool designed to help leaders see, measure, and communicate the real-time impact of AI on customer behavior. Use it to map AI interventions across the customer journey, monitor key metrics, and demonstrate how AI directly drives business value. Whether you're aiming to boost engagement, improve conversion, or align teams around customer success, this tool helps turn insight into action faster and with greater confidence. To illustrate how leaders can visualize AI's impact on customer experience, the Customer Experience Pulse is a powerful tool. In brief, it provides a real-time view of how AI interactions shape customer behavior, enabling informed decisions, team alignment, and accelerated implementation.

When transforming customer experiences through AI, leaders often struggle to demonstrate tangible impact across complex, multichannel journeys. Traditional metrics and static reports fail to capture the dynamic nature of AI-enhanced customer interactions. This is where the Customer Experience Pulse comes in - a dynamic visualization tool that brings AI's impact on customer behavior to life.

Think of it as a real-time mission control for your customer experience. Just as flight controllers monitor multiple systems simultaneously to ensure a successful mission, the Customer Experience Pulse enables leaders to track, analyze, and optimize AI-driven customer interactions across every touchpoint. This comprehensive view helps teams identify opportunities, address issues proactively, and measure the concrete business value of AI initiatives.

Customer Experience Pulse

Purpose:
Track and visualize how AI interactions shape customer behavior and business outcomes across the entire customer journey.

Key Elements

Data Points:

- Journey interaction metrics
  - Click patterns and navigation flows
  - Time spent per touchpoint
  - Abandonment points
  - Conversion paths by product category
  - AI recommendation acceptance rates
- Business impact metrics
  - Revenue per customer segment
  - Customer lifetime value trends
  - Return on AI investment
  - Market share movement

Display Format:

- Interactive journey map
  - Real-time customer flow visualization
  - Hotspots showing engagement intensity
  - AI intervention points highlighted
  - Outcome tracking at each stage
- Performance indicators
  - Success metrics (green)
  - Warning signals (yellow)
  - Critical issues (red)
  - Trending indicators (↑↓→)

Update Frequency:

- **Real-time:** Customer behavior metrics
- **Daily:** Performance aggregates
- **Weekly:** Trend analysis
- **Monthly:** Strategic insights

Sample Metrics

Engagement:
- **Click-through rate:** 25–35% target
- **Average session duration:** 8–12 minutes
- **Pages per session:** 4–6 target
- **Return visitor rate:** >40%

Conversion:
- **Cart completion:** >65% target
- **AI-influenced sales:** >30% of revenue
- **Average order value:** +15% vs. non-AI
- **Cross-sell acceptance:** >25%

Customer Success:
- **First-contact resolution:** >85%
- **CSAT scores:** >4.5/5
- **NPS:** >60
- **Customer effort score:** <2

Implementation Steps

1. Journey mapping
   - Document all customer touchpoints
   - Identify AI intervention opportunities
   - Map current performance baselines
   - Define success metrics
2. Data integration
   - Connect customer interaction data
   - Implement real-time tracking
   - Set up AI performance monitoring
   - Enable cross-channel visibility
3. Visualization setup
   - Design intuitive interface
   - Configure role-based views
   - Enable drill-down capabilities
   - Set up automated alerts

4. Feedback integration
   - Capture customer feedback
   - Monitor AI recommendation quality
   - Track team insights
   - Document improvement opportunities

Common Pitfalls

Data Overload:
- **Solution:** Progressive disclosure
- **Solution:** Role-specific views
- **Solution:** Clear hierarchy of metrics

Context Gaps:
- **Solution:** Include historical trends
- **Solution:** Show competitive benchmarks
- **Solution:** Highlight seasonal patterns

Delayed Response:
- **Solution:** Real-time alert system
- **Solution:** Clear escalation paths
- **Solution:** Automated intervention triggers

Success Indicators

Usage Metrics:
- 90% team adoption rate
- Daily active users trending up
- Positive feedback from stakeholders

Performance Impact:
- Consistent improvement in KPIs
- Reduced customer friction points
- Increased AI-driven revenue

Business Outcomes:
- Higher customer satisfaction
- Improved retention rates
- Growing market share

From Insight to Action

The Customer Experience Pulse transforms abstract customer data into actionable intelligence. By providing a clear, real-time view of how AI shapes customer behavior, it enables leaders to:

1. Make informed decisions
   - Spot emerging trends before they become apparent in traditional reports.
   - Identify high-impact opportunities for AI enhancement.
   - Validate the ROI of AI investments in customer experience.
2. Drive team alignment
   - Create a shared understanding of customer behavior across departments.
   - Enable data-driven discussions about AI strategy.
   - Foster collaboration between technical and business teams.
3. Accelerate implementation
   - Reduce time-to-value for new AI initiatives.
   - Quickly identify and address implementation issues.
   - Scale successful AI solutions with confidence.

Remember, the goal isn't just to collect data; it's to inspire action. When teams can see how AI impacts customer behavior in real-time, they're better equipped to make decisions that drive meaningful business outcomes. The Customer Experience Pulse turns this vision into reality, helping leaders move from insight to impact with speed and confidence.

APPENDIX B: Visualization Tool Example for Speed with Rigor

How to Use This Appendix

This appendix introduces the **AI Trust & Impact Navigator**: a visualization tool that helps leaders balance innovation speed with rigorous oversight. Use it to monitor AI governance, performance, and business outcomes in one clear, integrated view. Whether you're launching new initiatives or scaling existing ones, this tool helps you communicate progress, build stakeholder trust, and maintain compliance without slowing innovation. Follow the steps provided to tailor the Navigator to your organization's needs and keep AI efforts aligned, transparent, and accountable. Trust in AI isn't a box you check; it's something you earn and protect over time. Leaders today are walking a tightrope: pushing innovation forward quickly while ensuring that stakeholders feel confident that it's being done responsibly. The AI Trust & Impact Navigator helps maintain this balance. It shines a light where governance, performance, and business outcomes intersect so that you can move fast without losing control.

This visualization tool serves as your organization's trust hub. Like a pilot's cockpit display that integrates critical flight data, the Navigator combines key trust indicators with performance metrics to ensure your AI initiatives stay on course. It transforms complex governance requirements and impact measurements into clear, actionable insights that help leaders build and maintain trust while delivering business value.

AI Trust & Impact Navigator

Purpose:
Monitor and demonstrate how AI governance, performance, and business impact align to deliver sustainable value while maintaining trust and compliance.

Key Elements

Data Points:

- Performance metrics
  - Processing efficiency rates
  - Model accuracy scores
  - Response time tracking
  - Resource utilization
- Governance metrics
  - Compliance status
  - Risk assessments
  - Data quality indicators
  - Security posture

Display Format:

- Quad-view layout
  - Operational Excellence (top left)
  - Risk & Compliance (top right)
  - Business Impact (bottom left)
  - Trust Indicators (bottom right)
- Status indicators
  - Exceeding targets (green)
  - Meeting targets (yellow)
  - Below targets (red)
  - Insufficient data (gray)

Update Frequency:

- **Real-time:** Operational metrics
- **Daily:** Compliance checks
- **Weekly:** Business impact
- **Monthly:** Trust indicators

Sample Metrics

Operational Excellence:

- **Model accuracy:** >95% target
- **Processing time:** <5 minutes

- **Automation rate:** 60–70%
- **Resource efficiency:** >85%

Risk & Compliance:

- **Compliance score:** >98%
- **Data quality index:** >96%
- **Security status:** All green
- **Audit readiness:** >95%

Business Impact:

- **Cost reduction:** >20% YoY
- **Revenue growth:** >15% YoY
- **ROI:** >3× investment
- **Productivity gain:** >30%

Trust Indicators:

- **Stakeholder confidence:** >4.5/5
- **Employee adoption:** >85%
- **Customer trust score:** >90%
- **Partner satisfaction:** >4/5

Implementation Steps

1. Framework setup
   - Define governance standards
   - Establish performance baselines
   - Set measurement criteria
   - Configure monitoring systems
2. Integration
   - Connect data sources
   - Implement real-time tracking
   - Enable cross-system visibility
   - Set up alert mechanisms
3. Visualization
   - Design intuitive interfaces
   - Create role-based views
   - Enable detailed drilling
   - Configure automated reporting

4. Continuous improvement
- Implement feedback loops
- Monitor emerging risks
- Track improvement initiatives
- Document lessons learned

Common Pitfalls

Governance Gaps:
- **Solution:** Comprehensive compliance mapping
- **Solution:** Regular audit schedules
- **Solution:** Automated compliance checks

Performance Blind Spots:
- **Solution:** End-to-end monitoring
- **Solution:** Leading indicators tracking
- **Solution:** Early warning systems

Trust Erosion:
- **Solution:** Transparent reporting
- **Solution:** Stakeholder engagement
- **Solution:** Proactive communication

Success Indicators

Governance Excellence:
- Zero compliance violations
- High audit readiness
- Strong risk management

Operational Impact:
- Consistent KPI improvement
- Reduced operational costs
- Increased efficiency

Trust Metrics:
- Growing stakeholder confidence
- High adoption rates
- Strong satisfaction scores

Balancing Innovation and Trust

The AI Trust & Impact Navigator bridges the gap between AI governance and business performance. By providing a holistic view of trust metrics alongside operational indicators, it enables leaders to:

1. Build sustainable trust
   - Monitor trust indicators across stakeholder groups.
   - Identify potential trust risks before they escalate.
   - Demonstrate responsible AI deployment.
2. Optimize performance
   - Balance innovation speed with governance requirements.
   - Track the relationship between trust and business impact.
   - Identify opportunities to enhance both simultaneously.
3. Drive accountability
   - Create transparency around AI decisions and outcomes.
   - Enable proactive risk management.
   - Foster a culture of responsible innovation.

The Navigator shows that trust and performance aren't opposing forces; they're complementary elements of successful AI leadership. When organizations can measure and visualize both dimensions simultaneously, they're better equipped to build AI solutions that deliver lasting value while maintaining stakeholder confidence.

This integrated approach to trust and impact measurement helps leaders move beyond compliance-focused governance to create truly sustainable AI initiatives. By making trust visible and measurable, the Navigator transforms it from an abstract concept into a tangible asset that can be actively managed and improved.

APPENDIX C: Visualization Tool Example for Simplicity

How to Use This Appendix

This appendix introduces the **Human + AI Decision Map**: a practical tool designed to help teams visualize how AI supports, not replaces, human decision-making. Use this visualization to clarify roles, build trust, and simplify complex AI workflows for stakeholders across your organization. Whether you're leading operations, managing AI deployment, or supporting change adoption, this tool makes it easy to show where AI adds value and where human input matters most. Follow the implementation steps to map your own collaborative decision flows and demonstrate how AI enhances, not complicates, business outcomes. This tool shows how people and AI work together to make better decisions. Through clear visuals and real examples, it reveals how AI supports human expertise rather than replacing it. Instead of hiding AI's workings in a black box, it shows each step of the process, helping teams understand and trust their AI tools.

Human + AI Decision Map

Purpose:
To visually demonstrate how AI recommendations and human input work together to improve decision-making, optimize processes, and achieve measurable outcomes.

Key Elements

Data Points:

- **AI Outputs:**
  - Key insights or predictions (e.g., risk scores, recommendations, or optimized schedules)
  - AI confidence levels (e.g., "85% certainty")
- **Human Inputs:**
  - Validation feedback (e.g., "recommendation accepted" or "adjustments applied")
  - Contextual overrides or refinements made by experts

Display Format:

- **Collaborative Workflow Layout:**
  - **Left Column:** AI-generated insights, predictions, and recommendations
  - **Right Column:** Human decisions, overrides, and actions based on AI outputs
  - **Central Flow:** The iterative loop of collaboration (e.g., "AI Suggests → Human Validates → AI Refines")
- **Outcome Indicators:**
  - Direct impact metrics (e.g., time saved, costs reduced, or risks mitigated)
  - Visualized as progress bars, icons, or before-and-after comparisons

Visualization Style:

- Dynamic, role-based views tailored to specific users (e.g., executives, operations managers, frontline workers)
- Interactive layers allow users to drill down into the reasoning behind AI insights or explore human feedback loops

Sample Metrics

AI Outputs:

- **Predictions:** "Delivery delay probability: 70%"
- **Recommendations:** "Shift Route A to avoid congestion"
- **Confidence Score:** "85% accuracy"

Human Inputs:

- **Override Rate:** "15% of recommendations adjusted by on-site managers"
- **Validation Feedback:** "90% of suggestions accepted"

Outcome Indicators:

- **Delivery Time Saved:** "15% improvement"
- **Reduction in Downtime:** "20% fewer maintenance incidents"
- **Cost Savings:** "$200,000 annually"

Implementation Steps

1. **Data Integration:**
   - Aggregate AI outputs and human feedback from existing systems.
   - Ensure real-time data synchronization for accurate decision tracking.
2. **Mapping the Workflow:**
   - Identify key decision points where AI and human collaboration occurs.
   - Outline the flow of AI suggestions, human validation, and resulting actions.
3. **Visual Design:**
   - Use clear, intuitive visuals (e.g., icons, arrows, and timelines) to map the decision process.
   - Incorporate role-specific views to show how AI recommendations align with stakeholder needs.
4. **Iterative Refinement:**
   - Continuously refine the map based on user feedback.
   - Add new metrics or decision points as the process evolves.

Common Pitfalls

1. **Overloading Users with Details:**
   - **Solution:** Highlight key insights and actionable steps, leaving technical details for optional drill-downs.
2. **Neglecting the Human Role:**
   - **Solution:** Clearly show where human expertise enhances or refines AI outputs to foster trust in the collaboration.
3. **Lack of Real-World Context:**
   - **Solution:** Anchor the map in relatable scenarios or case studies, ensuring stakeholders can see its relevance to their work.

Success Indicators

1. **Trust in AI Outputs:**
   - High validation rates and low override rates
2. **Improved Decision Outcomes:**
   - Quantifiable metrics like time saved, costs reduced, or accuracy improved
3. **Stakeholder Confidence:**
   - Positive feedback from users across roles and functions

Bridging Simplicity and Collaboration

The **Human + AI Decision Map** is more than a visualization tool; it's a storytelling device that showcases the tangible value of the human + AI partnership.

How It Builds Simplicity:

1. **Clear Communication:** Transforms complex AI outputs into actionable, easy-to-understand insights
2. **Trust and Transparency:** Highlights the interplay between human judgment and AI logic, building confidence in the decision process
3. **Actionable Outcomes:** Connects AI recommendations to measurable improvements, ensuring stakeholders see the real-world impact

This decision map shows how humans and AI work together, turning complex data into clear actions people can trust. It's a practical example of how Bold AI Leadership helps teams embrace AI's power while valuing human expertise.

APPENDIX D: Visualization Tool Example for Human-Centricity

How to Use This Appendix

This appendix provides a practical example of how to visualize AI's impact through a human-centric lens. Use the **Human Impact Visualization** to highlight the real, measurable ways AI improves employee experience, enhances productivity, and supports organizational goals. Whether you're presenting to executives, engaging cross-functional teams, or tracking AI adoption, this tool helps you turn abstract AI benefits into a compelling visual narrative that drives trust, transparency, and alignment. Follow the implementation steps to customize the visualization for your organization and use the success indicators to track its effectiveness over time. The Human Impact Visualization provides a clear, engaging representation of how AI initiatives enhance human potential and improve organizational outcomes. By highlighting metrics that matter to employees, leadership, and stakeholders, this tool emphasizes the tangible benefits of Human + AI collaboration while fostering trust and alignment.

Human Impact Visualization

Purpose:
To visually communicate the tangible effects of AI on employee roles, team dynamics, and organizational performance, ensuring alignment with human-centric principles.

Key Elements

Data Points:

Employee Benefits:

Time saved through automation (e.g., "12 hours saved per team member weekly")

Increased capacity for innovation and strategic thinking (e.g., "25% more time dedicated to creative projects")

Engagement Metrics:

Adoption rates of AI tools (e.g., "% of employees using AI solutions daily")

Employee satisfaction scores related to AI integration

Organizational Outcomes:

Reduction in manual errors (e.g., "Data errors reduced by 40%")

Speed improvements in decision-making processes (e.g., "50% faster project approvals")

Visualization Format:

Outcome Representation:

Progress arcs or before-and-after comparisons showing improvements post-AI implementation

Infographics presenting key achievements in simple, digestible formats

Interactive Layers:

Touchpoints for exploring team-specific impacts (e.g., by department or role)

Real-world quotes from employees sharing their experiences with AI

Impact Highlights:

Visual overlays emphasizing critical metrics, such as time savings or productivity gains

Sample Metrics

Employee Benefits:

Time Saved: "12 hours per week saved on manual data entry"

Increased Strategic Focus: "20% of employee time redirected to high-value projects"

Engagement Metrics:

AI Adoption: "85% of employees regularly use AI tools in their workflows"

Employee Confidence: "90% report feeling equipped to use AI effectively after training"

Organizational Outcomes:

Error Reduction: "Manual processing errors reduced by 35%"

Decision-Making Speed: "Critical decisions made 40% faster post-AI implementation"

Implementation Steps

Define Key Metrics:

Collaborate with department leads to identify the most relevant and impactful metrics.

Ensure metrics reflect both employee experiences and organizational outcomes.

Aggregate and Process Data:

Collect data from AI tools, feedback surveys, and performance reports.

Regularly update insights to maintain accuracy and relevance.

Design the Visualization:

Use clear, human-friendly formats such as infographics, progress arcs, or heatmaps.

Include quotes or testimonials to add a personal narrative to the data.

Iterate Based on Feedback:

Present the visualization to pilot groups and incorporate their feedback for improvement.

Expand its use across departments, tailoring content as needed.

Common Pitfalls

Overcomplicating Data:

Solution: Focus on high-impact metrics that resonate with employees and leadership.

Neglecting Personal Stories:

Solution: Include real-life examples and testimonials to connect the data to individual experiences.

Infrequent Updates:

Solution: Establish a regular cadence for refreshing metrics and ensuring they reflect current performance.

Success Indicators

Higher Engagement:

Increased adoption and positive employee feedback on AI integration

Improved Productivity:

Quantifiable gains in efficiency, such as time saved and error reduction

Leadership Confidence:

Clear evidence of AI's contribution to strategic goals, driving continued investment.

Showcasing human impact with AI: visualizing what matters.

The Human Impact Visualization serves as a storytelling device that brings the benefits of AI to life. By combining data-driven insights with personal narratives and intuitive visuals, this approach ensures stakeholders at all levels understand and appreciate the transformative power of Human + AI collaboration.

How It Embodies Human-Centricity:

Empowers Employees: Demonstrates how AI supports their roles, fostering trust and adoption

Promotes Transparency: Provides a clear, relatable view of AI's impact across the organization

Encourages Collaboration: Highlights the partnership between AI tools and human expertise, reinforcing the synergy that drives compounding success

This visualization inspires confidence, builds alignment, and showcases the essence of human-centric AI in action, driving measurable results while amplifying human potential.

APPENDIX E: The AI Performance Flywheel

Four-Phase Momentum Check

Use this guide to assess your organization's position in the AI journey and identify the key actions needed to build and sustain momentum. The AI Performance Flywheel is a system for turning AI potential into measurable business results by moving through four distinct phases. Find your current phase to see what to focus on—and what red flags to avoid.

Phase 1: Foundation Momentum Primary Goal: Convert skepticism into trust and build credibility with an undeniable early win.

Key Actions/Checklist	Red Flags (You Might Be Stuck If. . .)
✓ Identify a high-impact, low-risk business problem that AI can solve.	Your AI initiative is stuck in debate with no clear return on investment (ROI).
✓ Secure stakeholder buy-in with clear, measurable success metrics.	There is significant resistance or skepticism from key stakeholders.
✓ Showcase the pilot's success with visual, impossible-to-ignore proof of value.	You lack clean, accessible data for your chosen use case.

Phase 2: Execution Momentum Primary Goal: Turn a successful pilot into a reliable, integrated part of daily operations.

Key Actions/Checklist	Red Flags (You Might Be Stuck If. . .)
✓ Move the AI solution from a controlled pilot to a standardized daily workflow.	User adoption by frontline teams is low.
✓ Establish robust feedback loops to ensure the AI continuously learns and improves.	The AI is producing inconsistent or unreliable results.

Key Actions/Checklist	Red Flags (You Might Be Stuck If. . .)
✓ Implement change management and training to build trust and drive adoption.	The new AI workflow is causing disruption or confusion.

Phase 3: Scale Momentum Primary Goal: Expand departmental success into enterprise-wide impact without creating silos.

Key Actions/Checklist	Red Flags (You Might Be Stuck If. . .)
✓ Expand proven AI solutions into adjacent, high-potential business units.	AI projects are siloed and disconnected from one another.
✓ Establish a cross-functional governance model to align priorities and standards.	Momentum stalls after the initial department rollout.
✓ Standardize data infrastructure and share best practices to accelerate adoption.	There are resource constraints or quality inconsistencies as you expand.

Phase 4: Innovation Momentum Primary Goal: Embed AI as a continuous, self-driving engine for business growth and competitive advantage.

Key Actions/Checklist	Red Flags (You Might Be Stuck If. . .)
✓ Empower teams to proactively identify and suggest new AI use cases.	There is a lack of new ideas coming from the front lines.
✓ Create a formal, lightweight process for rapid experimentation and learning.	Engagement with AI tools or initiatives is declining.
✓ Embed Human+AI augmentation principles into your long-term business strategy.	AI is seen as a cost center to be managed, not a growth driver to invest in.

Ready to dive deeper? *Access a comprehensive, multipage version of this diagnostic checklist and other exclusive book resources at* **DrLisa .ai/snt-book-resources**.

APPENDIX F: Selecting the Right Visualization Tool

Visualizations are powerful tools for translating complex AI concepts into tangible, actionable insights for your organization. However, not all visualization approaches serve the same purpose or audience. This guide is designed to help you select the most effective visualization tools for specific business challenges, organizational contexts, and audiences you'll encounter throughout your AI adoption journey.

The right visualization can transform confusion into clarity, resistance into support, and abstract potential into concrete action. Rather than presenting an overwhelming catalog of options, this appendix organizes visualization tools according to the leadership challenges they best address. Whether you need to build initial buy-in with skeptical executives, overcome resistance from frontline managers, scale successful pilots across the organization, or drive continuous innovation, you'll find targeted visualization approaches tailored to your specific needs.

Use this guide as a practical reference as you navigate each phase of AI adoption. By matching the right visualization tool to your current challenge, you'll significantly increase your ability to communicate effectively, align stakeholders, and accelerate your organization's AI transformation.

When to Use Each Visualization Approach

The following visualization tools are organized by common leadership scenarios you'll encounter during your AI journey. Each section pairs specific business challenges with the visualization approaches most likely to help you succeed. Start by identifying your current challenge, then select the visualization tools most relevant to your specific situation and audience. See also Table F.1 and Table F.2.

For Building Initial Buy-In (Foundation Momentum)

- **Demos:** Create interactive demonstrations of AI capabilities to show immediate value and potential. Most effective for skeptical stakeholders who need to "see it to believe it."

- **Interactive ROI Heatmaps:** Visualize financial impact across different departments, processes, or timeframes. Particularly compelling for CFOs and financial decision-makers.

- **Infographics:** Distill complex AI concepts into accessible visual narratives that explain the "why" behind AI initiatives. Ideal for broad organizational communication.

- **AI-Powered Explainer Videos:** Use AI-generated content to create engaging explanations of complex concepts. Perfect for asynchronous communication across distributed teams.

For Overcoming Resistance (Execution Momentum)

- **Before-and-After Comparisons:** Create clear visual contrasts between current state and AI-enhanced future state. Highly effective for demonstrating tangible improvements.

- **Bias Detection Maps:** Visualize where potential biases exist in data or algorithms and how they're being addressed. Critical for addressing ethical concerns transparently.

- **Journey Simulations:** Create interactive walkthroughs showing how AI transforms specific workflows or customer experiences. Helps stakeholders envision concrete benefits.

- **Stakeholder Impact Maps:** Illustrate how AI initiatives affect different stakeholders across the organization. Useful for identifying and addressing specific concerns.

For Scaling AI Adoption (Scale Momentum)

- **Digital Twins:** Develop virtual models of processes, systems, or environments to test AI implementations safely. Ideal for complex operational environments.

- **AI Governance Flowcharts:** Map decision rights, oversight mechanisms, and accountability structures. Essential for establishing trust in expanded AI deployments.

- **Flowcharts:** Document AI-enabled processes with clear decision points and handoffs. Helps standardize operations as AI scales across the organization.

- **Real-Time Predictive Dashboards:** Create live monitoring tools that showcase AI impact on KPIs. Builds confidence through continuous visibility into performance.

For Driving Innovation (Innovation Momentum)

- **Gaming Interfaces:** Develop interactive, game-like experiences to explore AI capabilities. Stimulates creative thinking and engagement with new possibilities.
- **AR/VR/MR Experiences:** Create immersive environments to interact with AI and data in new ways. Powerful for envisioning transformative future states.
- **Generative AI Visuals:** Use AI to create novel visualizations that inspire new thinking. Particularly effective for ideation sessions and innovation workshops.
- **AI-Driven Simulations:** Build scenario planning tools that show potential futures based on different strategic choices. Valuable for long-term strategic planning.

For Technical Audiences

- **3D Data Landscapes:** Visualize complex data relationships and patterns in three dimensions. Helps data scientists and engineers identify insights and anomalies.
- **Algorithmic Artifacts:** Create visual representations of how AI makes decisions. Essential for debugging, improving, and explaining AI systems.
- **Bias Detection Maps:** Highlight potential areas of bias in datasets or algorithms. Critical for responsible AI development and addressing technical debt early.
- **Heatmaps/Geographic Maps:** Visualize data patterns across physical or conceptual spaces. Useful for identifying clusters, outliers, and regional trends.

For Executive Leadership

- **Interactive ROI Heatmaps:** Provide dynamic financial impact visualizations that executives can manipulate to test assumptions. Builds confidence in investment decisions.
- **Stakeholder Impact Maps:** Show how AI initiatives affect different parts of the organization and value chain. Helps executives understand comprehensive business impact.
- **Real-Time Predictive Dashboards:** Deliver ongoing performance monitoring with predictive alerts. Gives executives confidence that AI systems are delivering expected value.
- **Before-and-After Comparisons:** Create clear visual narratives showing measurable improvements. Particularly effective for board presentations and investor communications.

TABLE F.1 Matching Visualization Tools to Your AI Maturity Stage

AI Maturity Stage	Recommended Visualization Tools	Why These Work
Foundation Momentum	Demos Infographics AI-powered explainer videos Before-and-after comparisons	Focus on building understanding, establishing the case for change, and visualizing potential value
Execution Momentum	Journey simulations Flowcharts Stakeholder impact maps Bias detection maps	Emphasize process integration, operational details, and addressing specific stakeholder concerns
Scale Momentum	Digital twins AI governance flowcharts Real-time predictive dashboards Heatmaps/geographic maps	Support standardization, governance, and organization-wide visibility into AI performance
Innovation Momentum	AR/VR/MR experiences Gaming interfaces Generative AI visuals AI-driven simulations	Enable exploration of new possibilities, creative thinking, and future-focused strategic planning

TABLE F.2 Selecting Tools Based on Communication Challenge

If You Need To. . .	Consider Using. . .	Example Implementation
Explain complex AI concepts to non-technical stakeholders	Infographics Demos AI-powered explainer videos	An infographic showing how machine learning works using a familiar business process as an example
Demonstrate financial impact	Interactive ROI Heatmaps Real-time predictive dashboards Before-and-after comparisons	A dynamic dashboard showing cost savings across departments with the ability to adjust variables
Address ethical concerns	Bias detection maps AI governance flowcharts Stakeholder impact maps	A visual map showing how AI decisions are monitored, audited, and corrected when necessary

If You Need To...	Consider Using...	Example Implementation
Build momentum for broader adoption	Journey simulations Digital twins Gaming interfaces	An interactive simulation allowing employees to experience how AI will transform their specific workflow
Foster innovation	AR/VR/MR experiences Generative AI visuals AI-driven simulations	A virtual reality environment where teams can collaboratively explore AI-generated business scenarios

This guide helps you select the right visualization approach based on your specific situation, audience, and objectives. Rather than overwhelming your stakeholders with data, these targeted visualization strategies help you communicate effectively at each stage of your AI journey.

Access the visualization tools, checklists, and other exclusive book resources at **DrLisa.ai/snt-book-resources**.

Acknowledgments

I am deeply grateful to the many brilliant minds and kind hearts who helped shape this book. Thank you to my clients, who entrusted me to guide their AI journeys and taught me just as much in return. To my mentors and colleagues who inspired me to think bigger and move faster, your influence is woven into every insight shared here.

To my incredible team and partners in the Dr. Lisa AI ecosystem, your relentless dedication and creativity made this work possible.

A special thanks to my family and friends for standing by me through every unsure moment, every "just one more AI story," and every all-night writing session.

To my amazing sons, Cody and Braden, you are my constant motivation. From the moment I knew you existed, being the best possible version of myself has been my goal. Showing you that life is what you make it has been my purpose. I am incredibly proud to be your mom.

Shannon, thank you for encouraging me to share my voice, to stand firm in what I believe, and to never make myself small to ease someone else's comfort. Without you, there would be no book.

Finally, to the AI community for challenging norms and pushing the boundaries of what's possible, this book is a tribute to all of you.

About the Author

Dr. Lisa Palmer helps business and public-sector leaders skip the AI hype cycle and land wins that show up on the P&L. A 25-year tech veteran and former Microsoft, Gartner, and Splunk executive, she now leads two ventures: Dr. Lisa AI, an applied-AI advisory firm, and NCX, a future-of-work disruption company that empowers experts to operationalize and monetize their knowledge through AI agents. She brings a rare, full-circle perspective earned through years as an IT practitioner and CIO, a trusted executive advisor, a technology seller, and a doctoral researcher.

Her 2023 doctorate in Applied AI produced the widely adopted Five Pillars of AI Success framework, and her strategy-to-action playbook has guided Fortune 500 boards, PE-backed firms, and government agencies to achieve revenue gains, cost savings, and risk mitigation.

A sought-after keynote speaker who moves fluidly between private boardrooms and 15,000-person arenas, she's featured by media outlets including NBC, Fox News, the Financial Times, and **CIO.com**. Dr. Lisa turns complex tech into plain-spoken business moves that resonate with decision-makers.

If you meet her on the street, ask about her kids, growing up on a farm, hitting a triple during walk-on tryouts to make the college softball team, or hurtling down from the Great Wall of China on a rickety roller coaster.

She brings that same mix of grit, bold moves, and unexpected joy to her work, because leading with humanity is how we get the best results from AI.

Index